ORGANIZATION BEHAVIOR IN ACTION
SKILL BUILDING EXPERIENCES

William C. Morris

*Formerly of The Center for Research on Utilization
of Scientific Knowledge, Institute for Social
Research, The University of Michigan*

Marshall Sashkin

*School of Business Administration
Wayne State University*

D1296555

WEST PUBLISHING CO.

St. Paul   New York   Los Angeles   San Francisco

The West Series in Management

Consulting Editors:
Don Hellriegel
and
John W. Slocum, Jr.

Hellriegel-Slocum	Organizational Behavior: Contingency Views
Huse	Organization Development and Change
Mathis-Jackson	Personnel: Contemporary Perspectives and Applications
Morris-Sashkin	Organization Behavior in Action: Skill Building Experiences
Newport	Supervisory Management: Tools and Techniques
Ritchie-Thompson	Organization and People: Readings, Cases and Exercises in Organizational Behavior
Whatley-Kelley	Personnel Management in Action: Skill Building Experiences

Library of Congress Cataloging in Publication Data
Morris, William Clinton, 1928-
    Organization behavior in action.

    Includes bibliographies
    1. Problem solving. 2. Communication in
organizations. 3. Small group. I. Sashkin,
Marshall, 1944-   joint author. II. Title.
HD31.M6298   658.3   76-490
ISBN 0-8299-0080-2

2nd Reprint—1979

To Floyd
Norm
Ron

*

Contents

Preface

This book is a result of a continuing barrage of questions from friends, students, and clients. After our friends find out that we are organizational psychologists, and after we explain what we do, they look at us questioningly and say, "But what do you really *do*?" Our students, on the other hand, after plunging into the literature about organizational behavior and theory will often ask, "How do we learn to put this knowledge, these new ideas, into action?" At the same time, our clients in real groups and organizations, during and after the process of benefiting (hopefully, *most* of the time) from our help and association with them, find themselves asking, "How can we continue the processes that you've helped us start? How can we learn to do *what* you do and *how* you do it?"

This book is designed to show our friends the kinds of things we really do, as well as why and how. For our students, and students elsewhere, we believe this book will help us and other teachers provide a guided learning experience directed toward developing the knowledge *and* skills needed for effective problem solving in real organizations. And we expect to share this book with our clients so that, believe it or not, they will need our help less and less.

In general, our aim is to help people develop problem solving skills in interpersonal and group situations in organizations. In each of Chapters Two through Ten there is a section titled "Conceptual Support Materials," in some cases there are also such materials included as part of the specific skill development exercises (the term we have used is "learning designs"). These materials give a conceptual background for understanding the skill learnings and their use. We have *not* attempted to provide a "complete" organizational behavior textbook.

This text, however, can be used as the basic format for a course in organizational behavior, organizational psychology, helping or consultation skills, or, in fact, any of a wide range of courses which are centered on behavior in organizations. Normally, we would expect that the instructor would provide additional concept-content material. For example, for organization behavior courses there are several good, inexpensive paperbound texts which can be used in conjunction with our book. We have appended extensive bibliographies to each chapter, specially indicating which references we consider the most basic or important.

Although we direct this text primarily toward a college-level classroom audience, we believe it will be of considerable benefit in two other areas: training of consultants, and working with organizational clients. The former activity may occur in college programs, or in professional development programs (such as those being offered by several organizations). The latter activity would usually involve use of those portions of the text which are directly relevant to the needs of particular client groups. Thus, we developed an index chart, which can be found in the Instructor's Guide, to help the consultant obtain an initial fix on the relevant portions of the text. To facilitate use of the text in the classroom, the Instructor's Guide contains detailed design timing charts which provide realistic structures for using each learning design in one-, two-, or three-hour class sessions. In some cases this is done by shortening the design — removing less essential elements — while in other cases the design is set up for use in two sessions.

In summary, we see this book as being useful in a wide variety of situations, and have tried to make it as flexible as possible. We have given primary consideration to its use in the classroom, devoting particular effort toward making it easy for the instructor to fit the text to his or her particular course, in both content and format.

We hope, in particular, that instructors who have heard of "experiential learning methods" (few today have not) and want to experiment with such methods will find our book useful. For those who have been using experiential methods, we believe that our text will add a new dimension. That is, our aim is not merely the development of increased understanding through experiential learning involvement; we go beyond this in our focus on *skill* learning, in the context of conceptual understanding through experience. For the past decade, students — and even professors — have been calling for learning which has greater relevance to the "real world." In our teaching, we have striven to achieve such relevance *without* losing sight of the conceptual understanding which, we believe, is required if "relevance" is to be linked to practical applications of learning. This book is one result of our efforts, which, in this way, we hope to share with others.

Much of what is in our book was created by us, in our teaching and consulting practice. In learning the concepts and skills needed to do this, we have benefited most from our associations with two unique individuals, our respective mentors, Floyd C. Mann and Norman R. F. Maier. Our experiences as their students, and more recently colleagues, have been the most significant aspects of our professional education, and no acknowledgement can adequately express the depth of our feelings and appreciation toward them. What is of value in this book is a direct reflection of what they have given us. Additionally, we have had the good fortune to work with and learn from Ronald Lippitt, from whom we gained much in terms of the skills of applying laboratory learning methods.

Many individuals have given us encouragement in this project, most significantly our families. Writing a book takes much time, but was for us greatly facilitated by the understanding and support of those we love. Our professional associates and co-workers have also been of considerable help to us. In particular, we want to thank John W. Slocum, Jr., and Don Hellriegel, consulting editors of this series, who spent many hours reviewing our work and supplying helpful feedback as we revised, corrected, and slowly moved toward a finished product. Our editor, Richard T. Fenton, has been a continuing source of encouragement and support. We are also grateful to our students and clients, many of whom participated in the learning designs of this book, and whose reactions and comments helped us refine and improve our methods. Finally, we thank Rita Wiegers and Marcie Freeman, whose superb technical skills produced our manuscript and its several revisions.

We wish to add, however, that this book — with whatever strengths and weaknesses it contains — is uniquely our own, a product of our own creative efforts. We cannot blame anyone else for its shortcomings, but neither do we credit anyone else with its specific assets. We must qualify this claim slightly: obviously, a number of the brief readings in each chapter are the product of their identified authors; when no author is given, you may assume that the piece is our own, written specifically for this book. Furthermore, David Nadler developed and prepared for this book the simulation game in Appendix II. Intended for use in conjunction with Chapter Ten, this material can provide an excellent integrative skill learning and practice experience.

Finally, a brief note on professional ethics. In the field of training, consulting, and management and organization development there exists a common practice of using materials created by others. Some see this as theft or even plagiarism; we do not. As social scientists, we are most concerned with the dissemination and use of helpful products. We do, however, find unethical the practice of use without credit. (See Sashkin's note in *Social Change*, 1973, *4*(3), for further elaboration.) We have tried to give full credit for all ideas and materials in this book which are not our own creation. If we have failed in places, it is most likely due to the fact that the original sources for many useful concepts and materials have been "lost in the shuffle" of widespread application by practitioners. While this does not excuse any potential failings, we hope it does explain what may seem to be an inconsistency — especially to those readers who, upon seeing a particular learning design, might say, "I did practically the same thing five years ago. These guys are common thieves!" All we can say is that we have made every effort to avoid such possibilities; if any instances occur, the reader might at least take some satisfaction in the knowledge that widespread use of his or her ideas is the cause.

Dalton, Missouri   *William C. Morris*
Ann Arbor, Michigan   *Marshall Sashkin*
December, 1975

†

CHAPTER ONE

An Introduction to the Integrated Problem Solving Process

INTRODUCTION

This book is about helping people learn to solve problems in groups and organizations. Our major goal is to help the user (student, manager, or consultant) learn, through guided experience, the skills and procedures that are needed to be an effective "helper" or agent of change. First, we will define what we mean by "problem solving," then examine in more detail how we plan to teach problem solving, and, finally, consider briefly why we want to do this.

PROBLEM SOLVING: PROCEDURES AND SKILLS

Over the past few thousand years, humanity has done a fairly effective job of mastering the physical environment. For all of this time, and the time before, life, for individuals and for species, has been a series of problems. Our success as a species lies in our high level of adaptability, which is a result of our general ability to solve problems. Only in the last two hundred years or so, however, has our problem-solving capacity been greatly increased, primarily through the development of the methodology of science. And only in the past thirty years or so has problem solving become an area of scientific study itself. Much of the knowledge in this book is a result of such careful study, particularly the work of Norman R. F. Maier.* His work, along with that of his associates and students, has resulted in a much greater understanding of the procedures and skills involved in effective problem solving, as well as an understanding of how people can best learn these skills and procedures.[†] This book represents a further extension of the knowledge and the application methods developed by Maier and others.

We begin with a new model of the problem-solving process, shown in Table 1-1, which is, in some ways, not new at all. In one sense, it is no more than an adaptation and elaboration of the basic scientific model: understanding and defining a problem; developing hypotheses; testing hypotheses; evaluating results; and returning to the problem, if necessary. But there is really a lot more involved in our problem-solving model, because we're dealing not only with information and ideas but with

*For details see Maier, 1940, 1963, 1967, 1970.

[†]See especially Maier (1952, 1973); Maier and McRay (1972); Maier and Sashkin (1971); Maier, Solem, and Maier (1957); Maier and Thurber (1969); and Mann (1967).

people as well. We call our model "Integrated Problem Solving" because it not only follows this basic scientific model, integrating a necessary sequence of phases or major steps, but it also integrates the sequence of rational "acts" or task elements with a related sequence of "interacts" or interpersonal relation elements, resulting in effective problem-solving actions. But why should the separation and integration shown in Table 1-1 be necessary?

Differentiating, separating acts and interacts, and integrating them in action is particularly important because when dealing with human or social problems even the best scientists often leave their understanding of scientific problem-solving methods in the laboratory and fall into the same traps as the rest of us, who may never have heard of the "scientific method." But what are these traps? Let's review them, as we go through a description of each of the six phases of Integrated Problem Solving.

Phase I: Problem Definition

The best place to begin problem solving is with the problem. Often we assume that we know what the problem is, but too often we're wrong; we may be missing the boat entirely, looking at a symptom, or seeing only part of the problem. For example, the supervisor who docks tardy workers, assuming that the problem is motivational, may be totally off base — tardiness might, for example, be due to emergencies at home, or to poor bus service on the route to the plant. *First*, the general problem area must be explored and identified. Information has to be obtained from all those involved in the problem situation.

Even when the problem area is determined, more detailed information and problem specification is needed. The supervisor who "solves" a problem of insubordination by firing a worker who has refused to do a job might never have considered that the problem could involve some unknown yet resolvable issue. For example, the secretary who refuses to take notes at a department meeting held on the twenty-fifth floor of the office building may really be expressing a fear of elevators. Or, she could be acting on a need to save face among a group of co-workers: "I'm *not* going to take that crummy assignment again; you people are always needling me about it and it's time you had your turn!" Often, it's hard for people to share this kind of information openly. Finally, we must also look at objectives or goals. Is the aim really to get *this* secretary to do this job, or is it to get the job done efficiently and effectively? Careful examination of desired ends can help in telling the difference between a symptom and a problem.

In summary, the traps in Phase I can be avoided by (1) digging for information: *not* assuming that "we all know what the problem is here," but rather encouraging people to share their problem-relevant information; and (2) taking a hard look at our goals, at how we'd like the situation to be if there were no problem, and trying to agree on a shared image or goal.

Phase II: Problem-Solution Generation

In general, people are solution-minded rather than problem-oriented. If we fall into one of the traps of Phase I, we may produce a fine solution, except that it has little or no relation to the real problem. But, if we do avoid those traps, there is still the issue of coming up with a good solution. Often we pick the first or second solution idea that comes up, without even bothering to consider that there might be several better solutions. This happens because people have a built-in tendency to see the factors that are immediately in front of them, rather than trying to look for all the important factors in a problem situation. Of course, it's really impossible to examine *all* viable solution alternatives for a real-life problem. But that doesn't mean that we should go to the other extreme and grab the first idea that comes along. Research (Maier, 1970) has shown very clearly

TABLE 1-1 The Process of Integrated Problem Solving

	Phase	ACT	INTERACT	ACTION
I	Problem Definition	obtaining information resources understanding the problem situation determining goals	involving all persons concerned sharing information openly developing consensus on goals	**S**earch for the problem
II	Problem-Solution Generation	generating solution ideas refining ideas into alternatives listing specific alternatives	encouraging everyone to give ideas accepting all ideas without criticism cooperating in listing alternatives	**O**riginate ideas
III	Ideas to Actions	evaluating solution alternatives modifying and combining alternatives selecting a trial alternative	supporting rather than attacking accepting and resolving differences developing solution consensus	**L**ook for the best
IV	Solution-Action Planning	listing and timing the action steps identifying all needed resources determining action responsibilities	involving all group members identifying resistances openly developing action commitments	**V**erify responsibilities
V	Solution-Evaluation Planning	developing measures for each step creating a timetable for evaluation determining action responsibilities	using all group member resources sharing concerns and resolving differences developing commitments to evaluation actions	**E**licit evaluation plans
VI	Evaluation of the Product and the Process	comparing outcomes with objectives looking for new problems created determining further actions needed	evaluating degree of participation evaluating openness and support evaluating process learnings	**D**etermine effects

that solutions can be improved by looking at many — or at least several — alternatives. Doing this can lead to even more alternatives, since often one new idea leads to related but different ideas.

So, to avoid the trap in Phase II, postpone choosing a solution for a while. In fact, don't even evaluate the ideas — just *get* them. This approach means encouraging everyone to give ideas, even ridiculous ones, and accepting them *all*, without any criticism, for the time being.

Phase III: Ideas to Actions

Now we're ready to evaluate the ideas and come up with a final solution alternative to actually try out. Careful analysis of the pros and cons of each idea allows us to avoid the trap of random empiricism, that is, "Let's run it up the flag pole . . .," etc. It pays to consider first whether the hoist can take the weight of the new flag. An experimental attitude is a good thing, but random, or trial-and-error, experiments can be very costly, much more so than taking the time to think through the consequences of actions.

The feelings of the idea-givers must be considered, too. We all feel some sense of identification with our ideas. People can help and participate in the idea-evaluation process more easily when they don't feel attacked or threatened. To avoid creating these feelings, it's usually good practice to avoid identifying the poor ideas (which would only make those who thought them up feel defensive) and, instead, concentrate on selecting the *best* ideas. For example, it's helpful to avoid saying things like, "That's certainly the worst idea I've heard of yet; Joe, you must be pretty uncomfortable sitting on your brains like that!" Such criticism is really counterproductive, because it wastes valuable time and may cause Joe to stop giving *any* ideas, even when he has a good one. It's much more productive to focus on identifying and clarifying *good* ideas. Then, work these over until everyone can agree on one or two they'd like to try.*

The traps in Phase III can be avoided, then, by first identifying the good ideas and then carefully exploring them, looking for information that supports or contradicts each idea. Everyone can then be involved in refining these ideas and coming up with the final solution, which will be tried out.

Phase IV: Solution-Action Planning

We often assume that when a decision is made and an action-alternative selected, the solution will then be simple to implement, or even that implementation will be automatic. While it's true that avoiding the above traps makes it much more likely that the solution will work, there are still some traps left. One is neglecting to make a detailed, step-by-step plan, including *who* will do *what when*. In a complex social system or organization, coordination of actions is usually *not* simple and straightforward. The actions involved as part of putting the solution into effect need to be carefully scheduled and coordinated. One person may be able to carry out certain action responsibilities only after another person's actions are effectively accomplished. Somehow, these people must know what has been done. Without a detailed action plan, it's even possible that no one will do anything, assuming, with the best intentions, that someone else will do it.

Part of this action-planning process involves accepting responsibilities and making commitments. The trap here is that we tend to take it for granted that the world will accept the better mousetrap; unfortunately, it's more likely that the inventor will have to live off the mice. In general, people just don't rush to change their behavior because of a brilliant new idea. In fact, they may

*These comments are based on ideas originated by Maier (1963).

even try to sabotage the idea to avoid the inconvenience and uncertainty caused by change. Joe may agree, "Gee, that's a great idea, I'll try it out right away!" But Joe might be working on his own problem: "How can I show that this dumb idea doesn't work at all without getting blamed myself?" This is one reason why the people who are going to be carrying out the solution must be involved in the problem solving process, and why as part of action planning everyone should make clear commitments to carrying out the solution.

The traps in Phase IV can be avoided by preparing a detailed, step-by-step schedule for the implementation of the solution, including who does what when, and by making sure that everyone agrees to and expresses commitment to the plan and to his or her own action responsibilities.

Phase V: Solution-Evaluation Planning

The primary trap in this phase is its omission. Most groups stop working at Phase IV, which is unfortunate, because the group greatly reduces its own opportunities for learning. In general, we assume that it will be obvious whether or not the solution is successful. And, it is true that solutions are sometimes tremendously successful. However, it would be even more useful to know exactly what it was about the actions that were taken which made the solution work so well. Of course, occasionally a solution is a total bomb, and we feel like hiding the fact that we had anything to do with it. However, it would be much more productive to know exactly what went wrong, so we could avoid making the same mistakes in the future.

In real life, though, solutions generally work moderately well or are just barely adequate – neither spectacular successes nor spectacular failures. How often have you or someone you know said something like, "Well, it worked pretty well, but not as well as we'd hoped. I guess I'm not exactly sure why; we're still trying to figure it out." If we keep track of exactly what happens, as it occurs, and have some clear ideas about what is supposed to happen, we can probably determine how to make some relatively minor improvements or adjustments that would make the solutions work much better. And, if the solution was a spectacular success or failure, we might learn how to repeat or avoid these outcomes.

Improving solutions once they have been implemented cannot be done by guesswork or trial and error, but is possible only on the basis of accurate information about the effects of solution-actions. This means planning a detailed schedule of evaluation actions, including assignment of responsibilities and specification of measures and how they are obtained. Of course, it's also important to obtain clear commitments to evaluation actions, just as was true for solution actions.

In sum, the trap in Phase V is avoided by carrying out the activities we have described as parts of this phase.

Phase VI: Evaluation of the Product and the Process

Since, in real life, we rarely do much evaluation planning (Phase V), it follows that we usually don't do too well at making final evaluations. Effective accomplishment of Phase V will help avoid the first trap in Phase VI – failure to make a detailed final evaluation of the effects of actions. In a group evaluation meeting, we can determine exactly what did happen and the degree to which the solution was effective. If the problem, or some part of it, remains, the group can "recycle" – examine evaluation information and refine the problem definition or even redefine the problem. New solution alternatives can then be generated, one of the previously determined alternatives may be selected, or some minor changes can be made in the solution that was tried. This means going back through Phases III, IV, and V, at least, and possibly returning to Phase I or II.

If the problem *was* solved, the group can consider whether any related new problems have been created and how to deal with these, as well as determine what further actions will be necessary in order to support the continued effectiveness of the solution.

The second trap in this phase is also an omission — failure to use the group's problem solving experiences to evaluate how well the group has learned to solve problems. Only by examining how the group members worked together can the group as a whole improve its problem solving capacities.

So, the two traps in Phase VI are (1) failure to evaluate, in detail, the effects of the solution and follow-through with changes or modifications, and (2) failure to examine, in detail, how the group members worked together and what they learned.

Problem Solving Procedures

We've outlined in some detail a model of problem solving — a set of steps or procedures to follow. Our model is based on the scientific model of inquiry but takes into account human nature and limitations. We have not, however, defined very well the *process* of problem solving; what we've been talking about is a procedure — the "rules of the game." Effective problem solving does require an understanding of the procedure, but also requires certain *behavioral skills.* The procedures we have examined and have yet to look at are, of course, important, but are much easier to learn about than are the skills. Research (Maier and Thurber, 1969) has shown that the straightforward application of good procedures is fairly simple and results in far more effective problem solutions than when such procedures are not used. However, with additional *skills*, on the part of the users, the results are still better. Let's outline briefly just what these skills are.

Problem Solving Skills

The skills we're talking about are represented in the chapter titles. These are skills most people can learn, and they are needed by anyone who plans to be an effective manager, administrator, or "helper."

We begin with the skills involved in building effective task-centered relationships — the skills of giving and receiving help. A second important set of skills concerns generating and sharing information. There are also skills in giving others feedback — helping them understand how they appear to others and what effects their behavior has on other people. There are several interrelated skills needed by members of a group if the group is to work well — skills concerned with attending to the way the group is operating (group process), communication, and leadership functions. Diagnostic skills involve interpreting information in ways that help one better understand the problem. Skills are needed for the development of clear, well-defined goals or objectives, and for evaluating the attainment of those goals. Often, one who is trying to help people learn to solve problems will have to use several of these skills at the same time.

Most of this book is about learning these skills and learning to help other people develop them. This leads us to the question of skill development method: how do we propose to help you develop these skills yourself and learn to help others develop them?

SKILL-DEVELOPMENT METHODS: LEARNING BY DOING

We have a basic orientation, or bias, in the way we, as teachers, help our students or clients to learn. Our bias pervades this entire book, and can be stated fairly concisely: we believe that people learn best doing. This is no new and brilliant concept. It wasn't new when John Dewey formalized it in his book *Democracy and Education* in 1916, and it's not new today. But the meaningful application of this concept, in educational settings such as schools, colleges, and universities, is fairly recent.

We believe that conceptual understanding is absolutely required for effective learning. But learning is *change*. The most relevant measure of change is behavior, and behavioral change is far more likely to occur and to be effective when it is based on both conceptual understanding *and* on behavioral experience. This statement is based on our personal values, our personal-professional experience, and our professional judgment, as scientists and teachers. We could proceed to outline a lengthy scientific argument, complete with research references, but we think that our basic position – "why" this book has the form it does – is clear enough. Let us proceed to a brief outline of the "how."

The problem solving steps outlined in Table 1-1 are best learned by *using* them in the context of real, or even simulated but specific and detailed, problem situations. This is how, we hope, the student will eventually help others learn to solve problems. In learning to do this – help others learn – we face a number of additional problems. The major problem centers on the development of a set of specific behavioral skills.

This book is aimed at helping the student learn from experience and at helping the teacher or practitioner design and conduct such learning activities. Learning from experience, however, can be a costly approach when it means trial and error. That is, errors can teach very well indeed, but on occasion they can also be disastrous, for the learner and for others. It is possible, though, to make two major changes in the trial-and-error learning process that will increase the probability of learning and greatly reduce the negative consequences of error.

First, we clearly define what the learning goals – skills and concepts – are. Each of the following chapters has a fairly specific learning aim, stated at the beginning. Each chapter contains a set of learning designs. Each design has a particular skill-development objective within the overall aim of the chapter.

Second, we cannot eliminate the possibility of making errors, but we can eliminate or at least greatly reduce the *negative consequences* of errors. We wouldn't want to eliminate the possibility of errors even if we could engineer it, for the experience one gains from making the "wrong" response, from doing the "wrong" thing, is just as useful (and sometimes more useful) as the experience gained from successful, "correct" behavioral actions. But the point here is that experiential learning situations can be designed to be low in risk. If I try to help a very close friend solve a problem, and do a poor job of it, the consequences are serious. I may have lost a valued friend, although I have, in the process, learned some useful and important things about helping people learn to solve problems. Similarly, I may as a manager try to help my subordinates work together to solve a problem but the outcome may leave us worse off than ever. Again, I will have learned from the experience, but at a considerable cost (decreased performance, loss of respect, etc.). The learning value of such experiences can, however, be retained and the negative consequences eliminated through the use of *structured simulations* – role play and task or discussion exercises. Each of the following chapters contains a variety of such simulations; some are role plays, and some are discussion task exercises. Each of these structured simulation exercises has a specific aim or purpose.

Most people find it difficult or unreal, at first, to become involved in such simulations or learning designs. With just a little practice, however, the difficulty and unreality usually disappear. When you realize that there really isn't any risk, that the worst risk is looking a bit foolish for a few moments, the major difficulty is overcome. When you realize that the hypothetical, imaginary situation is not real, but that your behavior *is* real, and that it's the behavior, not the situation, that is our real interest, the unreality of the situation quickly dissipates.

One final note to the student: the experiential learning designs in this book are, as we have mentioned, inherently "safe." There is no risk of failure, as there would certainly be if these situations were "real." However, some people, though not many, find it extremely difficult, if not impossible, to get into learning experiences like the ones in this book. If you consistently feel uncomfortable with or very hesitant about anything you are asked to do in these learning designs, then don't do it; it's as simple as that.

PROBLEM SOLVING AND CHANGE: CONCEPTS AND APPROACH

Obviously, helping people learn to solve problems is a good and useful thing. We felt, however, that some further explanation should be given about why this book was written.

Both authors are deeply interested in *change*. We, as scientists and researchers, want to learn more about the processes of change in groups and organizations — in all kinds of social systems. As practitioners, as applied behavioral scientists, we want to learn to help such social systems become more effective — more useful, productive, and satisfying for the people who make them up. Quite a few theories and approaches have been developed about the process and practice of changing social systems.*

FIGURE 1.1 Postulated Approaches to Change and Associated Intervention Targets

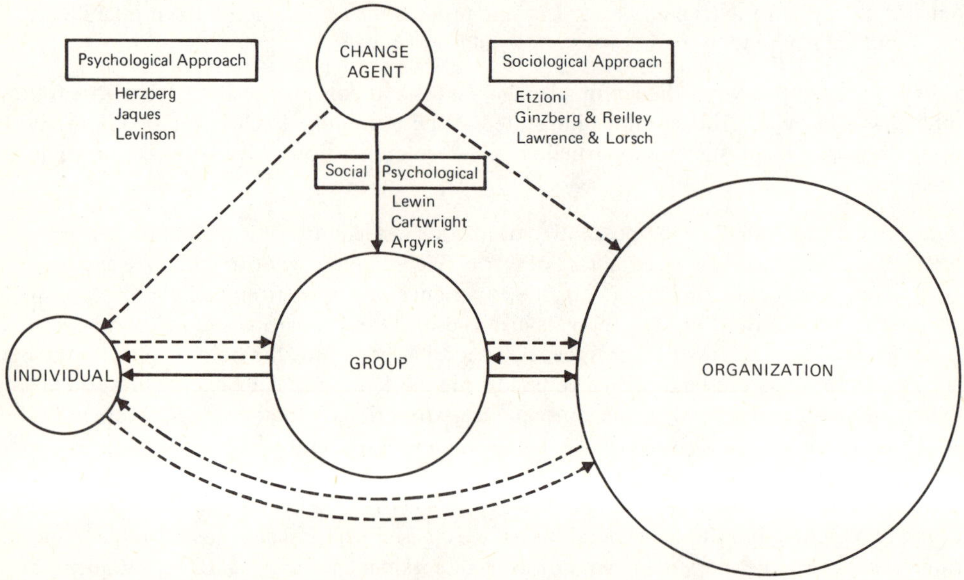

NOTE: See this chapter's references for the writings of persons referred to in this chart. Specific individuals named in Figure 1.1 are only some of the major exponents of the three approaches.

From a sociological perspective, one can argue that change is produced when the structure of the entire social system — an organization — is altered. Such change then affects the groups that comprise the system and the individuals who make up the groups, as well as having some direct effect on individual behavior.

*See, for example, Hornstein, Bunker, Burke, Gindes, and Lewicki (1971), or Sashkin, Morris, and Horst (1973).

From a psychological viewpoint, the process is seen almost reversed. By changing individuals, the behavior of individuals in groups is changed, which results in change throughout the social system or organization. There are also some direct effects as, for example, when a powerful or charismatic individual who has changed has a direct impact on change in the social system.

Our viewpoint, as noted in Figure 1-1, is that change is best achieved by working with groups. This approach stems from the work of Lewin (1947) and his students.* Cartwright (1951) explained that change in a social system is best achieved through groups, using the group as *target* of the change and also as the *source* and *method* of change. In this way, change in the group results in changes in individual behavior *and* promotes change in the entire social system or organization.

Actually, we don't deny that change can be attained in any of these three ways; the issue is, which approach is most *practical*? Which approach is easiest to carry out and which is most likely to attain results? We believe that the answer to these questions is that the *group* or social psychological approach is "best." This is why the primary focus of this book is on skills important for effective work in groups.

We need, however, to clarify our concept of change. We spoke earlier of helping social systems become more effective. To us, this means more adaptable, better able to confront, deal with, and resolve problems. If people can, in groups, learn how to solve problems more effectively, then the group and the organization of which it may be part will become more effective and more capable of producing change.

The basic thrust of this book is, then, as follows: by learning to help people, in groups, learn how to solve problems better, you will be acting as a change agent. The groups will become better at problem solving and will therefore become more adaptable and more effective; so will the individuals composing the group and so, in fact, will the organization or social system of which the group may be part. Our desire to see this kind of process occur more frequently, in the real world, is why we wrote this book.

REFERENCES

Argyris, C. (1970) *Intervention theory and method.* Reading, Mass.: Addison-Wesley.

Cartwright, D. (1951) Achieving change in people. *Human Relations* 4: 381-392.

Dewey, J. (1916) *Democracy and education.* New York: Macmillan.

Etzioni, A. (1968) *The active society.* New York: Free Press.

Ginzberg, E., and Reilley, E. W. (1957) *Effecting change in large organizations.* New York: Columbia University Press.

Herzberg, F. (1966) *Work and the nature of man.* Cleveland, Ohio: World.

**Hornstein, H. A.; Bunker, B. B.; Burke, W. W.; Gindes, M.; and Lewicki, R. J. (1971) *Social intervention.* New York: Free Press.

Hyman, R., and Anderson, B. (1965) Solving problems. *International Science and Technology* 45: 36-41.

Jaques, E. (1964) Social-analysis and the Glacier project. *Human Relations* 17: 361-375.

Jaques, E. (1951) *The changing culture of a factory.* London: Tavistock.

Kelley, H. H., and Thibaut, J. (1954) Experimental studies of group problem solving and process. In *Handbook of social psychology, Volume II*, ed. G. Lindzey. Reading, Mass.: Addison-Wesley.

Kepner, C. H., and Tregoe, B. B. (1965) *The rational manager: A systematic approach to problem solving and decision making.* New York: McGraw-Hill.

Lawrence, P. R., and Lorsch, J. W. (1969). *Organization development: Diagnosis and action.* Reading, Mass.: Addison-Wesley.

*One of the earliest applications of this work to industrial organizations was made by Maier (1946).

Levinson, H. (1972) The clinical psychologist as organizational diagnostician. *Professional Psychology* 3: 34-40.

Lewin, K. (1947) Frontiers in group dynamics. *Human Relations* 1: 5-42.

**Lippitt, R.; Watson, J.; and Westley, B. (1958) *The dynamics of planned change.* New York: Harcourt, Brace, & World.

Maier, N. R. F., and McRay, E. P. (1972) Increasing innovation in change situations through leadership skills. *Psychological Reports* 31: 343-354.

Maier, N. R. F. (1970) *Problem solving and creativity in individuals and groups.* Belmont, Calif.: Brooks/Cole.

**Maier, N. R. F. (1967) Assets and liabilities in group problem solving: The need for an integrative function. *Psychological Review* 74: 239-249.

**Maier, N. R. F. (1963) *Problem solving discussions and conferences.* New York: McGraw-Hill.

Maier, N. R. F. (1960) Screening solutions to upgrade quality: A new approach to problem solving under conditions of uncertainty. *Journal of Psychology* 49: 217-231.

Maier, N. R. F. (1952) *Principles of human relations.* New York: Wiley.

Maier, N. R. F. (1946) *Psychology in industry.* Boston: Houghton Mifflin.

**Maier, N. R. F. (1940) The behavior mechanisms concerned with problem solving. *Psychological Review* 47: 43-58.

Maier, N. R. F., and Sashkin, M. (1971) Specific leadership behaviors that affect problem solving. *Personnel Psychology* 24: 35-44.

Maier, N. R. F., and Solem, A. R. (1962) Improving solutions by turning choice situations into problems. *Personnel Psychology* 15: 151-157.

Maier, N. R. F.; Solem, A. R.; and Maier, A. A. (1957) *Supervisory and executive development.* New York: Wiley. (Reissued by Wiley Science Editions, 1966. Revised and reissued as *The role play technique.* La Jolla, Calif.: University Associates, 1975.)

Maier, N. R. F., and Thurber, J. A. (1969) Limitations of procedures for improving group problem solving. *Psychological Reports,* Monograph Supplement I-V25: 640-666.

Mann, F. C. (1967) Achieving an effective staff. In *The medical staff in the modern hospital*, ed. C. W. Eisele. New York: McGraw Hill.

Miles, M. B., ed. (1964) *Innovation in education.* New York: Bureau of Publications, Teachers College, Columbia University.

Osborne, A. F. (1953) *Applied imagination: Principles and procedures of creative thinking.* New York: Scribner's.

**Sashkin, M.; Morris, W. C.; and Horst, L. (1973) A comparison of social and organizational change models: Information flow and data use processes. *Psychological Review* 80: 510-526.

Scheerer, M. (1963) Problem solving. *Scientific American* 208: 118-128.

**References preceded by a double asterisk are those judged most basic or important.

CHAPTER TWO

The Helping Relationship: Learning to Give Help

Give a man a fish and he is fed for a day;
teach a man how to fish and he is fed for a lifetime.

INTRODUCTION

It is the second part of the above old saying that we mean by the term "helping relationship." But that's not all there is to it. There are more and less effective ways of helping; this chapter is about learning the skills needed to give help *effectively*. Certainly, one major principle is that people become more independent as a result of an effective helping relationship, not interminably dependent on the helper. But this does not mean that people should or can be completely independent of others. One of the most useful things a consultant, change agent, or helper can do is help the client learn how to ask for help, and how to give help when asked. Almost everyone has resources that can be used to help others at times. Almost everyone needs help from others at times. The first two skill learning designs in this chapter are designed to demonstrate how one can help others learn to ask for and give help to their peers. A more difficult situation exists when one of the parties has a position of status or authority above the other. The third learning design has two options, both of which are centered on such situations, the aim being to let you know how it feels to be in such positions and how you can help superiors and subordinates learn to ask for and give help to one another.

In sum, we have three objectives in this chapter: (1) learning how it feels to ask for and to give help; (2) developing of skills in giving and receiving assistance; (3) learning some methods for showing others how to accomplish the first two objectives. We suggest that you review the material in Section II carefully, and perhaps discuss it with others, before using the experiential designs in Section I.

I. SPECIFIC SKILL-DEVELOPMENT AND LEARNING DESIGNS

A. Design for Learning to Help Peers Consult with One Another (Classroom)

1. *Purpose.* In every organization, members are continually involved in a two-way process of giving help to and receiving help from their peers and colleagues. Some give help on problems more effectively than others and they may, in fact, be the informal consultants of the organization: those to whom others go most often when they need help. We believe that there are one-to-one consulting skills that can be learned and then spread throughout an organiza-

11

tion to support communication, openness, trust, and ultimately a more synergistic environment and a higher quality of output resulting from that environment.

The purpose of this learning design is to give individuals an opportunity to take a closer look at their own personal consulting skills by practicing those skills in front of others and then being critiqued on the process by their colleagues. We prepared this first learning design for use in classroom situations. However, since it is often the purpose of managerial training seminars to develop skills to solve real organizational problems when the participants return home, we have provided a second design similar to this one but for use in real organizational settings. (Design B in the present chapter.)

2.   *Materials needed.* The problem solving framework found in Chapter One.

3.   *Steps in using the design.*
    a.   Present brief talk on purpose of activity.
    b.   Arrange room for "client" and "consultant."
    c.   Choose volunteers for roles.
    d.   State the process rules for the interaction.
    e.   Stop the action for a critique.
    f.   Continue the process of interaction and stop-actions.
    g.   Summarize after last stop-action.
    h.   Divide group into pairs to practice client and consultant roles.
    i.   Reconvene and collect process data on activity.

4.   *Deriving learnings.* Some questions the group may wish to discuss during the summary period are:
    — Why, when asked for help, do we find it difficult to remain problem-, rather than solution-oriented?
    — Why is it difficult to define thoroughly an apparently simple problem?
    — Are there usually many other problems that relate to the one stated by the client? And, in fact, is the one the client originally states actually the one that he or she really feels is the most important to deal with first?
    — How can the consultant observe his or her own actions and keep on track with the client? What are the cues that indicate the consultant is going off the track of the problem?

B.   Design for Learning to Help Peers Consult with One Another (Organizational)

1.   *Purpose.* Seminars are often formed with the goal of increasing the interpersonal and managerial skills of those who participate. When these seminars are composed of people from the same profession or business and industrial background but from different locations or company settings, then a special kind of individual problem solving design may be used. For example, the laboratory directors from fifteen research and development labs might come together in such a seminar.* In addition to the above purpose, a common though usually unstated goal of each participant is to "get help on back-home problems from others who

*As actually happened in 1966-1967. For a brief summary of what occurred, see Mann (1968).

are somehow like me." Of course, within a single organization, the goal could be to *get* help on problems and to learn to *give* help more effectively.

People *do* bring their problems to seminars of this kind, often with little expectation that they will be helped. The value of such seminars on interpersonal relations and managerial skills can be considerably increased if opportunities are provided to work on "back-home" problems. Most of the problems that participants bring are directly related to some level of work in their home organizations. Problems may involve another individual on the staff, perhaps a peer with whom one has to work. They may involve the work-group or committee of which one is a member. Or, problems may involve another group in the system, or the total system, or perhaps changes needed in the whole organization. While the specific types of problems will depend upon the level of those participating in the seminar, surfacing and dealing with these problems in a seminar work session can often be a positive learning force in the process of applying new interpersonal and managerial skills.

The specific aim of this learning design is the creation of a situation in which the participants can give and receive help from one another on real organizational problems, while learning the skills involved in effectively doing this.

2. *Materials needed.* Meeting space for approximately fifteen persons, preferably open without tables and with movable chairs.

3. *Steps in using the design.*

    a. State purpose to group.

    b. Arrange room and choose participants.

    c. Give instructions to observers.

    d. Start the process and call the first stop-action.

    e. Continue the help-giving process.

    f. Present input on problem-solving steps.

    g. Derive learnings from activity.

4. *Deriving learnings.* Group discussion plus use of questions in part 4 of previous design.

C. Designs for Learning to Give and Receive Help

Purpose. Giving and receiving help, the learning aim of the first design in this chapter, is for several reasons easier with one's peers than when the helper and helpee are in an unequal status or power relationship. Often the relationship is unequal, always when the helper is a consultant — selected, hired, and paid for his/her recognized superiority in a certain area — and when the helpee is, in a formal organizational sense, subordinate to the helper. Such unequal relationships create communication barriers, since a person is unlikely to ask for help if he feels such a request or question will make him look foolish to his peers or will make him look bad in the eyes of the boss. The expertise of the consultant or superior is wasted, and the opportunity for learning on the part of the person needing help is reduced. Simple semantic problems — different ways of thinking and communicating — may compound the problem. Consultants, whether technical experts or behavioral scientists, often use jargon that adds to the problem. Supervisors and managers often have grossly incorrect ideas about the way subordinates think and the things they want.

The aim of the following two similar learning designs is to demonstrate effective and ineffective ways of giving help in such situations. The first concerns a teacher-student situation, a case not too far from the expert-consultant type of help relationship since the teacher is a "teaching assistant" without a great deal of direct authority over the student. The second case involves a superior and subordinate. The article reprinted in Section II is directly relevant and should be read over beforehand.

2. *Materials needed.* Role-play information sheets, newsprint, and markers.

3A. *Steps in using the design: "Consultant."*

   a.   Review the background of the case.

   b.   Form groups of three and read roles.

   c.   Start the interaction.

   d.   Stop action for feedback from observers.

   e.   Have group members switch roles and repractice.

   f.   Have each group discuss principles of help-giving.

   g.   Have groups report learnings to entire class.

3B. *Steps in using the design: "Supervisor-Subordinate."*

   a.   Read background information.

   b.   Form groups of three and have them take roles.

   c.   Start the interaction.

   d.   Have each participant fill out questionnaires.

   e.   Discuss observations of the experience (full group).

   f.   Discuss differences in interaction among role-play groups.

4. *Deriving learnings.* Design 3A is intended to focus attention on the process of asking for help and giving help in a fairly simple situation. Some questions for discussion are:

   — How can a helper make a client feel more comfortable in asking for help?

   — How can the helper avoid bias or prejudgment of the client?

   — Are there more and less comfortable ways for the client to ask for help?

   — How does the "power" the helper may have over the client affect their interaction? How can negative effects be reduced or avoided?

Design 3B brings out some of the specific characteristics of the client that make it easier or harder to ask for help. Some relevant questions for discussion are:

   — How can a subordinate ask for help in a way that does not make the subordinate look bad in the eyes of a "superior" helper?

   — Does the mere fact that the subordinate expects good communication actually help in achieving more open communication?

   — How can the superior encourage trust on the part of subordinates in asking for help, both in general and in the specific case that was used here?

5. *Support materials.* The background information and role orientation sheets needed for Design 3A and 3B follow.

ART HISTORY 101

Background

Joan/John Blake is a student in Professor Kurtz's Art History 101 course. The class is organized with two hours of lecture (one hour each Monday and Wednesday) and one hour of discussion in smaller groups with a teaching assistant (on Friday). Bob/Robin Sherman is the TA for the discussion section Blake is enrolled in. Blake has asked to talk with Sherman after class today. It is the end of the fifth week of classes.

ART HISTORY 101

Role for Joan/John Blake, Student

After five weeks of class, you are upset with the way the course is going. Kurtz's lectures are poorly organized, which makes it hard to take notes, and he uses a lot of jargon so you often miss what he's getting at, since there's no opportunity to ask questions during the lecture. The midterm exam, which Kurtz makes up and grades, is coming up in a week and you're worried! You decided to talk to your TA, Bob/Robin Sherman and see if (s)he can give you any help.

ART HISTORY 101

Role for Bob/Robin Sherman, Teaching Assistant

You are one of two TA's for Professor Kurtz's Art History 101 this term, and run two discussion sections. Joan/John Blake, who is in your Friday afternoon section, asked to talk to you after class today. From the questions (s)he's been asking in class, your impression is that (s)he's having some problems with the material. Class has just ended and (s)he's coming over. Since the midterm is coming up soon, you hope that you can help her/him.

ART HISTORY 101

Observer

As you watch the TA and student interact, look for behaviors that will clarify the following issues:

— Is the TA encouraging the student to ask for help? How? Or, how is the TA being unhelpful or discouraging?

— Is the student being open? Is he or she holding back information or feelings?

ALLIED ELECTRICAL PRODUCTS CORPORATIONS

Background

This case concerns the Small Retail Products Division of the Allied Electrical Products Corporation. Mike/Mary Dutton is Manager of this division, which has five product groups. One of the product group supervisors is Tom/Tana Watts. Dutton has asked Watts to meet with him/her in Dutton's office this morning, to discuss progress on a certain project.

ALLIED ELECTRICAL PRODUCTS CORPORATION

Role for Mike/Mary Dutton, Manager

You are Manager of the Small Retail Products Division of Allied Electrical Products Corporation. Five product group supervisors report directly to you; your boss is Mr. James Carney, General Manager of the Retail Products Division. You were formerly a product group supervisor, and were promoted two years ago to your present position, so you are familiar with the problems and pressures faced by your subordinates. There are, for instance, many technical hang-ups in getting a new product from the development lab out of the prototype stage and into actual production.

Tom/Tana Watts, one of your product group supervisors, is a bright young individual who was promoted to your old job. Right now his/her major project is getting a new small color television receiver, which uses a liquid-crystal display, into production. This process involves a brand-new technology, so you figure (s)he's been running into problems, especially since (s)he's requested two project extension dates. It's really important to get this project through, since the company could really be on top of a whole new market with tremendous potential. You know, from various sources, that RCA is working on a similar project, and if they break the market first, your efforts are likely to go down the drain. You've asked Tom/Tana to come see you this morning; if there are still hang-ups, you'd like to try and find out just what the trouble is, and maybe then you could give him/her some help.

ALLIED ELECTRICAL PRODUCTS CORPORATION

Role for Tom/Tana Watts, Product Group Supervisor

You are one of five product group supervisors in the Small Retail Products Division of Allied Electrical Products Corporation. You were promoted into this position two years ago to fill the vacancy caused by the promotion of Mike/Mary Dutton, who is now your boss (Manager of the Small Retail Products Division). You're a pretty ambitious individual, and you expect to go a lot further in management, probably in this company. You've learned a lot in the two years you've had this job. Dutton's a pretty good boss, but you don't expect him/her to go any higher in the organization. Thus, you've really got to show them you can perform.

Your best chance for this would be the success of one of your current major projects, a new miniature television receiver that uses a liquid-crystal display. With this product the company will be in on the ground floor of a whole new technology and will have an excellent chance of capturing the biggest share of the market. Since it involves a brand-new technology, there have been many more problems and hang-ups than is usual for your group; in fact, you had to ask Dutton for time extensions on two occasions. Things are going okay now, though, and you are confident you'll meet this latest deadline.

You are, however, a little concerned about an indirectly related problem. Joe Barnes, one of your engineers, is an awfully sharp guy, but he seems to have a hard time getting along with others, especially in the other four product groups. You're pretty sure that at least a couple of the minor delays on the new TV receiver display were due to Joe's inability to get some specialized help from people in the other groups.

Anyway, everything's okay for the moment. Mike/Mary asked to see you this morning. You're not sure what (s)he wants, but maybe you're starting to get some attention from the higher-ups. At least you'll have a chance to tell him/her how well the project is coming along.

ALLIED ELECTRICAL PRODUCTS CORPORATION

Role for Tom/Tana Watts, Product Group Supervisor

You are one of five product group supervisors in the Small Retail Products Division of Allied Electrical Products Corporation. You were promoted into this position two years ago to fill the vacancy caused by the promotion of Mike/Mary Dutton, who is now your boss (Manager of the Small Retail Products Division). Dutton is a pretty good boss; you've learned a lot in the past two years and have grown to have considerable trust and confidence in him/her..

For example, there's one very important project you're on now, a new miniature television receiver that uses a liquid-crystal display. With this new product the company will be in on the ground floor of a whole new technology and will have an excellent chance of capturing the biggest share of the market. Since it involves a brand-new technology, there have been many more problems and hang-ups than is usual for your group. On two occasions you had to go to Dutton and ask for time extensions. After you explained the problems, Mike/Mary gave you the extensions, and also came up with a couple of ideas that really helped (and, in one case, certainly helped you to avoid another minor delay). Things are going okay now, though, and you are confident you'll meet the latest deadline.

You are, however, a little concerned about an indirectly related problem. Joe Barnes, one of your engineers, is an awfully sharp guy, but he seems to have a hard time getting along with others, especially in the other four product groups. You're pretty sure that at least a couple of the minor delays on the new TV receiver display were due to Joe's inability to get some specialized help from people in the other groups.

Anyway, everything's okay for the moment. Mike/Mary asked to see you this morning. You're not sure what (s)he wants, but you'll have a chance to tell him/her how well the project is coming along.

ALLIED ELECTRICAL PRODUCTS CORPORATION

Role for Tom/Tana Watts, Product Group Supervisor

You are one of five product group supervisors in the Small Retail Products Division of Allied Electrical Products Corporation. You were promoted into this position two years ago to fill the vacancy caused by the promotion of Mike/Mary Dutton, who is now your boss (Manager of the Small Retail Products Division). The great advantage of having Dutton for a boss is that you and (s)he seem to think a lot alike. You've never had any trouble explaining things to him/her, as was true with your last boss...

For example, there's one very important project you're on now, a new miniature television receiver that uses a liquid-crystal display. With this new product the company will be in on the ground floor of a whole new technology and will have an excellent chance of capturing the biggest share of the market. Since it involves a brand-new technology, there have been many more problems and hang-ups than is usual for your group. On two occasions you had to go to Dutton, explain the problem, and ask for time extensions. Both times (s)he picked up on the nature of the problem almost immediately, and not only granted the extensions, but was able to give you some good ideas that helped to avoid further delays. Things are going okay now, though, and you are confident you'll meet the latest deadline.

You are, however, a little concerned about an indirectly related problem. Joe Barnes, one of your engineers, is an awfully sharp guy, but he seems to have a hard time getting along with others, especially in the other four groups. You're pretty sure that at least a couple of the minor delays on the new TV receiver display were due to Joe's inability to get some specialized help from people in the other groups.

Anyway, everything's okay for the moment. Mike/Mary asked to see you this morning. You're not sure what (s)he wants, but at least you'll have a chance to tell him/her how well the project is coming along.

ALLIED ELECTRICAL PRODUCTS CORPORATION

Observer

Watts, the subordinate, has been asked by Dutton, the superior, to meet with him/her. Watts may or may not bring up a problem concerning one of his/her subordinates, Joe Barnes. If (s)he does, make note of the time and context of the discussion, how (s)he raised the issue, and what Dutton did or said both before and after Joe's name came up.

Other questions you should have in mind while observing and taking notes are:

— Is Dutton encouraging Watts to ask for help? How? Or, how is Dutton being unhelpful or discouraging Watts?

— Is Watts being open with Dutton? Is Watts holding back information relevant to the discussion?

— Is the project Watts and Dutton are discussing really coming along well? What does Watts say or do that gives you an impression one way or the other?

ALLIED ELECTRICAL PRODUCTS CORPORATION

Post-Discussion Questionnaire

Your Name: _____

Your Role (circle one):   Dutton

Watts

1.   What was the net result or outcome of this discussion?

2.   How do you *feel* about the discussion, right now? (circle one)

Very negative . . .   1   2   3   4   5   6   7   . . . Very positive

3.   How *satisfied* are you with the discussion, right now? (circle one)

Very dissatisfied . . .   1   2   3   4   5   6   7   . . . Very satisfied

4.   Do you feel that the other person was being open with you in the discussion, or that (s)he was to some extent holding back or concealing some things? (check one)

(S)He was: □ completely open

□ generally open

□ somewhat open

□ not very open

□ not at all open

5.   For Dutton: Who is Joe Barnes?

6.   For Watts: What help was Dutton able to give concerning Joe Barnes?

II. CONCEPTUAL SUPPORT MATERIALS: THE HELPING RELATIONSHIP

IS HELP HELPFUL?*
Jack R. Gibb

People in the service professions often see themselves as primarily engaged in the job of helping others. Helping becomes both the personal style of life and a core activity that gives meaning and purpose to the life of the professional. The youth worker, the camp director, the counselor, the consultant, the therapist, the teacher, the lawyer — each is a helper.

Helping is a central social process. The den mother, the committee chairman, the parent, the personal friend, the board member, the dance sponsor — each is a helper.

Help, however, is not always helpful. The recipient of the proffered help may not see it as useful. The offering may not lead to greater satisfaction or to better performance. Even less often does the helping process meet a more rigorous criterion — lead to continued growth on the part of the participants.

To begin with, a person may have varied motivations for offering help. He may wish to improve performance of a subordinate, reduce his own guilt, obtain gratitude, make someone happy, or give meaning to his own life. He may wish to demonstrate his superior skill or knowledge, induce indebtedness, control others, establish dependency, punish others, or simply meet a job prescription. These conscious or partially conscious motivations are so intermingled in any act of help that it is impossible for either the helper or the recipient to sort them out.

Depending upon his own needs and upon the way he sees the motives of the helper, the recipient will have varied reactions. He may feel gratitude, resentment, or admiration. He may feel helpless and dependent, or jealous of the helper who has the strength or resources to be in the helper role. He may feel indebted, or pressured to conform to the perceived demands or beliefs of the helper.

We have all noticed that in certain cases the recipient of the help becomes more helpless and dependent, less able to make his own decisions or initiate his own actions, less self-sufficient, more apathetic and passive, less willing to take risks, more concerned about propriety and conformity, and less creative and venturesome. We have also seen circumstances in which, following help, recipients become more creative, less dependent upon helpers, more willing to make risk decisions, more highly motivated to tackle rough problems, less concerned about conformity, and more effective at working independently or interdependently. Help may or may not lead to personal growth and organizational health.

Under certain conditions both giver and the receiver grow and develop. In general people tend to grow when there is reciprocal dependence — *inter*dependence, joint determination of goals, real communication in depth, and reciprocal trust. To the degree that these conditions are absent, people fail to grow.

From the standpoint of the organization, help must meet two criteria: the job or program must be done more effectively, and the individual members must grow and develop. These two criteria tend to merge. The program and the organization are effective only as the participants grow. The same conditions that lead to personal growth further organizational health. The following table

*Reproduced with permission from *Forum*, February 1964, pp. 25-27.

presents a theory of the helping relationship. Seven parallel sets of orientations are presented. One set of conditions maximizes help and a parallel set of conditions minimizes help.

TABLE 2.1   The Helping Relationship

Orientations That Help	*Orientations That Hinder*
1. Reciprocal trust (confidence, warmth, acceptance)	1. Distrust (fear, punitiveness, defensiveness)
2. Cooperative learning (inquiry, exploration, quest)	2. Teaching (training, advice-giving, indoctrinating)
3. Mutual growth (becoming, actualizing, fulfilling)	3. Evaluating (fixing, correcting, providing a remedy)
4. Reciprocal openness (spontaneity, candor, honesty)	4. Strategy (planning for, maneuvering, gamesmanship)
5. Shared problem solving (defining, producing alternatives, testing)	5. Modeling (demonstrating, information giving, guiding)
6. Autonomy (freedom, interdependence, equality)	6. Coaching (molding, steering, controlling)
7. Experimentation (play, innovation, provisional try)	7. Patterning (standard, static, fixed)

Reciprocal trust. People accept help from those they trust. When the relationship is one of acceptance and trust, offers of help are appreciated, listened to, seen as potentially helpful, and often acted upon. The receiver accepts help from one whose perceived motives are congenial to him. He tends to reject offers from people whose offering is seen as a guise for attempts to control, punish, correct, or gain power. "Help" is most helpful when given in an atmosphere in which people have *reciprocal* feelings of confidence, warmth, and acceptance. When one feels that his worth *as a person* is valued he is able to place himself in psychological readiness to receive aid.

Distrust. When people fear and distrust each other, even well-intended help is resisted, resented, or seen as unhelpful. Offers of help are sometimes given in service of motivations that are unacceptable to the receiver. That is, one offers help in order to place the other person in a dependent position, elicit expressions of gratitude, assert one's superiority, or punish him. In distrust the recipient's guard is up. He is likely to project his distrusts into the helper and to resist or resent the help.

One often gives help to camouflage or assuage his desire to change another person — change his character, habits, or misconceptions. The desire to change another person is essentially hostile. At a deep level, one who genuinely accepts another person does not wish to change him. A person who is accepted is allowed *to be*, become, determine his own goals and follow them at his own pace. The person who genuinely wishes to help offers the help that *the recipient wishes*. Genuine help is not foisted upon the receiver. Neither the punisher nor the child really believes that the punishment is given "for the good of the child."

Punishment or censure may be given with a conscious desire to help but usually is accompanied by a deep component of retaliation, or by a desire to hurt, control, or assert superiority. The giver often speaks of his act as "helpful" in order to rationalize to himself and to the receiver acts that are done for other motivations.

Cooperative learning. People are helpful to each other when they are engaged in a cooperative quest for learning. The learning atmosphere is one of joint inquiry and exploration. Needs for help and impulses to give help arise out of the demands of the common cooperative task. Help is thus reciprocal. The helper and helpee roles are interchangeable. Each participant has the *intent* to learn and feels he can learn from the partners and from the common task. The boss and the subordinate, the teacher and the student, the professional worker and the youth — all are most helpful when each member of the pair sees the relationship as a quest with potential learning for each. An effective project team is guided by the task and not by the teacher. It is motivated by the shared potential for learning.

Teaching. When one participant in a project sets out to teach, train, advise, persuade, or indoctrinate the other members or is *seen* as wanting to do so, the learning of each member is reduced. People cannot be taught. People must learn. People cannot be trained. They grow and develop. The most deeply helpful relationship is one of common inquiry and quest, a relationship between co-learners and co-managers in which each is equally dependent upon the other for significant help and in which each sees and accepts this relationship.

Mutual growth. The most permanent and significant help occurs in a relationship in which both members are continually growing, becoming, and seeking fulfillment. Each member participates in a mutual assessment of progress, accepts this reality of growth, and participates in a way that will maximize the growth of both participants. In a fundamental sense one can only help himself. The helper can only participate with another in an effort to create a climate in which growth can occur.

Evaluating. Growth is often hindered when one member of the helping team sets out to appraise or remedy the defects in the other member. Help is most effective when it is seen as a force moving toward growth rather than as an effort to remove gaps, remedy defects, or bring another person up to a standard criterion. The limits of growth of any person are extremely difficult to foresee or to assess. The potential for growth is consistently underestimated by both participants in the helping relationship.

Reciprocal openness. One of the essential conditions for effective human learning is the opportunity for feedback or knowledge of progress. Feedback is essential in acquiring skills, knowledge, and attitudes. In the areas where professional help is most commonly sought or given, the essential progress in learning and growth is blocked most often by the failure to obtain adequate data on people's feelings and perceptions of each other. In order to do effective work one must know how others feel and how they see things. In the usual situations in which professional helpers find themselves, there are many pressures which camouflage or distort the relevant data necessary for efficient work and best learning. Many factors reduce the availability of the relevant data: differential status, differentially perceived power, and fears that one can hurt or be hurt.

Strategy. When some part of the helping process is closed or unavailable to all participants, people are likely to become anxious, resentful, or resistant. Neither participant in the helping process can "use" the other for his own needs. The helping process is most effective when one plans *with* another, not *for* another. One is not helped when he is maneuvered into some action which he does not understand. Gamesmanship and gimmicks are antithetical to the helping process.

Shared problem solving. The productive helping relationship focuses upon the problem to be solved. Problem solving involves a joint determination of the problem, continual redefinition of the problem as successive insights are gained, joint focus upon possible alternative solutions, joint exploration of the data, and continual reality testing of the alternatives. The expertness and resources of each person are shared. The aspect of the behavior about which help is given is seen as a *shared problem* — not as a defect to be remedied or as something to be solved by the helper as consultant.

Modeling. A common image of the helping relationship is one where the helper offers a model for the advisee to follow. The expert gives a demonstration of how the recipient may solve his problems. The problem is defined by the expert. Diagnosis is made by the expert. The expert is challenged to offer additional alternatives to the solution of the problem and perhaps even to test the solutions. The process is uni-directional. The limitations of modeling are many. Dependency is increased. The pupil seldom gets better than the model. The worker tries to conform to the image of the supervisor. Growth is limited.

Autonomy. The ideal relationship for helping is an interdependent one in which each person sees the other as both helper and recipient in an exchange among equals. It is essential that each participant preserve his freedom and maintain his autonomous responsibility for guiding himself toward his own learnings, growth, and problem solving. The helper must work himself out of the helping job. The supervisor, youth worker, and counselor must become decreasingly necessary to the people being helped. Psychological weaning, however painful to both helper and recipient, must continue if help is to be truly helpful.

Coaching. The coach molds, steers, or controls the behavior of the recipient, much as a tennis coach or physical education director molds the behavior of the athlete or skill-directed recipient of help. This is another uni-directional process in which the coach is assumed to have special diagnostic and observational powers which he applies in a skilled way to the behavior of the recipient, who puts himself in the hands of the coach. The recipient of help is encouraged to maintain respectful dependency upon the coach, to not challenge his authority or expertness, to put implicit trust in his abilities and powers, and to receive from the coach motivational or inspirational guidance. Both coach and pupil suffer under this pattern. Each *may* gain in skill. Neither grows *as a person.*

Experimentation. Tentativeness and innovative experimentation are characteristic of the most productive helping relationship. There is a sense of play, excitement, and fun in the common exploratory quest for new solutions to continually changing problems. The helping process is viewed as a series of provisional trials. Each participant joins in the game and adds to the general excitement. Errors can be made — and are perhaps expected. Help is a search. Finding creative solutions to newly defined problems is a game — full of zest and intrinsic drives that keep the game going.

Patterning. Help is limited when the process is seen as an attempt on the part of one person to help another meet a prescribed standard, come up to a criterion, or reach a goal specified in advance. Helping is a creative synthesis or growth and a continual search for new forms.

"Help" is not always helpful — but *it can be.* Both the helper and the recipient can grow and learn when help is given in a relationship of trust, joint inquiry, openness, and interdependence. Growth-centered helping processes lead to healthy groups and effective organizations.

REFERENCES

**Argyris, C. (1961) Explorations in consulting-client relationships. *Human Organization* 20: 121-133.
Argyris, C. (1965) Explorations in interpersonal competence — I. *Journal of Applied Behavioral Science* 1: 58-63.
Argyris, C. (1965) Explorations in interpersonal competence — II. *Journal of Applied Behavioral Science* 1: 255-269.

Argyris, C. (1962) *Interpersonal competence and organizational effectiveness.* Homewood, Ill.: Irwin-Dorsey.

**Avila, D. L.; Combs, A. W.; and Purkey, W. W. (1971) *The helping relationship sourcebook.* Boston: Allyn & Bacon.

Boyatzis, R. E. (1974) The need for close relationships and the manager's job. In *Organizational psychology: A book of readings.* 2nd ed., eds. D. A. Kolb, I. M. Rubin, and J. M. McIntyre. Englewood Cliffs, N. J.: Prentice-Hall.

Carkuff, R. R., and Truax, C. B. (1966) Toward explaining success and failure in interpersonal learning experiences. *Personnel and Guidance Journal* 45: 723-728.

Combs, A. W.; Avila, D. L.; and Purkey, W. W. (1971) *Helping relationships: Basic concepts for the helping professions.* Boston: Allyn & Bacon.

**Glidewell, J. C. (1959) The entry problem in consultation. *Journal of Social Issues* 15(2): 51-59.

Heider, F. (1958) *The psychology of interpersonal relations.* New York: Wiley.

**Kolb, D. A., and Boyatzis, R. E. (1970) On the dynamics of the helping relationship. *Journal of Applied Behavioral Science* 6: 267-289. (Reprinted in *Organizational psychology: A book of readings.* 2nd ed., eds. D. A. Kolb, I. M. Rubin, and J. M. McIntyre. Englewood Cliffs, N. J.: Prentice-Hall.

**Lippitt, R.; Watson, B.; and Westley, B. (1958) *The dynamics of planned change* (chaps. 5 and 7). New York: Harcourt, Brace, & World.

Mann, F. C. (1968) The researcher and his working environment: Research findings and their application. In *Vistas in Science*, ed. D. L. Alvin. Albuquerque, New Mexico: University of New Mexico Press.

Rogers, C. R. (1961) *On becoming a person.* Boston: Houghton Mifflin.

**Rogers, C. R. (1958) The characteristics of a helping relationship. *Personnel and Guidance Journal* 37: 6-16.

Rogers, C. R. (1967) The interpersonal relationship in the facilitation of learning. In *Humanizing education: The person in the process,* ed. R. R. Leeper. Washington, D.C.: National Education Association.

Soper, D. W., and Combs, A. W. (1962). The helping relationship as seen by teachers and therapists. *Journal of Consulting Psychology* 26: 288.

Zaleznik, A. (1965) Interpersonal relations in organizations. In *Handbook of organizations,* ed. J. G. March. Chicago: Rand McNally.

**References preceded by a double asterisk are those judged most basic or important.

CHAPTER THREE

Surfacing Problems—
Helping People
Learn to Generate
Information

"This creature is like a great snake."
"Are you mad! It is formed like a tree trunk!"
"You are both fools as well as blind! The thing
is obviously made of huge leaflike flaps!"

Three Blind Men
Encountering an Elephant

INTRODUCTION

Both the consultant-helping and the self-helping process, in groups and in organizations, must start with some kind of data-gathering process; information must be generated about the problems in that system. Action plans and specific interventions should *always* be based upon adequate diagnosis, so a good group problem solving process *always* starts with information gathering and diagnosis. The building blocks for diagnosis are the specific data about the group. Elsewhere, we have described several different models of *using* data, which change agents can apply in their consulting and change activities with organizations (Sashkin, 1974; Sashkin, Morris, and Horst, 1973). In this chapter, however, we are concerned only with making one basic point: *problem-specific data must be generated by the persons involved in the problem if relevant actions and appropriate interventions for change are to follow.* Of particular importance is the fact that the group(s) affected must be the one(s) to furnish the data in the first place.

There are many ways to collect data from groups. In this chapter, we will propose only three designs, one on interviewing, one on surveying, and one on surfacing data about values. In the interviewing design, the participant learns the skills of a consultant, who must collect data about a system that has requested help. In the surveying design, however, the participants play the roles of system members themselves, learning how to generate data about themselves that can then be used to initiate various problem-solving processes. In the third design, on values, participants also learn how to generate data about themselves, but in this case the data are individual rather than system-specific, and process- rather than content-oriented. The first design is the most appropriate for consultant-change agent training in the classroom, the second is best suited for real groups in an organization, and the third, though written here for use in the classroom, can also be used in real organizations. All three can easily be adapted to either situation.

There is a fourth, equally important, data-gathering methodology commonly used by change agents and consultants: observation of the client group. Chapter Five, "Group Process," provides some basic skill training for this information-generation approach.

I. SPECIFIC SKILL-DEVELOPMENT AND LEARNING DESIGNS

A.   **Design for Learning Data-Gathering Skills: Interviewing**

1.   *Purpose.* This exercise is designed to give skill practice in interviewing as a consultant. It is based on a format of practice and repractice, with peer consultation intervening between repractice times. The interview situation calls for the consultant to obtain general information from the interviewee, thus the primary focus is on how to establish a relationship with the respondent that will facilitate information-giving. The behavioral skills associated with this type of interview are the focus of this learning design. (Participants might find it helpful to read Gibb's paper on "Defensive Communication" in Chapter Four prior to this exercise.)

2.   *Materials needed.* Case background and role sheets, paper and pencils, small table and two chairs.

3.   *Steps in using the design.*

   a.   State purpose of the activity.

   b.   Read general background information.

   c.   Divide class into small groups.

   d.   Have groups devise plans of action for interviews.

   e.   Select the first consultant and set up the role-play situation.

   f.   Stop the action and discuss the interactions.

   g.   Have groups prepare new interviews.

   h.   If time is available, repeat until all group members have practice.

4.   *Deriving learnings.* Following this exercise, the instructor should explore in some depth with the group the reasons why this interview was difficult and the specific skills in interviewing that are needed to overcome this difficulty.

   The instructor may then wish to present a brief lecture on the various types of interview situations (personnel selection, exit, counseling, etc.) and have the group determine the similarities and differences among them, as well as the specific behavioral skill need implications for each type of interview. Some specific questions one might explore with the group are:

   — What different types of interview might an organization development consultant conduct?

   — Would the interview case used here have been done differently if this were the tenth or twentieth interview instead of the first?

   — How precisely can the behavioral skills needed for this interview to succeed be defined? Can we make a list?

   — When is it appropriate to focus on specific problems in an interview? Should the interviewer attempt to give help with such problems when trying to obtain general information is the primary purpose for the interview?

   — When is it appropriate to advise the interviewee of the confidential nature of the interview?

   — To what extent are the interviewing skills identified as necessary for the success of this interview also needed by the typical supervisor or middle-level manager?

5. *Support materials.* Following are some brief reading materials that are particularly relevant to this design, after which appear the materials needed for the role play.

INTERVIEWING SKILLS*

Generally, there are two significant factors in any interview situation. First, the interviewer must establish a degree of rapport with the interviewee. That is, the interviewee should be made to feel comfortable in the discussion. Perhaps the best way to do this is for the interviewer to present himself initially as openly as possible: who he or she is, why he is there, what he is doing, what he hopes to accomplish, what the information will be used for. At an appropriate time in the interview it is generally desirable to assure the respondent that he or she will not be quoted without explicit permission; that no one except the interviewer will be told what the respondent actually said.

Second, the interviewee should do most of the talking. While this principle is true for almost any interview situation, and seems obvious, it is surprising how often an interviewer will take up more air time than the interviewee. Afterward, the interviewer may even be puzzled to find that relatively little information was obtained. In a general information-gathering interview, this factor becomes extremely important. The interviewer should, at least during the first half of the session, avoid asking directive questions. A Rogerian, client-led type of interview style is most productive for general data gathering and is facilitated when the first factor noted above — the establishment of a good interviewer-interviewee relationship — is effectively attended to. For some specific details on the interviewer-interviewee relationship, in the context of a structured survey approach, see "Building a Good Interviewing Relationship" in Section II of this chapter.

STIMULATING DISCUSSION – PROBING[†]

One of the most challenging and important aspects of the interviewer's work is probing. The quality of the interview depends a great deal on the interviewer's ability to probe meaningfully and successfully.

What is Probing?

Probing is the technique used by the interviewer to stimulate discussion and obtain more information. A question has been asked and an answer given. For any number of reasons, the answer may be inadequate and require the interviewer to seek more information to meet the survey objectives. Probing is the art of getting this additional information.

Probes have two major functions:

1. Probes motivate the respondent to communicate more fully so that he enlarges on what he has said, or clarifies what he has said, or explains the reasons behind what he has said.

2. Probes focus the discussion on the specific content of the interview so that irrelevant and unnecessary information can be eliminated.

*Kahn and Cannell (1957) present an excellent overview of the methodology of interviewing, which the instructor may want to refer students to prior to this exercise. The paper by Jack Gibb in Chapter Two would also be good review material prior to this learning design and so are the following readings.

[†] Reprinted in abridged and modified form from the Survey Research Center *Interviewer's Manual* (Ann Arbor, Mich.: Survey Research Center, Institute for Social Research, The University of Michigan, 1969). Used by special permission.

Probes must perform these two functions without introducing bias by avoiding the introduction of unplanned and unwanted influences.

Kinds of Probes

Several different neutral techniques which should appear as a natural and casual part of normal conversation may be used to stimulate a fuller, clearer response.

- *A brief assertion of understanding and interest.* By saying such things as "uh-huh" or "I see" or "Yes" or "That's interesting," the interviewer indicates that she has heard the response given so far, that she is interested in it, and that she expects more. These things serve to stimulate the respondent to talk further.

- *An expectant pause.* The simplest way to convey to a respondent that you know he has begun to answer the question, but that you feel he has more to say, is to be silent. The pause — often accompanied by an expectant look or a nod of the head — allows the respondent time to gather his thoughts.

  Accepting pauses during an interview is often difficult for the new interviewer. She has the feeling that she must keep things moving. A few seconds of silence seem to last forever. Pauses are useful, however, in encouraging communication, and the art of using them should be acquired.

  One word of caution. The interviewer must be sensitive to each individual respondent in using this technique. Some respondents may be truly out of ideas, and a pause cannot stimulate them to further discussion. Instead of the "pregnant pause" you have an "embarrassed silence."

- *Repeating the question.* When the respondent does not seem to understand the question, when he misinterprets it, when he seems unable to make up his mind, or when he strays from the subject, it is often useful to repeat the question just as it is written in the questionnaire. Many respondents, hearing it for a second time, realize what kind of answer is needed. They may not have heard the question fully the first time, or missed the question's emphasis.

- *Repeating the respondent's reply.* Simply repeating, in your own words, what the respondent has said as soon as he has stopped talking is often an excellent probe. Hearing his idea repeated often stimulates further thought by the respondent.

- *A neutral question or comment.* Neutral questions or comments are frequently used to obtain clearer and fuller responses. Some examples are:

    "Could you tell me more about your thinking on that?"

    "I'm not sure I understand what you have in mind."

    "Why do you think that is so?"

    "Could you tell me why you feel that way?"

    "What do you think causes that?"

    "Anything else?"

Such questions indicate the interviewer is interested and they make a direct bid for more information. This technique takes a while for newer interviewers to master, but it is a dependable and fruitful technique when used correctly. It requires that the interviewer recognize immediately just how the respondent's answer has failed to meet the objective of the question, and that the interviewer then formulate a neutral type of question to elicit the information needed. The interviewer's manner of asking these neutral questions is important. Needless to say, a strident, demanding tone of voice can damage rapport.

● *Asking for further clarification.* In probing, it is sometimes a good technique for the interviewer to appear slightly bewildered by the respondent's answer, and intimate in her probe that it might be herself who failed to understand. (For example: "I'm not quite sure I know what you mean by that — could you tell me a little more?") This technique can arouse the respondent's desire to co-operate with a human being trying to do a good job. It should not be overplayed, however. The respondent should not get the feeling that the interviewer doesn't know when a question is properly answered, or can't understand the respondent. This approach is very useful in dealing with what appears to be an answer that is inconsistent with previous answers. For example, the interviewer might simply say, "I'm sorry, but I'm not sure I understand. Did you mention previously . . .?" and then briefly mention the respondent's earlier answer. It is most important that you appear to ask this question because you did not understand; do not appear to contradict or "cross-examine" the respondent in any way. If you feel you cannot ask for clarification of an inconsistent answer without upsetting the respondent, simply go right on with other questions.

Probing Methods Should Be Neutral

Remember that we have described probing as the technique that motivates the respondent to communicate more fully, and that focuses the discussion on specific topics. We also said these two things must be done without introducing bias.

The potential for bias is great in the use of probes. Under the pressure of the interviewing situation, the interviewer may quite unintentionally imply that some responses are more acceptable than others, or (s)he may hint that a respondent might wish to consider or include this or that in giving his responses.

BURTON ELECTRIC PRODUCTS CORPORATION

Background

R. G. Burton founded the firm back in 1919 to build electronic parts for the new radio industry. He was a very intense man and a strong leader, building a highly successful organization. Even during the Great Depression, very few of his employees were laid off their jobs. He was quite paternalistic toward his workers; he insisted on intense personal loyalty, and rewarded this with a rather progressive scheme of benefits and pensions.

Apparently because of his desire to retain personal control over the firm, old Burton never expanded as he might have; today the company is still of moderate size, about two thousand employees in all. Even when he retired ten years ago, he continued to exercise a large degree of control, which ended only at his death two years ago. His son, Thomas ("young") Burton has been president for ten years, but only since his father's death has he really had control over the firm.

In response to some problems that seemed to be getting worse rather than better Mr./Ms. Wylie, the Executive Vice-President of Personnel, contacted Dr. John/Joan Conners, an organization development consultant. After several discussions with Wylie and with young Burton, Conners agreed to begin preliminary work on the basis of one day per week for one month, after which s/he would meet with the top management group and decide what to do next.

Conners decided to interview first a number of upper- and middle-level managers. Wylie put out a memo last week informing all managers at these levels of the plan. We are going to observe one such interview, with Mr. Robert Burns, who is Assistant Manager of the Miniaturized Assembly Division (which employs some two hundred persons). This is Conners's first scheduled interview. It is Wednesday morning and Dr. Conners is about to enter Mr. Burns's office.

BURTON ELECTRIC PRODUCTS CORPORATION

Role for John/Joan Conners, Organization Development Consultant

You were recently contacted by Mr./Ms. Graham/Greta Wylie, Executive Vice-President of Personnel for the Burton Electric Products Corporation. In several discussions with you (s)he described some of the problems Burton is currently facing. His/her greatest concern has to do with recent unionization attempts. The founder of the firm, R. G. Burton (now deceased), had been fervently anti union all his life and had run his organization very much on his own, while expressing real concern for his workers, albeit in a rather paternalistic fashion. For example, even during the Great Depression no worker of more than one year's tenure had been laid off. Burton insisted that all of his management and supervisory staff display an equal regard for the workers, and this approach seems to have had much to do with his success in avoiding several unionization efforts over the past thirty years. Burton retired ten years ago, although he continued to exercise significant control over company policies until his death two years ago.

During the past year several unions have begun efforts to gain representation of the workers, including one particularly active and antimanagement local of an international union. While Wylie is not opposed to unionization per se, (s)he is very concerned lest the more extreme elements take over and win the upcoming election.

The organization employs some two thousand men and women, about half on routine assembly-line work involving electronic subassemblies for consumer products, and the remainder in a variety of jobs (e.g., a small R&D lab, a moderate-sized sales force, and several specialized product groups that construct equipment to order for the radio-TV industry). Pay is somewhat below the community average, but there is an excellent health and pension plan (developed many years ago by the founder).

After speaking with the current president, Tom Burton, you agreed to spend one day a week for the next month in preliminary data-collection and diagnostic activities, after which your findings will be reviewed with the top management group (ten persons, including the president). You decided to begin by holding some unstructured interviews with middle and top management. It is now Wednesday morning and you are to interview Mr. Robert Burns, Assistant Manager of the Miniaturized Assembly Division (which employs some two hundred persons). This is your first scheduled interview.

BURTON ELECTRIC PRODUCTS CORPORATION

Role for Robert Burns, Assistant Manager, Miniaturized Assembly Division

You are one of two assistant managers of this division of the Burton Electric Products Company, which employs some two hundred persons (about two-thirds female) in assembly-line production of miniaturized TV receiver components. You've been with the company for ten years, starting out of high school as a first-line supervisor and working your way up to your present position.

A lot of changes have occurred in the past five years, since old Burton retired and then passed on. You can recall a time when the line workers seemed generally pleased with their work, taking an almost professional pride in their jobs and expressing strong loyalty to the firm and to old Burton personally. Of course, a lot of those people are now retired, too. The younger workers seem to have none of their spirit or loyalty. In fact, there has been considerable conflict between the larger group of young workers and an older, smaller group. The latter frequently get into arguments with their younger co-workers over the younger workers' apparent lack of concern for the quality of their work. It especially infuriates the older people when, after carefully wiring a complex circuit, a younger worker makes an error in the final assembly that results in the assembly being rejected. The conflict is also reflected in the drive for the upcoming unionization election: older workers support a small local union, while many of the younger people are pushing hard for the radical local of a giant international.

Although you've always felt a strong dedication to, and enjoyment in, your job, these recent problems are beginning to get you down. You've been spending more time with your family than you used to, which is nice, but you can see where it's partly just an escape from the work tensions. If young Burton could only take a strong leadership role, like his father, things might work out, but he seems to be getting more and more confused and uncertain. In fact, he even hired some kind of consultant to try and clear up this problem, something his father would never have done. This Conners has decided (s)he wants to talk to a bunch of middle managers, including yourself, but you can't see what (s)he hopes to find out that Wylie (the Vice-President of Personnel) and young Burton haven't already told him/her. If (s)he's got some ideas, why doesn't (s)he just submit then to young Burton? You're kind of worried that (s)he might make things worse, especially in the union conflict, rather than better; at least you've been able to keep things under control between the old and young workers (though one pretty vocal older man was recently beaten up by a bunch of young fellows). Anyway you're not sure you should tell Conners anything about this, certainly not until you know where (s)he stands or what (s)he wants to do about the unionization problem.

B.   Design for Learning Data-Gathering Skills: Surveying

1.   *Purpose.* This design has two aims, when used with a real organizational group: (1) learning some elementary survey-development methods; (2) generating information around a specific real problem of concern to the group. In an organization, the group will come to the session with job-specific roles and content issues, thus no special materials will be needed.

In a classroom situation, only the first purpose is of real significance, although the class might choose to look on a real problem they have been experiencing, say in working to-gether as a group. However, we see it as of primary importance that the class focus on the *process* of survey data gathering, not on the *content* of a particular problem. Thus, the in-structor may use a case, and could even have students take on the roles of persons described in the case.

When used with "real" client groups, this activity is *always* used as *part* of a more complete problem-solving process, either as a start-up to a development process that will take place over time or as an activity that takes place after it becomes clear to the group that it cannot proceed very far until more relevant data about its organization have been gener-ated.

2.   *Materials needed.* Large group meeting space, areas for small groups of four to five to meet, movable chairs, paper and pencils, marking pens and newsprint, masking tape for posting newsprint, hand-held electronic calculator.

3.   *Steps in using the design.*
   a.   State the purpose for data collection.
   b.   Clarify the process for the meeting.
   c.   Have group brainstorm needed information.
   d.   Evaluate and combine information areas.
   e.   Form small groups to create survey questions.
   f.   Have small groups meet.
   g.   Reconvene and post question lists.
   h.   Conduct trial survey by all responding to questions.
   i.   Count responses and post results.
   j.   Plan for next steps.

4.   *Deriving learnings.* In an organizational setting, this design would be self-completing — it flows on to other issues and tasks, as indicated above. Still, it would be useful to set aside some time for a discussion of the group's process — how it went about accomplishing the design and how its process interaction could be improved. Some additional questions could be:

   — Which other groups in the organization would benefit by learning this methodology? Management? What levels?

   — How can we — this group — help others learn?

In a classroom setting, time should certainly be allowed for discussion of the implications for use of this design. Questions include:

— In what circumstances should this learning design be used in an organization?

— How could this be done with two different groups? What would be the value in doing so?

— How does the group decide which areas and items should go into a final survey instrument for use in the organization?

5. *Support materials.*

USING SURVEYS TO FACILITATE CHANGE*

Survey methodology has, in the past twenty years, developed to the point of a true science. This state has been facilitated by several research organizations, perhaps most prominently the Survey Research Center of the Institute for Social Research at the University of Michigan. ISR's Center for Research on Utilization of Scientific Knowledge has been prominent in the development of the use of survey methods to facilitate organizational change (Bowers, 1973; Neff, 1965). Their work has resulted in the publication of several basic resource books of survey questionnaires, which anyone interested in helping people in organizations should be familiar with. In fact, there are so many readily available questionnaire instruments that the user of this methodology need only rarely create a totally new instrument from scratch. Even so, it is also true that every group and every organization has its own, unique problems, or has unique ways of referring to organizational problems or concerns. For this reason, almost any survey instrument selected from those available would need some additions, modifications, or omissions. It is, then, extremely useful for clients to have the basic skills needed to develop well-constructed questionnaire items.

There are two aims in helping clients learn to use survey methods. First, the client should be able to determine the appropriate areas for investigation. Second, the client should know where to find useful questionnaire survey instruments and how to modify or extend an instrument to meet the needs of a particular situation.

C. Design for Learning to Help Groups Collect Information about Value Differences

1. *Purpose.* This design is an example of a specific technique that can be used to help a group elicit data about the members' attitudes toward particular aspects of the work situation. Equally important for some groups is the aim of looking closely at the assumptions group members have as they begin to help their group set objectives and goals for the future. And, a third purpose for collecting data about value differences may result from a suspicion that it is this kind of problem that is keeping that group from attaining its objectives or working together effectively. Thus, because of this latter objective, the design could also be considered part of Chapter Eight, on conflict management.

2. *Materials needed.* In order to conduct this learning design it is necessary to have an open room where participants can walk freely to any part of the room. Chairs, therefore, must be movable. Needed also are masking tape, newsprint and markers, or chalkboard.

---

*The basic reference sources for the use of survey methods to facilitate change in groups and organizations are Baumgartel (1959), Bowers (1973), Mann (1957), Neff (1965), and Taylor and Bowers (1972).

3.   *Steps in using the design.*

   a.   Choose the content area for discussion.

   b.   Brainstorm important values in this area.

   c.   Decide upon the most important values.

   d.   Post the agree-disagree scale categories.

   e.   Give instructions for next steps.

   f.   Have group members take stands on the first issue.

   g.   Record individuals' positions on the first value issue.

   h.   Repeat the process for all value statements.

   i.   Discuss differences and similarities in group members' positions.

   (The purpose of the design is achieved after this step. The following two steps begin the real problem solving process on value differences.)

   j.   Choose the statement on which group members differ most widely.

   k.   Stop the action and discuss learnings.

4.   *Deriving learnings.* Some questions that might be used with the group are:

   — How did you feel when you discovered that there were that many people with points of view different from your own?

   — In what kinds of groups or organizations would you use a design like this one?

   — As you began to discuss why you were where you were on the scale and heard why others were where they were, did you really feel you were as far apart as you first seemed to be?

   — Do you think that some of the differences are really misunderstandings and not real value differences between the groups?

   — What next steps would you take to work on the value differences if you decide that you really *can't* get together?

II. CONCEPTUAL SUPPORT MATERIALS: SURFACING PROBLEMS

THE IMPORTANCE OF GENERATING DATA

Effective helping is data-based. Without information, actions cannot be planned on sound, rational, grounds. At best, results would be hit or miss, without reliable information. For this same reason people cannot be expected to learn improved problem solving processes without also learning how to generate information. The generation of valid, reliable data is the first "primary task" of the interventionist, according to Argyris (1970), and in accomplishing this the interventionist is teaching client-system members how to do it themselves.

Like other elements of the helping and the problem-solving processes, information generation depends on both methods or procedures and skills. Interviewing is largely a matter of skill, although certain procedures have been developed that are of some help (see the *Interviewer's Manual* published by the Institute for Social Research). Noninterview questionnaire survey methods do not involve much skill, except in item construction. Often an appropriate survey questionnaire can be found, rather than created (several volumes of questionnaire instruments are generally available; see the reference list at the end of the chapter), and a very useful general organizational survey instrument was developed by Taylor and Bowers (1972). In most cases, however, it is necessary to add items of particular relevance to a particular group or organization. Thus, some understanding of and skill at questionnaire-item development is generally desirable for client groups and is certainly required for helpers or consultants.

Of course, the ability to gather data does not guarantee that the data will be used; using information to solve problems is a process that must be learned and practiced. Yet, information generation is a prerequisite for effective problem solving. If a helper does not leave a client with new or improved data-gathering skills and methods, the client cannot be expected to apply effectively any new problem solving process in the absence of the helper. In such a case, the helper has created a dependency situation and has failed in reaching the goal of increased client self-support and adaptive capacity.

LOCATING A PROBLEM*
Jacobo A. Varela

Locating the problem is essential to achieving a solution. Very often a group meets to solve a problem, arrives at a solution, and later learns, to the chagrin of all, that the problem did not lie where they had thought. A perhaps trivial, though interesting, case occurred when a group in a company got together to decide how to keep outsiders from going into the company washrooms, thereby keeping them neat. A solution was finally adopted: the washrooms would be locked and every employee given a key. In this way, no outsider could have access to the washrooms, and they would therefore remain clean. The locks were duly put in place, and keys carefully issued to all with the admonition that they were for personal use only. Later inspections showed that the washrooms continued to be just as messy as before. Obviously, the problem had not been solved. The elimination of outsiders had been thoroughly accomplished, to the discomfiture of clients, friends, and other visitors who found they could no longer make use of these facilities. When eventually a meeting was called to solve the problem of "What can be done to assure that our washrooms are tidy at all times?" an extremely simple solution involving brief training sessions

*Reprinted from Jacobo A. Varela, *Psychological solutions to social problems: An introduction to social technology* (New York: Academic Press, 1971), pp. 160-161. Used by permission.

was found. The washrooms are now perfectly tidy; they are open to the general public; and, most of the employees have misplaced or lost their keys, which had proved to be an utterly useless expense.

The problem described above was a minor one in which a minor expense and some discomfort to others was involved. Nevertheless, solving the wrong problem quite often proves to be very costly and embarrassing to many, and it can create conflict as well.

THE FIRST PRIMARY TASK OF AN INTERVENTIONIST: GENERATION OF VALID AND USEFUL INFORMATION*
Chris Argyris

First, it has been accepted as axiomatic that valid and useful information is the foundation for effective intervention. Valid information is that which describes the factors, plus their interrelationships, that create the problem for the client system. There are several tests for checking the validity of the information. In increasing degrees of power they are public verifiability, valid prediction, and control over the phenomena.

It is conceivable that a client system may be helped even though valid information is not generated. Sometimes changes occur in a positive direction without the interventionist having played any important role. These changes, although helpful in that specific instance, lack the attribute of helping the organization to learn and to gain control over its problem solving capability.

The importance of information that the clients can use to control their destiny points up the requirement that the information must not only be valid, it must be useful. Valid information that cannot be used by the clients to alter their system is equivalent to valid information about cancer that cannot be used to cure cancer eventually. An interventionist's diagnosis should include variables that are manipulable by the clients and are complete enough so that if they are manipulated effective change will follow.

THE SURVEY†

What is a Survey?

A survey involves collecting data from a sample of people who are often selected to represent accurately some larger population. Sometimes, as in an organization, the entire population is included in the survey. The data are collected by means of a carefully developed set of questions. The persons responding may be interviewed, or may fill out printed questionnaire forms. In either case, the questions are "standardized" — the same questions are asked of every respondent, in the same way. The answers are then put together in an organized fashion so that conclusions can be drawn. This information can then be made available for use in working on specific problems.

Types of Surveys

A survey of the use students make of a university library is one example of the many organizational topics which may be studied through the use of the survey method. Today, the survey is

*From Chris Argyris, *Intervention theory and method* (Reading, Mass.: Addison-Wesley, 1970), pp. 17-18. Reproduced with the permission of the author and publisher.

†Reprinted in abridged and modified form from Survey Research Center, *Interviewer's manual,* Chapter 3. Ann Arbor, Mich.: Survey Research Center, Institute for Social Research, The University of Michigan, 1969. Used by special permission.

being used to advantage in opinion polling, market research, government surveys, and social research. These types of survey activity and the various ways in which they are used are described briefly below.

The Public Opinion Poll

The polls are perhaps the most well-known branch of the survey field. The polls are outgrowths of the "straw" or informal votes conducted by newspapers for the purpose of forecasting elections as early as 1824. During the 1930s, a number of independent polling agencies were organized, such as Roper and Gallup polls. Since then, organizations have polled public opinion on elections, specific topics of interest, public affairs, etc. One of the contributions of the straw vote has been its success in arousing popular interest in survey work.

The Market Research Survey

Another type of survey activity is done by business in consumer market research. Each year, thousands of surveys are made by market research groups to determine consumer needs and the effectiveness of marketing programs. Market surveys are focused on the consumers' attitude toward current products on the market, consumers' demand for new products, the unsatisfied needs of consumers, etc. Work in the market research field has helped bring manufacturers closer to the needs of the consumer, and has helped contribute to public acceptance of results based on interviewing small samples of respondents.

The Government Survey

Government surveys are an old idea. From the earliest times governments have taken inventories of their human resources for taxing, military, and legislative purposes. In addition, democratic procedures in government brought forth a new need — the need for better communication between the people and their officials. Through the development of sampling and other survey techniques, it is now possible to get information about public opinions, desires, and problems with an ease never dreamed of by the framers of the Constitution. Various government agencies conduct or sponsor a wide variety of surveys designed to measure public opinion and to gather statistics about the various segments of the population.

The Social Survey

The social survey is used to gather information about the social and economic conditions of the population, or segments of the population. Social surveys are mainly an outgrowth of the European social reform movements of the 19th century. In France, England, and other countries, philanthropists and others interested in social welfare began to study prison conditions, treatment of mental patients, poverty, and other social problems. These early studies were grounded on the idea that until the size and nature of these problems could be measured, very little effective action could be taken to improve conditions.

The Organizational Survey

The methods so painstakingly developed over the past thirty or forty years have been applied with increasing frequency in organizations of all types. Originally, the aim was little more than providing management with accurate readings of how workers felt about their jobs, the organization, and the actions of management. More recently, survey methods have been used to gather information that points out problem issues and can be used to help define and then begin to solve problems. Often the respondents will be given the actual survey results, for use in actively working on problems in their own departments or work groups.

Conducting a Survey

To the casual observer, surveying may appear to be a simple procedure. The questions asked seem obvious enough and the tabulated percentage of responses add up to one hundred. The casual observer seldom suspects the detailed labors which lie behind the neat columns of figures. The fact is that a survey is carried out, step by step, with the utmost care.

Survey procedures in earlier days tended to be haphazard and impractical. Over the years, through experiment and experience, researchers have developed more scientific and systematic methods. Developments in social science and statistics were especially instrumental in speeding this progress. Researchers came to realize that they could reliably estimate conditions in large populations from careful observations of relatively small numbers.

Just as a chemist must follow a chemical formula exactly in order to make the desired product, so the researcher must follow the survey formula exactly in order to produce accurate information. Many people involved in the survey process must carry out their own work accurately and they must work together as a team if the survey is to be successful.

Steps in Conducting a Survey

Here are some general steps in the survey procedure:

   a.   defining the study objectives;

   b.   choosing the study design;

   c.   selecting the sample;

   d.   constructing and pretesting the questionnaire;

   e.   interviewing the sample or administering a written questionnaire;

   f.   coding the interview or questionnaire responses;

   g.   tabulating and analyzing the results; and

   h.   preparing a summary of the results.

BUILDING A GOOD INTERVIEWING RELATIONSHIP*

On first thought it might seem simple to go and ask another person questions about various topics. By their very nature human beings communicate with those around them — with family, friends, co-workers, casual acquaintances, sales clerks, etc. We all learn early to participate in the question-and-answer process, and it would appear that this constant training would simply facilitate the job of the interviewer.

Communication is not simple, however, and communication in interviewing is complicated by the personalities of the people involved. It has been found that respondents usually react more to their relationships with the interviewer than to the content of the questions they are asked. In other words, respondents may remember more about the interviewer and about how the interview was conducted than they will about the topics covered in the interview. This emphasizes the importance of the interviewer being an understanding person capable of accepting what the respondent says without apparent judgment or rejection of the respondent.

The intent of survey research interviews is to gather information. They are not intended to change or influence the respondent. The aim is simply to find out how things are and how people

*Reprinted in abridged and modified form from Survey Research Center, *Interviewer's manual,* Chapter 3. Ann Arbor, Mich.: Survey Research Center, Institute for Social Research, The University of Michigan, 1969. Used by special permission.

feel and think. In order to maintain an objective, information-gathering atmosphere, the respondent must find satisfaction in talking to a receptive and understanding person without fear of appearing inadequate.

Thus, the first step in the interviewing process involves setting up a friendly relationship with the respondent and getting him to cooperate in giving the needed information.

Increasing Respondent's Receptiveness

There are three factors which help bring about the respondent's receptiveness:

1. *The respondent needs to feel that his acquaintance with the interviewer will be pleasant and satisfying.*

2. *The respondent needs to see the interview as being important and worthwhile.*

The extent to which an interviewer might have to explain the survey will vary considerably from respondent to respondent. In some interview situations, a respondent knows what is expected of him; for example, in a job interview or in an interview with a doctor. This is not the case in most survey research interviews.

The full burden of the introduction is on the interviewer, for few respondents know what is expected of them. All respondents, even those who are least interested, should feel that the survey is important and that their cooperation will be meaningful not only to themselves, but to the survey results.

3. *Barriers to the interview in the respondent's mind need to be overcome.*

Usually the respondent will be polite enough to let the interviewer talk. The interviewer must use this time to advantage; and must be alert to doubts the respondent may feel, even if the respondent does not express them vocally.

The interviewer's own state of mind is often reflected in the respondent's reaction to the request for an interview. If the interviewer's approach is uncertain or uneasy, if the interviewer cannot answer the questions the respondent asks and appears unknowing about the work and its purposes, this feeling is communicated to the respondent who will react accordingly. The interviewer must approach the introduction with a view to the respondent's needs and goals.

"Rapport" is the goal. Rapport is the term used to describe the personal relationship of confidence and understanding between the interviewer and the respondent; rapport provides the foundation for good interviewing. The respondent's impression during the introduction, and the manner in which the interviewer adapts him or herself to the situation from the respondent's point of view, determines considerably the rapport that will develop.

Characteristics of a Good Interviewing Relationship

The characteristics of a good interviewing relationship can be described in the following terms:

Warmth and responsiveness on the part of the interviewer. The respondent needs to feel the interviewer is genuinely interested in him, and accepts him as a person.

A permissive atmosphere in which the respondent feels completely free to express any feeling or viewpoint. The interviewer's attitude is one of complete acceptance and understanding of the respondent's statements. The respondent should be entirely free to "let down his hair." By attitude and behavior, the interviewer demonstrates that no answer is out of place.

Freedom from any kind of pressure or coercion. The interviewer in no way states ideas, reactions, or preferences. Although permissive and understanding, the interviewer remains objective in the same manner as any professional person when dealing with clients.

In this kind of atmosphere, the respondent obtains much satisfaction in "opening up" without argument or hurry by the interviewer. The respondent gets the feeling that his ideas are acceptable to the interviewer. It is the feeling of "Here is that rare thing — a person to whom I can really talk." Nothing that the respondent says is too trivial for the attention of the interviewer. *Through his relationship with the interviewer, the respondent not only feels free to talk, but is actually stimulated to do so.*

Leaving the Respondent

The respondent should feel that his time has been well spent and that the interview has been worthwhile. Any questions or doubts he might have about the interview should be cleared up before the interviewer leaves. Finally, the respondent should be warmly thanked for his cooperation and time.

REFERENCES

**Argyris, C. (1970) *Intervention theory and method.* Reading, Mass.: Addison-Wesley.

**Bales, R. F. (1950) *Interaction process analysis.* Cambridge, Mass.: Addison-Wesley.

Baumgartel, H. (1959) Using employee questionnaire results for improving organizations: The survey "feedback" experiment. *Kansas Business Review* 12: 2-6.

Beckhard, R. (1967) The confrontation meeting. *Harvard Business Review* 45(2): 149-155.

Bowers, D. G. (1973) OD techniques and their results in 23 organizations. *Journal of Applied Behavioral Science* 9: 21-43.

Festinger, L., and Katz, D. (1953) *Research methods in the behavioral sciences.* New York: Holt, Rinehart & Winston.

Goode, W. J., and Hatt, P. K. (1952) *Methods in social research.* New York: McGraw-Hill.

Jones, J. E., and Pfeiffer, J. W. (1973) *The 1973 annual handbook for group facilitators.* Iowa City, Iowa: University Associates.

**Kahn, R. L., and Cannell, C. F. (1957) *The dynamics of interviewing.* New York: Wiley.

Kish, L. (1967) *Survey sampling.* New York: Wiley.

Libo, L. M. (1954) *Measuring group cohesiveness.* Ann Arbor, Mich.: Institute for Social Research, The University of Michigan.

Mann, F. C. (1957) Studying and creating change: A means to understanding social organization. In *Research in industrial human relations,* ed. C. Arensberg et al. New York: Harper & Brothers. (Industrial Relations Research Association Publication No. 17.)

Mellinger, G. D. (1956) Interpersonal trust as a factor in communication. *Journal of Abnormal and Social Psychology* 52: 304-309.

Merton, R. K.; Fisbe, M.; and Kendall, P. L. (1956) *The focused interview.* Glencoe, Ill.: Free Press.

Neff, F. W. (1965) Survey research: A tool for problem diagnosis and improvement in organizations. In *Applied Sociology,* eds. S. M. Miller and A. W. Gouldner. New York: Free Press.

**Oppenheim, A. N. (1966) *Questionnaire design and attitude measurement.* New York: Basic Books.

Patchen, M.; Pelz, D. C.; and Allen, C. W. (1954) *Some questionnaire measures of employee motivation and morale.* Ann Arbor, Mich.: Institute for Social Research, The University of Michigan.

Pfeiffer, J. W., and Jones, J. E. (1972) *The 1972 annual handbook for group facilitators.* Iowa City, Iowa: University Associates.

Richardson, S. A.; Dohrenwend, B. S.; and Klein, D. (1965) *Interviewing: Its forms and functions.* New York: Basic Books.

**Robinson, J. P.; Athanasiou, R.; and Head, K. B. (1969) *Measures of occupational attitudes and occupational characteristics.* Ann Arbor, Mich.: Survey Research Center, Institute for Social Research, The University of Michigan.

**Robinson, J. P., and Shaver, P. R. (1973) *Measures of social psychological attitudes.* Rev. ed. Ann Arbor, Mich.: Institute for Social Research, The University of Michigan.

Sashkin, M. (1974) Models and roles of change agents. In *The 1974 annual handbook for group facilitators,* eds. J. W. Pfeiffer and J. E. Jones. San Diego, Calif.: University Associates.

Sashkin, M.; Frohman, M. A.; and Kavanagh, M. J. (1976: in preparation) *Organization development: Research and practice.* Homewood, Ill.: Irwin.

Sashkin, M.; Morris, W. C.; and Horst, L. (1973) A comparison of social and organizational change models: Information flow and data use processes. *Psychological Review* **80**: 510-526.

**Selltiz, C.; Jahoda, M.; Deutsch, M.; and Cook, S. W. (1959) *Research methods in social relations.* 2nd ed. New York: Holt, Rinehart, & Winston. (1st ed., New York: Dryden Press, 1951.)

Simon, S. B., and Kirschenbaum, H., eds. (1973) *Readings in values clarification.* Minneapolis, Minn.: Winston Press.

Simon, S. B.; Howe, L. W.; and Kirschenbaum, H. (1972) *Values clarification: A handbook for teachers and students.* New York: Hart.

**Survey Research Center, Field Office. (1969) *Interviewer's manual.* Ann Arbor, Mich.: Institute for Social Research, The University of Michigan.

Taylor, J. C., and Bowers, D. G. (1972) *Survey of organizations.* Ann Arbor, Mich.: Institute for Social Research, The University of Michigan.

**References preceded by a double asterisk are those judged most basic or important.

CHAPTER FOUR

Feedback: Helping Others Learn to Share Information

"What! Me, improve? How, I ask you, could I improve?"

INTRODUCTION

The quote above is an example of ineffective use of feedback by the recipient. But, it *might* have been provoked by poor skill on the part of whoever was *giving* the feedback. In this chapter we examine the skills of giving, receiving, and using *feedback* — information about your own behavior, others' behavior, the perceptions you have of others, and the perceptions others have of you.

More specifically, the following learning designs are centered on how you can better understand yourself by getting and using feedback, from others, about your own behavioral skills of giving and receiving feedback. We will also examine a variety of methods for giving and receiving feedback, and how to use these techniques.

Through knowing how to give, receive, and use feedback about our own behavior we gain *control* over our behavior. In this way we can change our own behavior in specific ways that are likely to be more beneficial to us. If someone says to me, "The tone of voice you're using makes me feel defensive," I can argue that I had no such intention and try to convince the other person of this — all in the same, defensiveness-provoking tone of voice. Or, I can ask for more information and then try to *change* my tone of voice to make the other person feel more comfortable. This is a small example, but a very important one. If you want to help others, in any kind of helping relationship (manager, consultant, counselor, etc.), you must be able to understand the effect your behavior has on others and be able to alter your behavior accordingly. Helping others learn to do this is also a basic part of the problem solving process.

I. SPECIFIC SKILL-DEVELOPMENT AND LEARNING DESIGNS

A. Design for Learning to Give and Receive Feedback: How Others See Me; How I See Others

1. *Purpose.* This design should be used only after the group has met for several sessions or when group members have some basic information about each other. The aim is to provide a "mini-T-group" as a means of sharing self-perceptions and perceptions of others in the group.

2. *Materials needed.* Newsprint and markers, or chalkboard, blank paper for everyone, reading materials in part 5.

3. *Steps in using the design.*
    a. Review the conceptual materials.
    b. Present and discuss the Johari Window.
    c. Present and explain the ABC Procedure.
    d. Have each person write information about self — List 1.
    e. Divide group into three subgroups (A, B, C), and have them sit as diagrammed in part 5.
    f. Have each person write information about others in own subgroup — List 2.
    g. Have A's give List 1 to alter egos (B's).
    h. Have A's exchange List 2's with other A's.
    i. Have A's and B's feed back information; C's meet separately.
    j. Begin interaction among A's; B's consult with A's as desired; C's observe.
    k. Stop action for A's — consultation with B's; C's meet with instructor.
    l. Resume interaction among A's.
    m. Conclude interaction among A's.
    n. Have C's report on observations to group.
    o. Repeat cycle for B's (B's become A's, C's become B's, A's become C's) and then for C's.
    p. Discuss learnings (entire group).

4. *Deriving learnings.* At least half an hour, possibly more, is needed for adequate discussion of this experience. Since more individuals will have a chance to participate in a small, as compared with a large, group, the class could be split into groups of four or five. This division would be particularly appropriate if the class contains twenty or more persons. Another approach could be to begin the discussion and continue it at the next meeting. The group might generate a list of questions or issues raised by this experience for participants to review and consider during the time before the next group meeting. Such a list might be based on the following questions:
    — What have I learned about myself that I didn't know before?
    — How well have I been able to share some "hidden" aspects of myself?
    — Was I able to receive feedback nondefensively and to give feedback supportively?
    — Was I giving nonjudgmental feedback?
    — Did I get better at giving and receiving feedback as the group went through successive "rounds"?
    — How much feedback really came through my "internal filters"?
    — How do I use this feedback *now*?

5. *Support materials.*

THE JOHARI WINDOW

The Johari Window (developed by Joe Luft and Harry Ingram) is often used as a tool or a framework to focus on the giving and receiving of feedback about one's self. In effect, it allows both you and others (maybe me) to consider separately the different parts of yourself that are both known and unknown.

FIGURE 4.1 The Johari Window

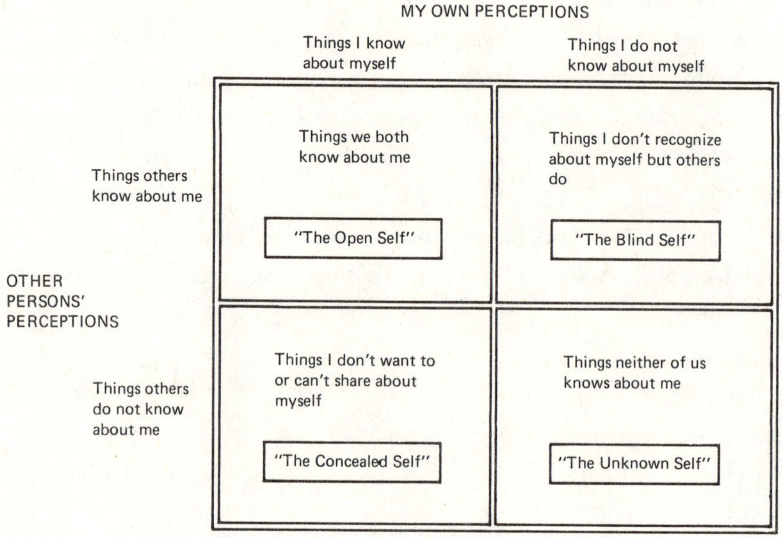

MY OWN PERCEPTIONS

	Things I know about myself	Things I do not know about myself
Things others know about me	Things we both know about me "The Open Self"	Things I don't recognize about myself but others do "The Blind Self"
Things others do not know about me	Things I don't want to or can't share about myself "The Concealed Self"	Things neither of us knows about me "The Unknown Self"

OTHER PERSONS' PERCEPTIONS

MONOLOGUE TO A FRIEND

Through the "Open Self" pane of the window both you and I see things about you. The pane is clear and free of dust as we look at you. We both see, for example, that you have long hair, wear glasses, stammer a little when you're excited, talk more than you should in a group, and usually come late for activities.

For you the "Blind Self" pane of your window is cloudy and unclear, but for me it is not. I see things through it about you that you don't seem to know anything about; some of them I like about you and some I don't. If only you could see these things about yourself, maybe you could help others better than you do *or* maybe you wouldn't turn me off sometimes. Sometimes, for example, I watch you jump in to get the group moving off dead center and it's very appropriate. Then again, you do this sometimes when we're not really finished with what we've been doing. I wish you wouldn't interrupt me so often. Have patience, friend. If I could only tell you these things, I know they would help.

On the other hand, I know that you know a lot more about yourself than I ever will. For me your "Concealed Self" pane is cloudy and dark while for you I know it must be very clear. There must be some things about yourself that you would like to tell me. When will you trust me enough to deal kindly with that information? I'm really ready to help if you'll let me see through the window there.

I guess there's no way to talk about the "Unknown Self" pane of your window. I'm not a therapist and neither are you. Anyway, both of us are getting along fine without seeing through that pane. Perhaps it's better left dark for now. Who knows, if we *really* get to know each other well, we may both catch a glimpse through there once in a while.

This has really been interesting, thinking about you, but you know what — I think I'll start again now and think about my own window.

THE ABC FORMAT

This exercise and its many variations have been used extensively at National Training Laboratories (NTL) and other training centers and by individual practitioners. The aim is to provide a taste of what a T-group is like without actually delving into the complete experience (which would, normally, require from one full weekend up to a three-week laboratory program). Figure 4-2 shows the physical arrangement using the ABC format.

FIGURE 4.2 The ABC Format

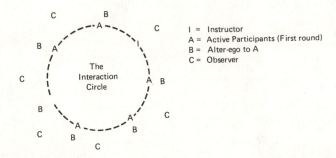

    I = Instructor
    A = Active Participants (First round)
    B = Alter-ego to A
    C = Observer

B.   Design for Learning to Give Helpful Feedback

1.   *Purpose.* Design A provides some experience in giving feedback in a carefully constructed, relatively nonthreatening situation, while Design C gives practice in using a variety of structured feedback methods or techniques. The present design is different and more difficult, in that it requires a "consultant" to give feedback to a "client" in a much less structured (role-play) situation. The aim is to practice the *skills* involved in giving helpful feedback. It will be useful to review the reprinted article by Jack Gibb in Section II of this chapter, as well as the "Rules for Helpful Feedback" (also in Section II), prior to the exercise.

2.   *Materials needed.* Role-play orientation sheets (in part 5).

3.   *Steps in using the design.*

   a.   Read background material and review principles of role playing.

   b.   Divide group into trios and read role information.

    c.   Explain how to begin role play.

    d.   Stop role play; observers give feedback.

    e.   Have trio members switch roles.

    f.   After three rounds, discuss learnings.

4.   *Deriving learnings.* We have found that it is useful to spend some time after this exercise discussing what happened in the context of the conceptual materials regarding feedback. Thus, the group might review the conceptual materials in Section II of this chapter, showing how each of the "rules of helpful feedback" were illustrated (or violated) in the role play, as well as how Gibb's suggestions for creating a nondefensive, supportive communication climate were or could be applied to the role-play situation. Some relevant questions for discussion are:

   — How can "positive" (or "negative") feedback be given in *nonevaluative* ways?

   — How realistic and situation-specific should the consultant be, and how does he do this without being punishing?

   — To what extent should the consultant help the client to use the feedback in planning changes in the client's actions?

5.   *Support materials.* The role-orientation sheets and the observers' guideline forms are on the following pages.

CORWIN FAMILY SERVICES AGENCY

Background

James/Jan Corwin is director of a small private family services agency that (s)he organized about two years ago. Three others work with Corwin in providing family-counseling services to residents of a moderate-sized, middle-class community. Due to certain organizational problems that Corwin perceived, (s)he hired Leslie Kregar, an organizational consultant. Kregar is an experienced consultant with an MBA from UCLA. (S)he has been talking to the staff and observing some meetings over the past month. A staff meeting, with Kregar attending, has just ended and (s)he and Corwin are walking out of the room.

CORWIN FAMILY SERVICES AGENCY

Role for James/Jan Corwin, Director

You are director of a small private agency that offers family-counseling services to the residents of a moderate-sized, middle-class community. You have an MSW and training in guidance and counseling. Your staff consists of three salaried counselors, all with master's degrees, and a small office staff (one secretary, one clerical worker). You have been operating now for almost two years and have been doing pretty well. Your biggest problem, lately, seems to be in coordinating decisions with the other three staff members. You, therefore, asked an organizational consultant, Leslie Kregar, to help work with your group on this issue. The consultant has interviewed all of the agency personnel and has attended three staff meetings, including one you just adjourned. You're feeling pretty good about this meeting; a lot got accomplished. It is puzzling, though; in only an hour you had the week's case assignments clear. Your meetings with the staff seem to go more smoothly over time, yet this coordination problem keeps getting worse. You feel it's about time that the consultant and you reviewed the organization's problems. (S)he should have had enough time, by now, to get a good fix on the situation and make some recommendations.

CORWIN FAMILY SERVICES AGENCY

Role for Leslie Kregar, Organizational Consultant

You were hired by James/Jan Corwin, director of a small private agency offering family-counseling services to residents of a moderate-sized, middle-class community. There are three staff counselors in addition to the director, a secretary, and one clerical worker. Corwin felt that there were problems with their coordination and decision making and asked if you would help. You've interviewed all personnel and attended three staff meetings, including the one that has just ended. The basic problem seems to be centered around Corwin's rather authoritarian-directive leadership style. While the director's leadership does have the effect of producing logically sound decisions with a minimum of meeting time, resentment seems to have built up among the other three counselors, who are less and less committed to Corwin's decisions. The meeting you just observed was typical: in less than an hour Corwin reviewed client cases for the upcoming month and assigned specific cases to individuals and, in some cases, teams. The decisions seemed good, but it was clear that the others resented the way (s)he went about it. You doubt that the teams (s)he appointed will coordinate their efforts effectively. You are now faced with the task of providing the director with some feedback on the nature of the problems you have uncovered.

CORWIN FAMILY SERVICES AGENCY

Observation Guidelines

The consultant is going to attempt to give feedback to the client. Take particular note of the following:

1.   Is the feedback *descriptive* or *evaluative?*

2.   Is the feedback *specific* or *general?*

3.   Is the feedback appropriate to the needs of the receiver?

4.   Is the feedback directed toward behavior the receiver can do something about?

5.   Did the consultant check to see if the client wanted feedback?

6.   Was the timing of the feedback appropriate; that is, in the context of the discussion?

7.   Did the consultant check with the receiver to make sure that the client heard and understood what the consultant was saying?

C.   Design for Learning a Variety of Methods of Giving Feedback

1.   *Purpose.* Anyone who plans to help others learn to solve problems should be familiar with a number of methods or techniques for facilitating the giving and receiving of feedback that is helpful. Ultimately, of course, you will create or develop your own such techniques. It is also useful for real-life groups to be able to use certain techniques for facilitating feedback. In this design our aim is to provide some experience in using several different feedback methods.

2.   *Materials needed.* Newsprint, markers, and questionnaire forms (in part 5).

3.   *Steps in using the design.*

    a.   Present short lecture on the variety of feedback techniques.

    b.   Have individuals fill out internal dialogue forms.

    c.   Form small groups and have them meet.

    d.   Reconvene full group; have members fill out individual feedback forms and deliver the forms.

    e.   Reconvene full group; have members select others to fill out and return feedback on participation forms.

    f.   Reconvene full group; have members review feedback received, using individual feedback summary forms.

    g.   Form new small groups for discussion.

    h.   Halt discussions; in each group have members give nonverbal feedback, then discuss.

    i.   Reconvene full group; review methods of feedback used.

    j.   As they leave, have group members write feedback comments about session on newsprint.

4.   *Deriving learnings.* Rather than have a further discussion of learnings (beyond the discussion mentioned in step i) at the end of the session, it will generally be more appropriate to begin the next meeting with a short discussion about the various methods of giving feedback, attempting to derive some learnings for the whole group from the previous experience. Group members might, however, be informed of this plan and asked to think about their own learnings from this session, both in terms of the specific feedback they received and in terms of what they learned about giving and receiving feedback.

5.   *Support materials.*

TECHNIQUES FOR GIVING AND RECEIVING FEEDBACK

The first two designs in this chapter concentrated on the skills involved in giving and receiving feedback. There are also many techniques or procedures within which these skills are used. The most obvious and general such procedure simply involves the "giver" and "receiver" in direct verbal discussion. But this is not always the most practical or comfortable technique to use. In a large group with a limited amount of time, it is impossible for everyone to engage in interpersonal discussion with each of the other persons he or she wants to give feedback to. Or, sometimes, we'd like to give some feedback to another person but have fears or uncertainties about doing so in direct verbal contact — for example, fears that the other person may react unfavorably to us, or uncertainties about our ability to give the feedback in a supportive way on a direct verbal level.

Of course, feedback is appropriate and useful not only with regard to individual behavior, but in terms of relationships between individuals or among individuals in groups. We can think of four specific feedback situations:

1. *The individual alone.* This would involve reflection or analysis of one's own behavior; giving feedback to yourself.

2. *Interpersonal dyadic.* This is the most common feedback situation, involving two persons.

3. *Small group.* This situation exists for most of us — a small group of three to eight persons who interact on a regular basis. We are all part of work groups, social groups, family groups, etc., but we only occasionally use these situations for giving and receiving feedback about how the group is functioning or how individuals in the group are helping or hindering the functioning of the group.

4. *Large group.* At times, we are all part of a large group — a class, an organization (or some part of one, as a department) — in which the people share certain goals. Very rarely, however, do we try to use such a large group setting for giving and receiving feedback.

In interpersonal dyadic situations we often do give and get feedback. Most of the time, such feedback does not involve the skills and principles discussed in this chapter. Sometimes we *don't* give feedback in such situations — at least not overtly — because we find it too difficult or are in some way afraid of possible outcomes. Of course, these are the times when feedback could probably be most helpful. The above reasons also apply to the small group situation, but here and in the other two situations we often do not give or receive feedback simply because we don't know of any practical ways of doing so. What follows is a limited list of techniques or procedures that can be used to facilitate the giving and receiving of feedback. Some are appropriate only to one of the four situations defined, while others could be used or adapted for some or all of the situations. All are fairly simple and are aimed at making it practical or easier to give and receive feedback in certain situations.

Feedback Techniques and Procedures

1. Self-dialogue. On an individual basis, it can be very helpful to give ourselves feedback. This is particularly true when we are of two minds on some issue. In a self-dialogue, the individual alternates between two positions, arguing first for one, then for the other — an internal role play. Often it helps actually to write down the dialogue, or to tape-record it, and then review the "discussion." At the least, such a dialogue tends to clarify the individual's ideas or problem. Actually, it is quite easy to talk out the two parts; the hard part is *listening* to yourself. That's why it's so helpful to record and review this kind of dialogue.

2. Self-analysis. Sometimes it is not too difficult to observe, record, review, and analyze one's own behavior. For example, if I just did poorly on an exam, I might sit down and review my behavior that relates to the situation. What were my study behaviors the past week and the night before? What were my in-class behaviors during the past week? How did I act while actually taking the exam? One makes notes, then reviews these, looking for strengths and weaknesses.

On a more general and immediate level, one can examine the gestalt or wholeness of the situation one is in, asking one's self, "What am I aware of *now*? What am I feeling *now*? What do I want *now*?" If careful attention is given to each of these three critical questions, the individual will certainly receive from himself much valid and usable feedback.

3. Colors. When time is short and the members of a small group want to give one another some immediate feedback, one useful "game" is to have prepared small slips of paper in a variety of colors. Each person then selects colored slips at the end of the meeting, signs each, and gives one (of the "appropriate" color) to every person he or she wants to give feedback to. The group may then spend a few moments discussing the reactions of members, or verbalizing the intended messages. Or, receivers can reflect on what they interpret the intent of each giver to be. At the next meeting, group members can check out their assumptions about the feedback with the senders. Similar procedures can be used for quick feedback, such as "give each person you want to give feedback to the name of an animal." (A simplified variation of this technique would be to dichotomize the feedback by using categories, such as drawing pictures of orchids and onions and distributing these.)

4. Questionnaire forms. Questionnaires can, of course, be used in a limitless number of ways for individual and group feedback. When such a form is used for feedback to individuals, the most generally useful items are questions like "I see your strengths/contributions (to the group, to my own achievement, etc.) as . . ." and "I would like to see you change (grow, develop, etc.) in these ways . . ." Questionnaires can also be designed for feedback on very specific behaviors and skills. When this type of feedback technique is used, the recipients should have the opportunity to question the givers about their comments. It is also extremely useful for the recipients to review and summarize the feedback given to them and consider what actions, if any, they could take based on the feedback.

For small groups, questionnaires can be used to develop group feedback when time is short. The Post-Meeting Reaction (PMR) form is one generally useful example (see Chapter Five).

In large groups, the questionnaire items should involve response scales, rather than open-end written responses. Data can then be conveniently analyzed and reported back to the group for discussion.

5. Gummed labels. In a small or large group, this quick feedback technique involves distribution of gummed labels to all members. Each person writes a brief feedback message — perhaps just a word or phrase — on the label and gives it to the receiver. The receiver can easily categorize the feedback comments and paste them on one sheet for personal review.

6. Nonverbal. As a feedback technique, this is best for either small groups up to twenty in size or for very large groups (over fifty). Individuals are asked to find someone they want to give feedback to and express this feedback in any (nondestructive) way they wish without using words. In a small group this can be done with one person giving feedback and others observing, or the group may form a circle with the giver of feedback going from one person to the next. In a somewhat larger group (twenty or so), two concentric circles can be formed, with the inner circle rotating clockwise until each person has had an opportunity to give nonverbal feedback to each person in the outer circle. The circle would then reverse. It is usually important to allow time for verbal discussion after this sort of exercise is concluded.

7. Mailbox. In a moderate- to large-sized group, individuals can give one another written feedback using the mailbox technique. For a group around twenty in size, large manila envelopes

can be prepared, one for each person. These are then attached to a wall with masking tape, in alphabetical order. Group members then write their feedback and deposit the message in the mailbox of the appropriate individual. For large groups, make newsprint indications for alphabetical division (e.g., A-C; D-F; etc.), post these around the room, and have those giving the feedback write the recipient's name on the back of a feedback sheet, which is then attached to the wall beneath the appropriate alphabetical designation. Obviously, this technique can be used with questionnaires as well.

8.   Adjective call-out. For large groups, some feedback about people's feelings at the close of the meeting can be obtained by asking group members to call out adjectives describing their feelings about or reactions to the meeting or the group. Someone can serve as recorder and the adjectives can later be categorized for discussion at the start of the next meeting.

9.   Newsprint closure. This technique is best suited to large groups. During the session large pieces of blank newsprint should be posted by the main exit. At the close of the meeting, group members are asked to write a word, phrase, or symbol on the newsprint as they leave. (Be sure to have a number of marking pens on hand.) The sheets can be analyzed later and presented as feedback at the start of the next session.

The above techniques do not, of course, make up for a lack of skill in the giving and receiving of feedback. They are aimed at one or another of three basic goals: (1) to provide a structure that permits feedback to be given and received in situations where this is normally very difficult or impossible (e.g., a very large group pressed for time, yet the facilitator or instructor is aware of a real need for some feedback on the session); (2) to act as a structural aid while people are in the process of learning the skills involved in giving and receiving feedback (e.g., a questionnaire designed specifically for use by observers of a role play that focuses the feedback and helps the observer be more effective in giving feedback); (3) to actually reduce the personalization of the feedback — to make the situation less personal — and thus ease the anxiety of those who are giving the feedback (e.g., the mailbox technique used with a group of ten people).

The third point deserves some further comment. Obviously, feedback is more effective when it is *more*, not less, personal, in terms of specifying the feelings of the giver and allowing the receiver to ask the giver for more details and clarification. Yet, there *are* occasions on which the giver would rather remain silent than run the risks he or she may perceive associated with speaking directly to the receiver. This is one situation in which a reduced degree of personalization — and some feedback — is often preferable to increased personalization — and no feedback. Another type of situation is when the individuals clearly do not have the skills needed for the giving and receiving of helpful feedback, yet when some feedback is desirable. Individuals may even be willing to give and receive feedback, although it is evident that they lack most of the skills needed to do so effectively.

We do not suggest that the above list of techniques is either complete or the best possible one. Also, each technique can be modified or altered in many ways.

Internal Dialogue

Purpose. To provide a time for introspection to gain clearer perceptions of dilemmas within ourselves that lead to ambiguous or inconsistent behavior.

Dialogue within Ourselves. We belong to groups of people, but in one sense, each of us is a group, within himself or herself, a private world of many interesting parts. We each are a "complex society." We need practice in listening to and making use of our internal voices just as we need practice in listening to and participating more effectively with the other persons in our external society.

In this session, you are asked to tune in on one of your internal dialogues. Select a topic of great interest to you — a dilemma, a self-examination. Write a brief dialogue of the conversation between the internal voices.

For example, you might want to record a discussion:

Between your optimistic self and your pessimistic self on how effective you are as a
    consultant (group member, leader, trainer, etc.).
Between your desire to help a friend with a specific problem and your reluctance to do so.

Before you start, see whether you can "hear" the two sides of the conversation. If you can, write it down as the dialogue of a play or the script of a conversation. Be sure the conversation is focused on some issue or confrontation between the two selves that are involved.

Me 1	Me 2

Individual Feedback Sheet

FROM: _____   TO: _____

While interacting with you, I've observed the following:

1.   Strengths; things you did that were helpful to me/the group.

2.   Areas for growth or further development; things I think you can learn to do better.

NOTE: In writing feedback comments, refer back to the "Rules for Helpful Feedback" in
       Section II.

Individual Feedback Sheet

FROM: _____   TO: _____

While interacting with you, I've observed the following:

1.   Strengths; things you did that were helpful to me/the group.

2.   Areas for growth or further development; things I think you can learn to do better.

NOTE: In writing feedback comments, refer back to the "Rules for Helpful Feedback" in
        Section II.

Individual Feedback Sheet

FROM: _____   TO: _____

While interacting with you, I've observed the following:

1. Strengths; things you did that were helpful to me/the group.

2. Areas for growth or further development; things I think you can learn to do better.

NOTE: In writing feedback comments, refer back to the "Rules for Helpful Feedback" in
       Section II.

Feedback on Participation Questionnaire

Name: _____

Reviewed by: _____

1. How well have the opportunities for learning provided by the activities we have engaged in been used by this participant? Please comment on *why* you check where you do, on the reverse side of this form.

VERY WELL	QUITE WELL	FAIRLY WELL	FAIRLY POORLY	QUITE POORLY	VERY POORLY

2. How effectively has this participant contributed to the learning of others, e.g., helpful confrontation, support, feedback, consultation, group membership? Please comment on *why* you check where you do, on the reverse of this form.

VERY EFFECTIVELY	QUITE EFFECTIVELY	FAIRLY EFFECTIVELY	FAIRLY INEFFECTIVELY	QUITE INEFFECTIVELY	VERY INEFFECTIVELY

3. How effectively has this participant used the resources of the staff for his/her learning? Please comment on *why* you check where you do, on the reverse of this form.

VERY EFFECTIVELY	QUITE EFFECTIVELY	FAIRLY EFFECTIVELY	FAIRLY INEFFECTIVELY	QUITE INEFFECTIVELY	VERY INEFFECTIVELY

4. How effectively has this participant used the resources of peers for learning? Please comment on *why* you check where you do, on the reverse of this form.

VERY EFFECTIVELY	QUITE EFFECTIVELY	FAIRLY EFFECTIVELY	FAIRLY INEFFECTIVELY	QUITE INEFFECTIVELY	VERY INEFFECTIVELY

Feedback on Participation Questionnaire

Name: _____

Reviewed by: _____

1. How well have the opportunities for learning provided by the activities we have engaged in been used by this participant? Please comment on *why* you check where you do, on the reverse of this form.

VERY WELL	QUITE WELL	FAIRLY WELL	FAIRLY POORLY	QUITE POORLY	VERY POORLY

2. How effectively has this participant contributed to the learning of others, e.g., helpful confrontation, support, feedback, consultation, group membership? Please comment on *why* you check where you do, on the reverse of this form.

VERY EFFECTIVELY	QUITE EFFECTIVELY	FAIRLY EFFECTIVELY	FAIRLY INEFFECTIVELY	QUITE INEFFECTIVELY	VERY INEFFECTIVELY

3. How effectively has this participant used the resources of the staff for his/her learning? Please comment on *why* you check where you do, on the reverse of this form.

VERY EFFECTIVELY	QUITE EFFECTIVELY	FAIRLY EFFECTIVELY	FAIRLY INEFFECTIVELY	QUITE INEFFECTIVELY	VERY INEFFECTIVELY

4. How effectively has this participant used the resources of peers for learning? Please comment on *why* you check where you do, on the reverse of this form.

VERY EFFECTIVELY	QUITE EFFECTIVELY	FAIRLY EFFECTIVELY	FAIRLY INEFFECTIVELY	QUITE INEFFECTIVELY	VERY INEFFECTIVELY

Feedback on Participation Questionnaire

Name: _____

Reviewed by: _____

1. How well have the opportunities for learning provided by the activities we have engaged in been used by this participant? Please comment on *why* you check where you do, on the reverse of this form.

VERY	QUITE	FAIRLY	FAIRLY	QUITE	VERY
WELL	WELL	WELL	POORLY	POORLY	POORLY

2. How effectively has this participant contributed to the learning of others, e.g., helpful confrontation, support, feedback, consultation, group membership? Please comment on *why* you check where you do, on the reverse of this form.

VERY	QUITE	FAIRLY	FAIRLY	QUITE	VERY
EFFECTIVELY	EFFECTIVELY	EFFECTIVELY	INEFFECTIVELY	INEFFECTIVELY	INEFFECTIVELY

3. How effectively has this participant used the resources of the staff for his/her learning? Please comment on *why* you check where you do, on the reverse of this form.

VERY	QUITE	FAIRLY	FAIRLY	QUITE	VERY
EFFECTIVELY	EFFECTIVELY	EFFECTIVELY	INEFFECTIVELY	INEFFECTIVELY	INEFFECTIVELY

4. How effectively has this participant used the resources of peers for learning? Please comment on *why* you check where you do, on the reverse of this form.

VERY	QUITE	FAIRLY	FAIRLY	QUITE	VERY
EFFECTIVELY	EFFECTIVELY	EFFECTIVELY	INEFFECTIVELY	INEFFECTIVELY	INEFFECTIVELY

Feedback Skills Questionnaire

Instructions:

Rate each member of your group, including yourself, by placing their initials on the scale. Indicate for each question the rating (1-7) that most nearly describes your own direct experience of the person. She or he:

1. Takes time to find out what the problem really is.

    Hardly ever   1   2   3   4   5   6   7   Always

2. Gives evidence of listening to and trying to understand my point of view.

    Hardly ever   1   2   3   4   5   6   7   Always

3. Picks up and describes the feelings I may be experiencing.

    Hardly ever   1   2   3   4   5   6   7   Always

4. Asks me to repeat, asks me to clarify.

    Hardly ever   1   2   3   4   5   6   7   Always

5. Repeats and clarifies what I have said before she or he makes own statement.

    Hardly ever   1   2   3   4   5   6   7   Always

6. Asks the kind of questions that help me think things through.

    Hardly ever   1   2   3   4   5   6   7   Always

7. Shares own feelings and discusses own strengths and weaknesses appropriately.

    Hardly ever   1   2   3   4   5   6   7   Always

8. Supports and encourages me.

    Hardly ever   1   2   3   4   5   6   7   Always

9. Gives me a chance to talk and opens the door for me to contribute.

    Hardly ever   1   2   3   4   5   6   7   Always

10. Helps me explore alternatives without pushing her or his own solutions.

     Hardly ever   1   2   3   4   5   6   7   Always

11. Sets out to find the facts.

     Hardly ever   1   2   3   4   5   6   7   Always

12. Takes time to set goals and objectives.

     Hardly ever   1   2   3   4   5   6   7   Always

13. Takes time to evaluate how we are doing individually and as a team.

      Hardly ever   1   2   3   4   5   6   7   Always

14. Gives evidence of putting talk and decisions into action.

      Hardly ever   1   2   3   4   5   6   7   Always

15. Seeks and accepts help from others.

      Hardly ever   1   2   3   4   5   6   7   Always

16. Provides different functions to the team at different times (e.g., leader, clarifier, opinion giver, summarizer, gatekeeper, etc.).

      Hardly ever   1   2   3   4   5   6   7   Always

17. Says clearly what she or he expects from me.

      Hardly ever   1   2   3   4   5   6   7   Always

18. Faces disagreements directly and seeks to understand them.

      Hardly ever   1   2   3   4   5   6   7   Always

19. Is concrete, direct, and nonevaluative in giving me feedback.

      Hardly ever   1   2   3   4   5   6   7   Always

20. Seems to care about me and whether I accomplish my best goals.

      Hardly ever   1   2   3   4   5   6   7   Always

Individual Feedback Summary Sheet

Name: _____

The major points of the feedback I received, as I read them, are:

STRENGTHS	WEAKNESSES

Any other interpretative comments you feel help summarize your feedback:

In light of this feedback of professional direction, the implications for my personal growth are:

II. CONCEPTUAL SUPPORT MATERIALS: FEEDBACK

"DEFENSIVE COMMUNICATION"*

Jack R. Gibb

One way to understand communication is to view it as a people process rather than as a language process. If one is to make fundamental improvement in communication, he must make changes in interpersonal relationships. One possible type of alteration — and the one with which this paper is concerned — is that of reducing the degree of defensiveness.

Definition and Significance

"Defensive behavior" is behavior which occurs when an individual perceives threat or anticipates threat in the group. The person who behaves defensively, even though he also gives some attention to the common task, devotes an appreciable portion of his energy to defending himself. Besides talking about the topic, he thinks about how he appears to others, how he may be seen more favorably, how he may win, dominate, impress, or escape punishment, and/or how he may avoid or mitigate a perceived or an anticipated attack.

Such inner feelings and outward acts tend to create similarly defensive postures in others; and, if unchecked, the ensuing circular response becomes increasingly destructive. Defensive behavior, in short, engenders defensive listening, and this in turn produces postural, facial, and verbal cues which raise the defense level of the original communicator.

Defensive arousal prevents the listener from concentrating upon the message. Not only do defensive communicators send off multiple value, motive, and affect cues, but also defensive recipients distort what they receive. As a person becomes more and more defensive, he becomes less and less able to perceive accurately the motives, the values, and the emotions of the sender. The writer's analyses of tape recorded discussions revealed that increases in defensive behavior were correlated positively with losses in efficiency in communication.[1] Specifically, distortions became greater when defensive states existed in the groups.

The converse also is true. The more "supportive" or defense reductive the climate the less the receiver reads into the communication distorted loadings which arise from projections of his own anxieties, motives, and concerns. As defenses are reduced, the receivers become better able to concentrate upon the structure, the content, and the cognitive meanings of the message.

Descriptive speech, in contrast to that which is evaluative, tends to arouse a minimum of uneasiness. Speech acts which the listener perceives as genuine requests for information or as material with neutral loadings are descriptive. Specifically, presentations of feelings, events, perceptions, or processes which do not ask or imply that the receiver change behavior or attitude are minimally defense-producing. The difficulty in avoiding overtone is illustrated by the problems of news reporters in writing stories about unions, Communists, Negroes, and religious activities without tipping off the "party" line of the newspaper. One can often tell from the opening words in a news article which side the newspaper's editorial policy favors.

*Reprinted from the *Journal of Communication* XI (September, 1961): pp. 141-48, by permission of the author and the publisher.

[1] J. R. Gibb, "Defense Level and Influence in Small Groups," in *Leadership and Interpersonal Behavior*, ed. L. Petrullo and B. M. Bass (New York: Holt, Rinehart & Winston, 1961), pp. 66-81.

Control and Problem Orientation

Speech which is used to control the listener evokes resistance. In most of our social intercourse someone is trying to do something to someone else — to change an attitude, to influence behavior, or to restrict the field of activity. The degree to which attempts to control produce defensiveness depends upon the openness of the effort, for a suspicion that hidden motives exist heightens resistance. For this reason attempts of non-directive therapists and progressive educators to refrain from imposing a set of values, a point of view, or a problem solution upon the receivers meet with many barriers. Since the norm is control, non-controllers must earn the perceptions that their efforts have no hidden motives. A bombardment of persuasive "messages" in the fields of politics, education, special causes, advertising, religion, medicine, industrial relations, and guidance has bred cynical and paranoidal responses in listeners.

Implicit in all attempts to alter another person is the assumption by the change agent that the person to be altered is inadequate. That the speaker secretly views the listener as ignorant, unable to make his own decisions, uninformed, immature, unwise, or possessed of wrong or inadequate attitudes is a subconscious perception which gives the latter a valid base for defensive reactions.

Methods of control are many and varied. Legalistic insistence on detail, restrictive regulations and policies, conformity norms, and all laws are among the methods. Gestures, facial expressions, other forms of non-verbal communication, and even such simple acts as holding a door open in a particular manner are means of imposing one's will upon another and hence are potential sources of resistance.

Problem orientation, on the other hand, is the antithesis of persuasion. When the sender communicates a desire to collaborate in defining a mutual problem and in seeking its solution, he tends to create the same problem orientation in the listener; and, of greater importance, he implies that he has no predetermined solution, attitude, or method to impose. Such behavior is permissive in that it allows the receiver to set his own goals, make his own decisions, and evaluate his own progress — or to share with the sender in doing so. The exact methods of attaining permissiveness are not known, but they must involve a constellation of cues, and they certainly go beyond mere verbal assurances that the communicator has no hidden desires to exercise control.

Strategy and Spontaneity

When the sender is perceived as engaged in a stratagem involving ambiguous and multiple motivations, the receiver becomes defensive. No one wishes to be a guinea pig, a role player, or an impressed actor, and no one likes to be the victim of some hidden motivation. That which is concealed, also, may appear larger than it really is, with the degree of defensiveness of the listener determining the perceived size of the suppressed element. The intense reaction of the reading audience to the material in the *Hidden Persuaders* indicates the prevalence of defensive reactions to multiple motivations behind strategy. Group members who are seen as "taking a role," as feigning emotion, as toying with their colleagues, as withholding information, or as having special sources of data are especially resented. One participant once complained that another was "using a listening technique" on him!

Categories of Defensive and Supportive Communication

In working over an eight-year period with recordings of discussions occurring in varied settings, the writer developed the six pairs of defensive and supportive categories presented in Table 1. Behavior which a listener perceives as possessing any of the characteristics listed in the left-hand column arouses defensiveness, whereas that which he interprets as having any of the qualities designated as supportive reduces defensive feelings. The degree to which these reactions occur depend upon the personal level of defensiveness and upon the general climate in the group at the time.[2]

TABLE 4.1   **Categories of Behavior Characteristic of Supportive and Defensive Climates in Small Groups**

Defensive Climates	Supportive Climates
1. Evaluation	1. Description
2. Control	2. Problem orientation
3. Strategy	3. Spontaneity
4. Neutrality	4. Empathy
5. Superiority	5. Equality
6. Certainty	6. Provisionalism

Evaluation and Description

Speech or other behavior which appears evaluative increases defensiveness. If by expression, manner of speech, tone of voice, or verbal content the sender seems to be evaluating or judging the listener, then the receiver goes on guard. Of course, other factors may inhibit the reaction. If the listener thinks that the speaker regards him as an equal and is being open and spontaneous, for example, the evaluativeness in a message will be neutralized and perhaps not even perceived. This same principle applies equally to the other five categories of potentially defense-producing climates. The six sets are interactive.

Because our attitudes toward other persons are frequently, and often necessarily, evaluative, expressions which the defensive person will regard as non-judgmental are hard to frame. Even the simplest question usually conveys the answer that the sender wishes or implies the response that would fit into his value system. A mother, for example, immediately following an earth tremor that shook the house, sought for her small son with the question: "Bobby, where are you?" The timid and plaintive "Mommy, I didn't do it" indicated how Bobby's chronic mild defensiveness predisposed him to react with a projection of his own guilt and in the context of his chronic assumption that questions are full of accusation.

Anyone who has attempted to train professionals to use information-seeking speech with neutral affect appreciates how difficult it is to teach a person to say even the simple "Who did that?" without being seen as accusing. Speech is so frequently judgmental that there is a reality base for the defensive interpretations which are so common.

When insecure, group members are particularly likely to place blame, to see others as fitting into categories of good or bad, to make moral judgments of their colleagues, and to question the value, motive, and affect loadings of the speech which they hear. Since value loadings imply a judgment of others, a belief that the standards of the speaker differ from his own causes the listener to become defensive.

A large part of the adverse reaction to much of the so-called human relations training is a feeling against what are perceived as gimmicks and tricks to fool or to "involve" people, to make a person

[2] J. R. Gibb, "Sociopsychological Processes of Group Instruction," in *The Dynamics of Instructional Groups,* ed. N. B. Henry (Fifty-ninth Yearbook of the National Society for the Study of Education, Part II, 1960), pp. 115-35.

think he is making his own decision, or to make the listener feel that the sender is genuinely interested in him as a person. Particularly violent reactions occur when it appears that someone is trying to make a stratagem appear spontaneous. One person has reported a boss who incurred resentment by habitually using the gimmick of "spontaneously" looking at his watch and saying, "My gosh, look at the time — I must run to an appointment." The belief was that the boss would create less irritation by honestly asking to be excused.

Similarly, the deliberate assumption of guilelessness and natural simplicity is especially resented. Monitoring the tapes of feedback and evaluation sessions in training groups indicates the surprising extent to which members perceive the strategies of their colleagues. This perceptual clarity may be quite shocking to the strategist, who usually feels that he has cleverly hidden the motivational aura around the "gimmick."

This aversion to deceit may account for one's resistance to politicians who are suspected of behind-the-scenes planning to get his vote; to psychologists whose listening apparently is motivated by more than the manifest or content-level interest in his behavior, or to the sophisticated, smooth, or clever person whose "oneupmanship" is marked with guile. In training groups the role-flexible person frequently is resented because his changes in behavior are perceived as strategic maneuvers.

Conversely, behavior which appears to be spontaneous and free of deception is defense reductive. If the communicator is seen as having a clean id, as having uncomplicated motivations, as being straightforward and honest, and as behaving spontaneously in response to the situation, he is likely to arouse minimal defense.

Neutrality and Empathy

When neutrality in speech appears to the listener to indicate a lack of concern for his welfare, he becomes defensive. Group members usually desire to be perceived as valued persons, as individuals of special worth, and as objects of concern and affection. The clinical, detached, person-is-an-object-of-study attitude on the part of many psychologist-trainers is resented by group members. Speech with low affect that communicates little warmth or caring is in such contrast with the affect-laden speech in social situations that it sometimes communicates rejection.

Communication that conveys empathy for the feelings and respect for the worth of the listener, however, is particularly supportive and defense reductive. Reassurance results when a message indicates that the speaker identifies himself with the listener's problems, shares his feelings, and accepts his emotional reactions at face value. Abortive efforts to deny the legitimacy of the receiver's emotions by assuring the receiver that he need not feel bad, that he should not feel rejected, or that he is overly anxious, though often intended as support giving, may impress the listener as lack of acceptance. The combination of understanding and empathizing with the other person's emotions with no accompanying effort to change him apparently is supportive at a high level.

The importance of gestural behavioral cues in communicating empathy should be mentioned. Apparently spontaneous facial and bodily evidences of concern are often interpreted as especially valid evidence of deep-level acceptance.

Superiority and Equality

When a person communicates to another that he feels superior in position, power, wealth, intellectual ability, physical characteristics, or other ways, he arouses defensiveness. Here, as with the other sources of disturbance, whatever arouses feelings of inadequacy causes the listener to center upon the affect loading of the statement rather than upon the cognitive elements. The receiver then reacts by not hearing the message, by forgetting it, by competing with the sender, or by becoming jealous of him.

The person who is perceived as feeling superior communicates that he is not willing to enter into a shared problem-solving relationship, that he probably does not desire feedback, that he does not require help, and/or that he will be likely to try to reduce the power, the status, or the worth of the receiver.

Many ways exist for creating the atmosphere that the sender feels himself equal to the listener. Defenses are reduced when one perceives the sender as being willing to enter into participative planning with mutual trust and respect. Differences in talent, ability, worth, appearance, status, and power often exist, but the low defense communicator seems to attach little importance to these distinctions.

Certainty and Provisionalism

The effects of dogmatism in producing defensiveness are well known. Those who seem to know the answers, to require no additional data, and to regard themselves as teachers rather than as co-workers tend to put others on guard. Moreover, in the writer's experiment, listeners often perceived manifest expressions of certainty as connoting inward feelings of inferiority. They saw the dogmatic individual as needing to be right, as wanting to win an argument rather than solve a problem, and as seeing his ideas as truths to be defended. This kind of behavior often was associated with acts which others regarded as attempts to exercise control. People who were right seemed to have low tolerance for members who were "wrong" – i.e., who did not agree with the sender.

One reduces the defensiveness of the listener when he communicates that he is willing to experiment with his own behavior, attitudes, and ideas. The person who appears to be taking provisional attitudes, to be investigating issues rather than taking sides on them, to be problem solving rather than debating, and to be willing to experiment and explore tends to communicate that the listener may have some control over the shared quest or the investigation of the ideas. If a person is genuinely searching for information and data, he does not resent help or company along the way.

Conclusion

The implications of the above material for the parent, the teacher, the manager, the administrator, or the therapist are fairly obvious. Arousing defensiveness interferes with communication and thus makes it difficult – and sometimes impossible – for anyone to convey ideas clearly and to move effectively toward the solution of therapeutic, educational, or managerial problems.

RULES FOR HELPFUL FEEDBACK

From Jack Gibb's paper, reprinted above, and from other sources,* we can extract several specific guidelines which, if followed, make feedback much more likely to be helpful for the receiver. We will discuss briefly each of these guidelines.

Description vs. Evaluation

Helpful feedback is descriptive, not evaluative. Evaluation – positive *or* negative – creates automatic blocks to effective communication. Good descriptive feedback is also "owned" – it is

---

*In this discussion we draw on materials that have appeared in a wide variety of sources, in particular the treatment of feedback in the 1971 NTL *Reading Book*, and the writings of Jack Gibb and Carl Rogers.

clearly attributed to the describer, rather than presented as some omniscient pronouncement. "Your reaction to my comment seemed out of character and not at all like you," may be descriptive, and is not overtly evaluative, yet a far better feedback statement would be, "Your reaction to my comment really surprised me, because I'd expected a very different response based on our past contacts." The second statement, while probably not a tremendous example of good feedback (see below, for discussion of *specificity*) at least does not imply that the giver understands perfectly the "true" character of the receiver, in some godlike fashion.

Specificity vs. Generality

Useful feedback is specific. If I'm trying to help you learn Morse code, and I say, "Your last message contained three errors," this is a descriptive and, in itself, not necessarily evaluative comment, but it is not specific enough to be of much help. "In your last message you substituted an 'A' for a 'D' twice, and a 'P' for an 'L' once" is even less likely to be seen as evaluative and is specific enough to be useful — the receiver can practice A's, D's, P's, and L's. On a more interpersonal level, the statement "I saw your interactions with me in this group as being quite brief so that I didn't really understand what you were trying to say" is descriptive, nonevaluative, and owned by the giver but is also far more general (and, proportionately less helpful) than the statement "Joe, you made that point about Bill's next assignment too quickly for me to grasp what you're getting at."

Needs of the Receiver vs. Needs of the Sender

Helpful feedback is given on the basis of the receiver's needs, not simply the needs of the sender to be heard or to "help." Such "help" is the kind of false help Gibb refers to in his paper "Is Help Helpful?" (see Chapter Two). This factor is closely related to the next one listed: is the feedback desired? Obviously, the recipient may not desire feedback yet may need it very much. In this case the helper has a difficult task, which is probably best begun by exploring with the receiver just why it is that he or she doesn't want feedback. It can also happen that the receiver may want feedback yet not appear to need it. In this case, it would probably be easiest to give feedback and ask to explore why the recipient feels a need for such feedback. Of course, the giver of feedback cannot ignore his or her *own* needs, but to give feedback solely on this basis, without considering the needs of the receiver, is not likely to be helpful to the receiver.

Asked vs. Imposed

Most of the time, people do want feedback; most of us have learned, at least, that such information can be useful at times. It is also true that most of us could learn to make better use of feedback, yet the use (or disuse) we make of this information is also directly related to the manner and format in which it is given — the *process* of giving feedback. Most people give cues, verbal and nonverbal. The helper must always be attuned to and on the lookout for negative cues, such as body position (turned away) or a verbal effort to redirect the conversation by the potential recipient. When such cues are perceived, it is *then* important to refrain from imposing feedback. If the helper sees the feedback as particularly important or of great value at that moment, he or she should always *ask* the recipient whether the feedback is permissible. This need not be done in so many words, but it should certainly be done. If the feedback is then clearly *not* desired, the helper can try to explore why this is so.

Timely vs. Out of Context

Helpful feedback is of immediate relevance, as seen by the recipient. Often, but not always, this means that specific feedback is best given in the particular context in which the behavior that the feedback concerns took place, and as soon after that behavior as possible. Naturally, this is not *always* true; it would be not only foolish but dangerous to give an automobile driver feedback on his steering wheel grip while he is concentrating on applying proper braking pressure to avoid a rear-end collision with a suddenly decelerating vehicle ahead of him. Such feedback could be useful *after* the car is safely stopped and the driver has calmed down. Accurate behavioral records, such as audio- and videotape, can extend considerably the length of the period within which feedback is timely; these methods also preserve much of the context. In general, however, the closer in time and context that the feedback is to the behavior on which it is based, the more helpful it will be.

Applicable vs. Useless

Useful feedback concerns behavior over which the recipient has some degree of control. The movie director tells the actor that his frequent eye blinks will distract viewers from the romance of the scene, but such feedback is pointless if the actor cannot control his eye blinks. The therapist may relate to his client the precise details of certain obsessive behaviors, but such feedback is useless if the client cannot control these behaviors. There are other types of useless feedback, for example, "You're so physically powerful that I'm afraid of you" is feedback the recipient cannot use directly, since few of us can change our physical appearance at will. A similar feedback statement is "I tend to ignore advice from people with advanced educational degrees," when said to an instructor with a Ph.D. These two examples illustrate cases in which the problem is the sender's, not the receiver's, and in which actions are more properly the responsibility of the sender. That is, the feedback could be helpful to the sender (e.g., "How can I become more open to advice from people I categorize as my superiors?") but is not useful to the recipient. In general, then, feedback that cannot be used by the receiver fits the old saying, "A difference that doesn't make any difference is no difference," and is not helpful.

Of course, feedback can also be useless to the receiver because it is too general, out of date, or irrelevant to the needs of the receiver. These problems have already been discussed.

Conclusion

We have outlined above six problem areas that can render feedback ineffective and unhelpful. We have also tried to suggest ways to avoid these problems. Our comments can be summed up in six "Rules for Helpful Feedback":

1. Helpful feedback is descriptive, not evaluative, and is "owned" by the sender
2. Helpful feedback is specific, not general.
3. Helpful feedback is relevant to the self-perceived needs of the receiver.
4. Helpful feedback is desired by the receiver, not imposed on him or her.
5. Helpful feedback is timely and in context.
6. Helpful feedback is usable, concerned with behavior over which the receiver has some control.

One final general rule concerns the communication process itself. Feedback cannot be helpful if it is not heard or is misunderstood. Thus, it is generally useful for the person giving feedback to check, explicitly, with the receiver, to make sure that the receiver actually heard and understood what the sender was trying to communicate.

REFERENCES

**Anderson, J. (1970) Giving and receiving feedback. In *Organizational change and development,* eds. G. W. Dalton, P. R. Lawrence, and L. E. Greiner. Homewood, Ill.: Irwin-Dorsey.

Culbert, S. A. (1967) *The interpersonal process of self-disclosure: It takes two to know one.* Fairfax, Va.: Learning Resources Corporation/NTL.

Goffman, E. (1959) *The presentation of self in everyday life.* Garden City, N. Y.: Doubleday.

Harris, T. A. (1969) *I'm OK – you're OK.* New York: Harper & Row (Avon, 1973).

Howard, R. D., and Berkowitz, L. (1958) Reactions to the evaluators of one's performance. *Journal of Personality* **26**: 494-507.

Jenkins, D. H. (1948) Feedback and group self-evaluation. *Journal of Social Issues* **4**: 50-60.

Jones, J. E., and Pfeiffer, J. W. (1973) *The 1973 annual handbook for group facilitators.* Iowa City, Iowa: University Associates.

Jourard, S. M. (1972) *The transparent self.* 2nd ed. New York: Van Nostrand Reinhold.

Leavitt, H. A., and Mueller, R. (1951) Some effects of feedback on communication. *Human Relations* **4**: 401-410.

Lorr, M., and McNair, D. (1963) An interpersonal behavior circle. *Journal of Abnormal and Social Psychology* **67**: 68-75.

Luft, J. (1973) *Group processes.* 2nd ed. Palo Alto, Calif.: National Press.

**Luft, J. (1969) *Of human interaction.* Palo Alto, Calif.: National Press.

**Maier, N. R. F. (1958) *The appraisal interview.* New York: Wiley.

Mehrabian, A., and Reed, H. (1968) Some determinants of communication accuracy. *Psychological Bulletin* **70**: 365-381.

Meyer, H. H.; Kay, E.; and French, J. R. P., Jr. (1965) Split roles in performance appraisal. *Harvard Business Review* **43**(1): 123-129.

**Miles, M. B.; Hornstein, H. A.; Callahan, D. M.; Calder, P. H.; and Schiavo, R. S. (1969) The consequences of survey feedback: Theory and evaluation. In *The planning of change.* 2nd ed., eds. W. G. Bennis, K. D. Benne, and R. Chin. New York: Holt, Rinehart, & Winston.

NTL Institute for Applied Behavioral Science. (1970) *Reading book: Laboratories in human relations training.* Rev. ed. Fairfax, Va.: Learning Resources Corporation/NTL.

Rogers, C. R. (1952) Barriers and gateways to communication (Part I). *Harvard Business Review* **30(4): 46-49.

Scheidell, T. M. (1966) Feedback in small group communication. *Quarterly Journal of Speech* **2**: 273-278.

Smith, E. E., and Knight, S. S. (1959) Effects of feedback on insight and problem solving efficiency in training groups. *Journal of Applied Psychology* **43**: 209-211.

Stoller, F. H. (1966) The use of focused feedback via videotape in small groups. *Explorations in Human Relations Training and Research.* No. 1. Fairfax, Va.: NTL Institute.

Tesch, F. E.; Lansky, L. M.; and Lundgren, D. C. (1972) The one-way/two-way communication exercise: Some ghosts laid to rest. *Journal of Applied Behavioral Science* **8**: 664-673.

Wiener, N. (1954) *The human use of human beings: Cybernetics and society.* Garden City, N. Y.: Doubleday.

**References preceded by a double asterisk are those judged to be most basic or important.

CHAPTER FIVE

Group Process: Helping People Learn to Work More Effectively in Groups

"A camel is a horse designed by a committee."

Anon.

INTRODUCTION

In Chapter One we discussed our primary orientation to learning, that is, the use of group methods. Many books have been written on the dynamics of behavior in groups; some of the most useful of these are listed at the end of this chapter. We are not trying to summarize what all of these other authors have said. Our more limited aim is helping you learn some of the most basic and important skills of group dynamics. These skills are needed by anyone who tries to help people learn to work together more effectively in groups.

The learning designs in this chapter are, perhaps, more tightly sequenced than for any other chapter in this book. That is, we start at a very basic level and build upward: to work at developing the skills that the fourth learning design is aimed at, one must first have some experience with the skills presented in the first three learning designs.

The first design explains the most basic processes, or ways things happen, in groups and provides some methods and skill in observing and understanding these processes. The second design aims at further developing the skill to do this through observing patterns of communication in a group. How these communication patterns can effectively be put together — integrated — to serve the group's goals is the subject of the third learning design. Finally, we look at patterns of integration that can help the group make better decisions. All of the learning designs in this chapter are directed toward the development of skill in helping people in group situations learn to work together better.

I. SPECIFIC SKILL-DEVELOPMENT AND LEARNING DESIGNS

A. Design for Learning to Observe What Is Happening in a Group

1. *Purpose.* The purpose of this design is to help people learn and understand behaviorally the difference between WHAT the group is working on and HOW the group is working on its tasks — the *content* (what) and *process* (how) work of the group. Groups have objectives to achieve. As such, they tend to be task-oriented. They often ignore work that needs to be done to maintain good *process* in the groups. In this exercise we attempt to make the distinction between these two levels of interaction.

2. *Materials needed.* In each of the three sets of steps that follow it is valuable to have news-print and markers available to record specific content and process comments coming from the group. In addition, observer sheets for use in 3B and a post-meeting reaction form to be used with 3C can be found in part 5, "Support Materials."

3A. *Steps in using the design: Informal activity.*

    a.   Present conceptual input on Content and Process.

    b.   Suggest discussion topics to be used.

    c.   Propose stop-action to discuss process and then begin discussion.

    d.   Stop the work on WHAT to look at HOW.

    e.   Critique the total process of the groups.

3B. *Steps in using the design: Using observers.*

    a.   Present conceptual input on Content and Process.

    b.   Appoint observers.

    c.   Start the work of the group.

    d.   Stop the work for observers' reports, then resume task work.

    e.   Appoint new observers.

    f.   Stop the work for observers' reports, then resume task work.

    g.   Critique the process of the entire session.

3C. *Steps in using the design: Using a post-meeting reaction (PMR) form.*

This design's purpose is best achieved in an ongoing group with a continuing purpose and a continuing existence, for example, a real staff group in an organization, or a class of students meeting throughout a school term, semester, quarter, etc.

    a.   Have group members fill out PMR's at end of meeting.

    b.   Review PMR data between meetings of groups.

    c.   Have group review results at beginning of second meeting.

    d.   Present conceptual input on Content and Process and consideration of suggested improvements.

4. *Deriving learnings.* Just learning the difference between the content and process work of the group does not mean that group members will immediately continue from that point to use that knowledge for the benefit of the group. Several questions need to be answered before any kind of success in using this new idea is likely. Some of these that can be used at the close of the exercises are:

— Are there those of us that are better at observing the HOW work than others; can we ask them to play a stronger leadership role in the future?

— Can we establish a norm in our group that it is okay to make a *process* comment whenever it seems relevant to the *content* going on at the time, and that anybody in the group can do this?

— Do we need to continue the stop-action technique in a few more of our upcoming meetings in order to gain confidence in integrating the *process* with the *content* work?

— Can we think of other positively reinforcing things we can do to make commenting on the process a legitimate activity at our meetings?

5. *Support materials.*

DISTINGUISHING BETWEEN PROCESS AND CONTENT IN A PROBLEM-SOLVING GROUP

All small groups meet to fulfill some common objective. This goal may be explicitly stated, as in the case of an organizational team charged with the development of a new work procedure, or it may be implicit, as in the case of a group of neighborhood couples getting together once a week to "have fun." At either extreme and at all points in between one might say that groups meet together to solve problems. The nature of the problem may in turn influence the life span of the group. Some groups are formed to meet only once or maybe just several times to work on and solve a specific problem. Others require regularly scheduled meetings over an extended period of time to achieve their stated objective, working on many related problems in the process.

Groups then, work on tasks. They work toward getting a job done. Proposing and then discussing the bits and pieces that come together to get the job accomplished is the *content* work of the group. Working together in a cohesive, achieving climate where all members share in the inputs needed, feel satisfied with their roles, and communicate effectively in the task flow is the *process* work of the group. Figure 5-1 makes this distinction between the *content* and the *process* work of a group.

FIGURE 5-1 The Process-Content Work Distinction in the Life Span of a Group

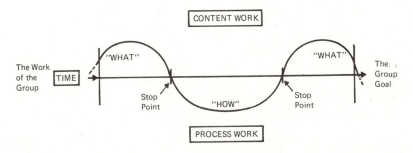

When a group is involved in its content work on the tasks needed to get the job done, it is concerned with the WHAT of its discussion. Group members are defining and clarifying the problem at hand, listing and evaluating possible solutions to the problem, choosing a solution that seems most relevant to them, and developing action steps to try out the solution. They are actively involved in getting the job done. When doing content work, group members are providing all of the relevant task functions needed to solve the problem: functions such as initiating ideas, giving suggestions and opinions, clarifying issues, doing the group record keeping, and summarizing what the group has done at any given moment.

When a group is involved in its process work, it is concerned with the HOW of its discussion. Group members are now providing all of the relevant group "development and maintenance" functions needed to insure that the group will function effectively as it goes about working on its task. Group members concerned with the HOW make sure that others have an opportunity to contribute to the discussion; they mediate differences and relieve tensions when it is appropriate to do so; and they encourage and praise, show warmth, and accept the contributions of others.

Working on the WHAT is relatively easier than working on the HOW. One way that a group can learn to increase its process competence is to stop the action on the content work for a few minutes' discussion on the process, on HOW they have been working together. After they have "processed" themselves for a few minutes, another stop point may be reached and they may again continue their work on the WHAT, or content dimension. They may continue like this, stopping from time to time to check on how they're doing as a group.

In this way, group members may learn that process skills are an important dimension in the life of a problem-solving group. They may also learn how to develop these important skills by practicing them, using the stop-action procedure. Ideally, both content and process work should be done at the same time, with good process work acting to facilitate the content work flow toward the group's objective. Figure 5-2 points to this ideal juxtaposition of the process and content dimensions of group problem-solving work.

FIGURE 5-2　The Ideal Process-Content Work of a Group

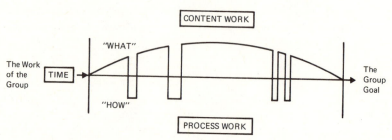

Group members have now learned to integrate the process and content dimensions in group problem solving, offering process comments not at specific regulated times, but in an ongoing fashion and *when* they are needed, facilitating and making more effective the content work of the group.

The stop-action procedure — stop work on content, work on process for a time, return to work on content — is suggested as a way to learn the distinction between process and content work of a problem-solving group and to use this knowledge to enhance and facilitate the work of the group as it moves toward the achievement of its objective. Basic developmental steps in learning are:

1. Distinguishing between process and content work with a basic conceptual input to the group and THEN

2. Stopping the action periodically to look at process:

   a. practicing and repracticing observing and making comments on the process dimension AND ALSO

   b. setting a few minutes aside at the end of the meeting to critique the process of the whole meeting and THEN moving on to

3. Practicing making process comments *without* the stop-action technique:

   a. continuing to practice making comments on the process dimension while content work is being done AND

   b. continuing to set aside a few minutes at the end of the meeting to critique the total process.

Process Observation Form: 1

Group Members' Names

Type of Behavior									
Giving ideas or suggestions									
Expanding and clarifying ideas or suggestions									
Putting together various parts of various ideas; integrating									
Summarizing the discussion									
Keeping track of the group's work — recording									
Asking for ideas or suggestions									
Critiquing ideas or suggestions									
Attempting to compromise one's own position or arguments with those of other group members									

NOTE: Write group members' names in spaces at top. Keep a tally of the number of times each group member engages in each type of behavior and, if possible, a few notes about each group member's behavior.

Process Observation Form: II

Group Members' Names

Types of Behavior						
Encouraging or praising; expressing support or warmth; recognizing the value of group members' ideas or suggestions						
Harmonizing; mediating differences; helping to relieve tensions between or among group members						
Helping "quiet" group members to get heard — have "air time" — by the others; keeping all communication channels open						
Making comments or observations on *how* the group is working; how the members are working together						
Expressing acceptance of others' contributions						
Helping to set standards or norms for the way the group will work together						

NOTE: Write group members' names in spaces at top. Keep a tally of the number of times each group member engages in each type of behavior and, if possible, a few notes about each group member's behavior.

Post-Meeting Reaction Questionnaire

1. Overall rating: let "1" be the very worst meeting you have attended and "7" the very best. Using the scale below, rate *this* meeting.

1	2	3	4	5	6	7
one of the very worst	very poor	poor	average	good	very good	one of the very best

2. In a few sentences, describe what happened, in terms of the interactions between and among group members and leader(s), as you saw it.

3. What do you feel was the *best* aspect of this meeting?

4. What do you feel was the *worst* aspect of this meeting?

5. How could it have been improved?

6. Additional comments:

B.   Design for Learning to Observe Patterns of Communication in Groups

1.   *Purpose.* This exercise aims to provide an opportunity for group members to learn and practice a very basic diagnostic skill in the problem-solving process: determining the structure of
communications at work in an ongoing group.

2.   *Materials needed.* Appropriate meeting space for the group, newsprint and markers for the
observers, tape to post the newsprint, and a table upon which the observers can spread
newsprint and record their observations. In part 5 is a suggested observation scheme for the
two group observers to transfer to their newsprint sheets. An alternative observation form is
provided and may be used either instead of or in addition to the observer outline.

3.   *Steps in using the design.*
    a.   Choose discussion topic and observers for first part of session.
    b.   Have group observers prepare newsprint sheets.
    c.   Begin the group discussion.
    d.   Stop action and have the observers report.
    e.   Briefly discuss the process of the group's interaction.
    f.   Continue the group discussion; new observers may be used.
    g.   Stop action and have the observers report.
    h.   Summarize learnings and derive ways to practice the skills.

4.   *Deriving learnings.* Some questions that the participants might wish to deal with in their discussion period include where and how to use the skill and variations of use. For example:
    — How can observing patterns of communication help us to get clues to other things that may
    be going on in our group?
    — Can we get information on who influences whom, who leads whom, or how leadership
    shifts depending upon the situation?
    — How do the situation and the particular content area under discussion influence group
    leadership behavior?
    — Would it be helpful to understand what styles people use when they communicate — like
    assertions, questions, deference, support, or the like?
    — What kinds of messages do people send *non*verbally — interest-disinterest, agreement-dis-
    agreement, support-nonsupport?
    — Would other groups in which we are members benefit from a general discussion of com-
    munication patterns or shifting discussion-leadership patterns?
    — How could I help others become better observers of group process?

5.   *Support materials.*

Suggested Observer Outline

Here are some suggestions for how the group observers can organize their observations from the
short content work periods of the group. One newsprint sheet could be prepared like this (with
only the circle of names — not the lines inside the circle):

FIGURE 5-3

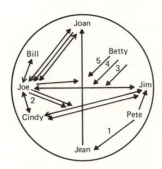

After preparing the sheet, one of the observers can act as recorder, using arrows to show: who speaks to whom (arrow 1 shows that Pete spoke once to Jean); who spoke first in an exchange (arrow 2 shows that Joe spoke to Cindy, who then responded); who spoke to the group in general (arrows 3, 4, and 5 show that most of Betty's communications were addressed to the group as a whole).

Only the longer comments — sentences, etc. — should be recorded, since the observer would find it too difficult to keep track of all the uh-huhs, yesses, etc.

The second observer may wish to help the first observer or keep a separate record. By doing the latter the group can then compare the observations of two people. Instead, the second observer may wish to record just a basic count of comments, both short and long, and the basic content under discussion at the time, perhaps using the form below.

Group Member Comments Tally Form

Name	Questions	Opinions	Ideas	Other	Content	Process

C.   **Design for Learning to Observe Leadership Functions in Groups**

1.   *Purpose.* The purpose of this design is to develop a framework that will allow us to better recognize what functions are needed in a group and then to supply the behaviors necessary to fulfill these functions.

2.   *Materials needed.* Newsprint and markers.

3A.   *Steps in using the design: Concept to practice.*

    a.   Post newsprint for listing of leadership functions.

    b.   List and review the three sets of leadership functions.

    c.   Add specific functions to lists.

    d.   Have group members select functions to practice.

    e.   Choose topic for group discussion.

    f.   Begin group discussion; members practice the new behaviors they selected.

    g.   Stop action and have group members report on effects of behavior.

    h.   Have individuals select different functions to practice; resume group discussion.

    i.   Derive implications for use.

3B.   *Steps in using the design: Practice to concept.*

    a.   Prepare behavior descriptions on slips of paper.

    b.   Arrange chairs in small circles, with a slip of paper on each chair.

    c.   Have group members read slips (no sharing of information), and begin discussion.

    d.   Stop action and have the group share perceptions of one another's behavior.

    e.   Exchange instruction slips; resume discussion.

    f.   Convene full group; discuss and attempt to define the various functions.

4.   *Deriving learnings.* Some questions that the group might wish to deal with in its discussion period are:

— Because of the type of content that our group usually works on, which of the leadership functions are most important for us?

— What new behavior that I've learned about today will I commit myself to use during the next week outside of the group?

— How can we (I) help a member recognize that he or she is acting dysfunctionally in our group?

— Can we set a group norm to stop the action for a few moments when we see someone provide a very helpful function and just call it to everyone's attention?

— How can we use this new observational framework that we have learned today in other groups in which we hold membership?

— And how, in fact, can we make some formal group leaders that we know understand that we are trying to help them with group leadership work and not competing with them for power or status?

5.   *Support materials.*

LEADERSHIP FUNCTIONS IN GROUP PROBLEM SOLVING

All small problem solving groups have various leadership functions that need to be fulfilled if work is to be done and effective solutions are to be found to group problems. The quality of group discussion is the responsibility of each of the members of the group, not just of the elected or appointed leaders. Groups in different stages of work in a problem-solving sequence have different functional role requirements for the members. The ideal objective of each group member should be to learn to diagnose the role requirements at different times and then do that "thing" when it is appropriate and needed. This is not easy to do, particularly since most people have developed one or two particular kinds of behavior over the years that seem to work well for them in groups in which they have membership. Sometimes they continue to provide these functions even when a particular one is inappropriate or not needed. This habit can and often does hinder the work of the group. But new behaviors can be learned. The purpose of this discussion is to suggest an initial framework of functional behaviors that can be used by group members to increase and enhance their skills of group membership. Using this framework, group members can learn to become better observers of these functions and, ultimately, to supply them when they are needed in the problem solving process.*

Types of Behavior Relevant to the Group's Fulfillment of Its Task

These kinds of functions are related to the task being performed; their purpose is to facilitate and coordinate group effort toward defining the problem, developing alternative solutions to the problem, evaluating these solutions, choosing a testable solution, and developing action steps to implement the chosen solution. Some of the various task functions that need to be supplied in this problem solving process are:

a.   Initiating. Giving new ideas or new directions; proposing tasks or immediate objectives; defining a group problem; suggesting a procedure or an idea for solving a group problem.

b.   Elaborating and clarifying. Expanding and exploring ideas of others; interpreting ideas or suggestions; defining, indicating alternatives; and clearing up confusions.

c.   Coordinating. Ideas need to be integrated and various concepts need to be put together, particularly when group members are evaluating and preparing to choose a solution to their problem.

d.   Summarizing. Drawing the work together and keeping the work flow focused and on track; offering a decision or conclusion for the group to accept or reject.

e.   Technical and recording. Work needs to be done for the group, such as arranging the physical setting, using newsprint, or in other ways recording the work of the group. Providing this function adequately becomes increasingly important when the group is developing alternative solutions to problems by brainstorming — to insure that no one's idea will be lost.

f.   Other task functions needed at different times are: the giving and seeking of information relevant to the task at hand; and the giving and seeking of opinions about the ideas that others have proposed.

*The substance of this discussion draws primarily on the original concepts of Benne and Sheats (1948) and Bales (1950).

Types of Behavior Relevant to the Group's Maintenance

These functions are related to group-centered activities and behaviors; their purpose is to build cohesiveness, maintain good relationships, and provide a climate in which members' resources are effectively used as the group goes about working on its task of problem solving. Some of these various maintenance functions in the problem solving process are:

a.   Encouraging and supporting. Members need praise and warmth. They need to feel that they themselves are relevant and that their contributions have been accepted. Remarks, gestures, or facial expressions indicate this acceptance of others.

b.   Harmonizing. There are times when differences need to be mediated and worked through, especially during the solution-evaluation phase of problem solving. A part of this function is also the ability to relieve tensions in the group so that work on the task can continue (e.g., making brief, humorous comments or jokes).

c.   Gatekeeping. Some find it easier to share ideas and participate in discussion than do others. Providing opportunities to share the stage or air time and keeping communication channels open for others is an important function in group problem solving.

d.   Process observing. Feedback on how the group is working together needs to be given from time to time so that hang-ups may be avoided or dealt with, and task work may proceed with more facility.

e.   Following. Everyone cannot lead all the time. Sometimes a very positive function is to follow, not sharing, but giving passive acceptance to the ideas of others, perhaps even showing acceptance with nonverbal behavior.

f.   Other maintenance functions needed at different times are: helping to set standards or norms for the group; compromising one's own conflicts or differences with others.

Types of Behavior That are Individual in Nature

Rather than being facilitative in the problem solving process, there are other functions that are sometimes irrelevant to the task or negatively oriented to building good group interaction. Some of these behaviors that are often visible in groups are:

a.   Aggression. Attacking others, being openly envious of the contributions of others, and disrupting the group's need to do task work.

b.   Blocking. Being negative and resistant without cause and in opposition most of the time is another visibly negative function, particularly disruptive when the group is doing evaluation on the solutions they have proposed.

c.   Attention seeking. Boasting and calling attention to oneself and constantly pleading a special interest can be negative influences on a problem solving process.

d.   Dominating. Often someone attempts to take over and lead the group in a different and nonappropriate direction, manipulating the group for his or her own purposes. It is apparent here also that this form of behavior can be extremely disruptive when the group is attempting to solve a common problem.

e.   Diverting. Inappropriately joking and indulging in horse-play is also a form of idiosyncratic behavior that does not facilitate problem solving work.

These, then, are examples of various kinds of functions that need to be supplied in problem solving groups, and some that are supplied but are dysfunctional and should be avoided. There are, of course, many others that could be added. What is important to observe will vary with what the group is doing, the observer's purposes, his needs, and other factors. Perhaps it is possible to see oneself providing one or more of these functions. Perhaps also, one can see improvements that he or she can make, either in eliminating in oneself a disruptive behavior or in learning to provide additional facilitative behaviors to the group. The key is practice.

D. Design for Learning to Help Develop Shared Leadership in Groups

1. *Purpose.* This learning design demonstrates the effects of different leadership processes in group problem solving. More specifically, it is intended to show how the leadership functions we worked with earlier can be used in different ways.

2. *Materials needed.* Post-discussion questionnaires and leader instruction sheets (in part 5) will be needed, plus newsprint and markers. A small hand-held calculator would be useful.

3. *Steps in using the design.*
    a. Review leadership functions material.
    b. Choose group discussion task.
    c. Form groups of four.
    d. Select a leader for each small group.
    e. Begin the group discussion.
    f. Have group members fill out post-discussion questionnaires.
    g. Collect questionnaires and compute means.
    h. Convene full group; each small group gives feedback on solutions arrived at.
    i. Present criteria for "correct" decision or solution.
    j. Post questionnaire results for each group.
    k. Read samples of process-observation statements from questionnaires.
    l. Have full group attempt to identify leader instruction differences.
    m. Review and discuss results.

4. *Deriving learnings.* The instructor may wish to use some of the following issues in the review discussion mentioned above:
    – To what extent were the directive (1/0) leaders actually able to fulfill the leadership functions?
    – How were the participative (.5/.5) leaders able to decide which group members should be asked or encouraged to perform which functions? Are there identifiable characteristics for making such functional role assignments?
    – To what extent were the leadership functions actually performed in the laissez-faire (0/1) groups?
    – How was leader approach related to task effectiveness? To process results?
    – How does task effectiveness relate to group process outcome?
    – Which leadership approach was most satisfying? Least satisfying?
    – Which groups took longest to reach decisions? Shortest? Why?
    – In which groups were the decisions most likely to be carried out?

5.   *Support materials.*

SHARED LEADERSHIP FUNCTIONS IN GROUP PROBLEM SOLVING

Part I: Leadership Functions, Power, and Style

Earlier we described three sets of leadership functions in small group discussions: task functions (initiating, elaborating, or clarifying, coordinating, summarizing, recording); positive or functional process functions (encouraging or supporting, harmonizing and tension-reducing, gatekeeping, process observing, following); and negative or dysfunctional process (individual) functions (aggressing, blocking, attention-seeking, dominating, diverting). Since it is hardly desirable to practice the negative functions, we concentrated on the task and the positive process functions. The previous exercise was used to demonstrate behaviorally these ten leadership functions.

We have, you will note, called these *leadership* functions, yet we have also said that *anyone* in the group can perform them. We can put this even more strongly, for a leader who tried to do all of these things would probably not be very effective. Of course, there *are* a few "great men" who can, and do, accomplish all of these functions themselves.* But such persons are really quite rare; less than five percent of all group leaders fit this great man description. The other ninety-five percent of leaders can, however, be just as effective as the great man by concentrating on *getting the leadership functions accomplished* rather than by trying to accomplish them all by themselves.

How this goal is achieved can best be conceptualized in terms of *power* and the extent to which power is *shared*. (This is an oversimplification, which we will explain further later on.) In any working group, we can say that interactions and decisions illustrate the amount of power each individual has. Often, the amount of power any person has depends on: his or her position in the organization (legitimate power, or authority); status or prestige in the group; special expertise or competency that others attribute to the person; liking or personal feelings toward the person (referent power); that person's ability to provide or administer rewards or punishments to others; or some combination of these five power bases.†

We can make a crude assessment of the power exerted by each person in a group by thinking of the total power in the group as one "power unit." In the three diagrams below (Figure 5-4), we show three different ways this power might be distributed.

FIGURE 5-4 Three Different Power Distributions in a Small Group

We can, then, think of this total unit of power as the sum of the power of all persons in the group. Of course, there are an infinite number of precise distributions, some of which are indicated on the scale on the next page (Figure 5-5).

*See Borgatta, Couch, and Bales (1954).

†For a detail discussion see French and Raven (1959).

FIGURE 5-5

Leader	1	.9	.8	.7	.6	.5	.4	.3	.2	.1	0	Leader
Members	0	.1	.2	.3	.4	.5	.6	.7	.8	.9	1	Members

| 1/0 | .5/.5 | 0/1 |

Our interest is in the *relative* distribution of power in the group. A leader who tries to do every-thing, to accomplish all of the group leadership functions, is exercising "1/0" (one-oh) power. We've all probably been in a group, at one time or another, with a leader like this. The leader dominates completely, there is no sharing of leadership functions. If you've been very fortunate, your experience with this type of directive or "authoritarian" leader *might* have been a good one — he or she could have been one of the five percent of all leaders who roughly fit the great man stereotype. It is, however, a lot more likely that the leader — and the group — were not very effective.

At the opposite extreme is the leader who refuses to take any of the power — or responsibility. Everything is dumped on the group members in a "0/1" (oh-one) power balance. Of course, this isn't really leadership at all; it is what has been called laissez-faire (let them alone) or do-nothing leadership. In general, the chances of any productive group work in this situation are even worse than in the 1/0 case.

The mid-range power distributions — from .6/.4 to .4/.6, roughly, might be called "participative" leadership styles. Without abdicating all power or responsibility, and without demanding all power and responsibility, the leader is able to share power, to involve the group members — and him or herself — in carrying out the leadership functions. This .5/.5 style is, in general, the most likely to yield positive results in terms of group performance. Unless the leader is truly a charismatic great man the 1/0 style will make group members feel hostile, frustrated, and unwilling to accept fully the leader or the leader's decisions. Unless the leader is a total nincompoop *and* an informal leader develops, is recognized, and performs some or all of the leadership functions, the 0/1 style will make group members feel uninvolved and uncommitted to do anything.

Two other even less desirable situations can arise — in fact are likely to arise — with the 1/0 or 0/1 power situations. In either case, if it is at all possible the group members will try to emulate the leader's model. Thus, a 1/0 situation can easily develop into a 1/1 impossible conflict, resolvable only when one or the other is defeated totally. Such win-lose conflicts are rarely, if ever, benefi-cial. Similarly, in the 0/1 case no one may be willing to accept power or responsibility for doing anything. When this happens, the group may dissolve or members may occupy themselves with irrelevant, time-killing activities. It is fairly certain that no work will be accomplished.

Since so few of us are "great men" and since most of us would like to be reasonably effective as leaders and in helping others learn to be reasonably effective as leaders, it is important to under-stand, first, the functional behavior patterns involved in each of the three leadership power styles and, second, how the leadership functions can be shared with group members in the participative or .5/.5 style.

This conclusion raises a final point of interest. We've been talking about power as a fixed quantity of something, which may be shared or kept to oneself. In reality, groups differ in the *total amount* of power, control, or influence* that exists among members of a particular group. One group may have only a small amount of power, while another group has a great deal of power. The greater the total amount of power, control, or influence in a group, the more likely it is that the group members will be satisfied with the group *and* that the group will perform effectively. Power is *not* a fixed and limited quantity — any given group can have more (or less) power. In fact, *each person* in a group can have more power, and this will mean that the group as a whole will have more power. You may see, now, that our point is that the .5/.5 style is likely to generate a greater degree of total power (or control, or influence) in the group; the group may, in fact, go from "one unit" of power to a total of 2, 5, or even 10 units of power! In other words, *everyone* can gain more power, control, and influence. This gain is, then, an added benefit of shared leadership functions in problem solving groups.

Part II: Leader Approach and Group Processes

In Chapter One we presented an outline of the problem solving process (see Table 1-1). While the proper phases may very well be used in all three of the leader approaches we have just described, the way this is done may vary quite a bit, particularly in terms of the *time* needed to *reach* a solution or decision, and the *commitment* to the decision by the group members, which is directly related to the *time* required to *implement* the solution or decision.

Looking simply at the time required to work through a problem solving meeting, it is clear that when the leader takes full power and responsibility in decision making the task will get done sooner, compared with a leaderless or participative group. The leaderless group spends much time in working through the phases of a problem solving discussion, particularly in the first, problem-definition, phase. In a shared leadership group time is needed for full involvement of and discussion by all group members; this, however, does not usually take quite so long as with the leaderless situation.

The time required to reach a solution or decision may *not*, however, be the most significant time requirement in problem solving. Ordinarily, the time required to *implement* the solution or decision is ignored. Of course, time-to-solution may, sometimes, be critical. The army officer in charge of a company in battle does *not* have the time to involve all of his subordinates in a critical decision, nor does the airplane pilot faced with an emergency landing. Yet these occasions are not normal — they are, in fact, quite out of the ordinary. Much of the time the instant decision pressure illustrated by the above examples does *not* exist, and the issue of solution implementation *is* significant.

In such cases, acceptance of and commitment to the solution by those who will have to carry it out may be a critical and time-costly factor. Table 5-1 shows both the decision-making and the implementation time-frames for each leader approach.

Thus, we suggest that although a *solution* can be reached quickly when the leader is very directive, takes all the power, and makes all the decisions, the actual implementation time will be far longer than when group members are actively involved in the problem solving and decision-making processes. A group that lacks effective leadership may fare slightly better, since the decision will obviously be that of the group, yet without effective attention to group processes it is unlikely that full group-member commitment to the solution will be achieved. Only in the participative, shared leadership case is the commitment developed that will free the leader from the time-consuming

---

*Technically, these terms do not mean exactly the same thing. Practically, however, we see no major need to differentiate among them. For futher, more detailed discussion, see Tannenbaum (1968).

TABLE 5-1   Comparison of Three Group Decision Approaches*

Leader Approach	Time to Reach a Decision through Group Problem Solving	Time to Develop Commitment to the Decision by Group Members	Time Required to Implement the Decision	Average Expected Total Time
Leader-Directed Decision	Short	Long	Long	Long
Group Decision with Leadership	Moderate	Short	Short	Moderate
Group Decision without Leadership	Long	Moderate	Moderate	Long

task of persuading group members to accept his decision and keeping a close check on them to insure effective implementation.

In summary, the shared leadership approach is generally more efficient than alternative approaches. Both the time required to reach a decision or solution in a problem solving group *and* the time needed to implement the decision depend on the part played by group members in the decision-making process. This affects directly the degree of satisfaction group members feel with the solution and the commitment they will develop toward carrying out the decision reached. The shared leadership approach increases somewhat the time initially needed to arrive at a decision but reduces drastically the time required to develop the kind of commitment that leads to effective, rapid implementation.

*This table, and discussion, is based in part on Maier (1965, 1973).

LEADER INSTRUCTIONS

In the discussion that is about to begin you are to be the formal leader. You are to try to practice as many of the functions of leadership as possible (*task* functions: initiating, elaborating, or clarifying, coordinating, summarizing, recording; and *process* functions: encouraging or supporting, harmonizing and reducing tension, gatekeeping, process observing, following). Although no one can be expected to do everything at once, try to practice as many of these leadership functions as you can. Your task is to develop skill in doing as many of these functions as you can.

LEADER INSTRUCTIONS

In the discussion that is about to begin you are to be the formal leader. In addition to carrying out some of the leadership functions, you should try to get group members to carry out some of the functions, so that *all* of them get performed. The functions are: *task* — initiating, elaborating, or clarifying, coordinating, summarizing, recording; *process* — encouraging or supporting, harmonizing and reducing tension, gatekeeping, process-observing, following. You should, then, perform whichever of these functions you feel you do best and try to get the group members to perform the other functions. Don't try to do too much yourself, but don't expect them to do everything, either.

LEADER INSTRUCTIONS

In the discussion that is about to begin you are to be the formal leader. Your real job, however, is to get the group members to practice leadership functions (*task* functions: initiating, elaborating, or clarifying, coordinating, summarizing, recording; *process* functions: encouraging or supporting, harmonizing and reducing tension, gatekeeping, process observing, following). Your task, then, is not to perform *any* of these functions, but to get the group members to try them and practice them.

DISCUSSION TASK

The four of you are all good friends and are together watching TV and about to have some beer and pizza. Joe (whose house you're at) ordered a large pizza for lunch but ate only a small part of it. Taking it out of the oven, you see that the pizza is square, instead of round, and Joe had one quarter of it. While there's still plenty left, you want to divide it equally among the four of you (if there are only three of you in the group assume that Joe is cleaning up in the kitchen). You've decided that you can only do this by making each person's share exactly the same size and shape. How to cut it up is the problem.

Here is what the pizza looks like. Assume the ingredients are equally distributed over the surface.

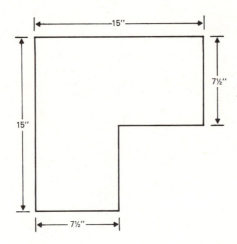

POST-DISCUSSION QUESTIONNAIRE

1. Indicate how you are now feeling about the group discussion that has just taken place by drawing a circle around the number that best represents your feelings.

    a. Objectives of the discussion were

        | very clear | 1 | 2 | 3 | 4 | 5 | 6 | 7 | not at all clear |

    b. My own feelings about these objectives is

        | very negative | 1 | 2 | 3 | 4 | 5 | 6 | 7 | very positive |

    c. The abilities, knowledge, and experience of the persons in the group were used

        | fully and effectively | 1 | 2 | 3 | 4 | 5 | 6 | 7 | poorly and inadequately |

    d. The level of involvement of all group members in the discussion was

        | very low | 1 | 2 | 3 | 4 | 5 | 6 | 7 | very high |

    e. Control, power, and influence in the discussion were

        | imposed on group members | 1 | 2 | 3 | 4 | 5 | 6 | 7 | shared by all group members |

    f. Leadership functions were

        | concentrated in one or two persons | 1 | 2 | 3 | 4 | 5 | 6 | 7 | shared by all group members |

2. Taking all things into consideration, how satisfied were you with this discussion?

    | not at all satisfied | 1 | 2 | 3 | 4 | 5 | 6 | 7 | very satisfied |

3. How committed do you feel to the conclusion or decision arrived at by the group?

    | fully committed | 1 | 2 | 3 | 4 | 5 | 6 | 7 | not at all committed |

4. Were you the *formal* (appointed) leader?

    [   ] Yes
    [   ] No

5. Briefly describe the process of the discussion.

II. CONCEPTUAL SUPPORT MATERIALS: GROUP PROCESS

GROUP OBSERVATION*

Warren G. Bennis and Herbert A. Shepard

The following discussion reviews in rough outline four basic approaches to the systematic collection of data about what is happening in a group. All four approaches are based on the direct, visual observation, recording, and categorization of data. These approaches do differ in several ways, mostly because an observer cannot watch everything. There is a lot of activity going on in most groups, and what the observer perceives depends on what he attends to, as well as on the acuity of his perception. Hence, the observer has to start by being sensitive only to certain aspects of the situation. The differences among the four approaches are, then, due mostly to what different researchers (who developed these approaches) believe to be the most significant factors in group interaction.

I. The Interactionists

The observer might begin by concentrating on one aspect of the situation that is basic to any kind of group activity: who interacts with whom. The interactionists say: "Group life is the outcome of interaction among organisms."[1] The most extreme interactionists undertake to observe only the patterns of interaction, without reference to the content of communication. From the interaction patterns, whether of a two-person relationship, a small group, a large organization, or a whole society, it is possible to make predictions about other aspects of the group — its power structure, for example. There are some areas of disagreement among the various authors who use interaction analysis. However, all interactionists share the view that much can be inferred from habitual patterns and changes in the interaction of members of a group.

When we chart the interaction of a group we are not interested in who hates whom and who loves whom, we are interested primarily in who interacts with whom. An interactionist observing a group is not concerned with what people are saying or how they are saying it. He is concerned only with the frequency of interaction, the participants in interaction, the initiation of interaction, the ordering of interaction, the duration of actions, and the interruption of actions.

Studies using interaction-analysis methods range from studies of decision making in small groups to studies of the communication systems of large industrial organizations.[2] Strodtbeck, in his study of the family as a three-person group, found that "the most-speaking person wins the largest share of decisions and in all cases the least-speaking person wins least."[3] In his study of clerical workers engaged in repetitive work, Homans showed that high interaction was closely correlated with personal popularity and productivity.[4]

*From W. G. Bennis and H. A. Shepard, *Group observations* (Boston, Mass: Boston University Human Relations Center, Research Papers and Technical Notes, No. 7). Abridged and used by permission.

[1] C. Arensberg. Behavior and organization: Industrial studies. In Rohrer & Sherif (Eds.), *Social Psychology at the Crossroads*. New York: Harper & Brothers, 1951.

[2] F. L. W. Richardson & C. R. Walker. *Human relations in an expanding company.* New Haven, Yale University Labor and Management Center, 1948. Also see E. D. Chapple (with the collaboration of C. M. Arensberg). Measuring human relations: An introduction to the study of the interaction of individuals. *Genetic Psychology Monograph*, 1940, **22**: 3-147.

[3] F. L. Strodtbeck, The family as a three-person group. *American Sociological Review,* 1954, **19**: 23-29.

[4] G. Homans. The cash posters: A study of a group of working girls. *American Sociological Review,* 1954, **19**(6): 724-733.

II. Interaction Process Analysis

As a social scientist, the interactionist is interested in predicting behavior and in correlating inter-action patterns with other aspects of the situation. As an observer, however, he is interested only in systematically recording an aspect of the situation that is obvious and unambiguous.

Some of the interactionists are interested in observing more than interaction patterns, however, and place enough emphasis on feelings and meanings for them to earn consideration as a separate group. R. F. Bales has developed a system for categorizing behavior known as interaction process analysis. This is an ingenious method for analyzing not only the interactions among group members, but also the sentiments accompanying interaction. It is "a way of classifying direct, face-to-face interaction as it takes place, act-by-act, and a series of ways of summarizing and analyzing the result data so that they yield useful information."[5]

As Bales points out, his selection of the set of categories is a practical compromise among demands of theoretical adequacy, ability of observers to categorize, and simplicity. In the first three and last three categories are recorded "social-emotional" units of interaction — positive and negative reactions of the group members to one another and to the group's task. The middle six categories are "task-oriented" — they cover exchanges of information among the group members related to the job of solving some problem under discussion.

Bales' studies indicate that in small discussion groups, where the group has a problem to solve, the process typically tends to follow a sequence of four phases. First, there is the "adaptive" phase of pooling information and other resources, and seeing how they can be used to accomplish the task. Second, is the "goal-attainment" phase of actually working out the decisions and taking the ac-tion that completes the task. Third, there is an "integrative" phase of reestablishing group solidar-ity, which may have been disturbed in the second phase. The fourth phase, which overlaps the third, is a period of "tension-release," which consists of joking, laughter, and other expressions of relief that the job has been accomplished.

Applying Bales' observation system requires more skill than that of merely counting interactions. Hence his observers are carefully trained in the details of scoring method so that their records agree.

III. Analysis of Group Mentality

It is a short step from common sense to Bales' category system. But it is a transatlantic hop from Bales to W. R. Bion,[6] a British psychiatrist who has formulated group process in quite different terms. Bion takes seriously the statement that a group is more than the sum of its members — that it has a life of its own.

In Bion's view groups are essential to man's mental-emotional life. Participating in group mental life is essential to a full life for the individual; man seeks his fulfillment through group member-ship. To the group he brings his private needs and desires, and attempts to derive corresponding satisfactions from the group. Picture now the several members, each attempting to exploit the group for the fulfillment of his desires. The resultant product of this tangle of desires Bion calls the group mentality.

As in an economic system, there is a disparity between what the individual wants from the group, and how much of the emotional pie the group is going to accord him. The group's method of

[5] R. F. Bales. *Interaction process analysis.* Cambridge, Mass.: Addison-Wesley, 1950, (pp. 5-6).
[6] W. R. Bion. Experiences in groups: I-VII. *Human Relations*, 1948, 5(1-4).

organization for settling this dispute Bion calls the group culture: "I employ the phrase 'culture of the group' in an extremely loose manner: I include in it the structure which the group achieves at any given moment, the occupation it pursues, and the organization it adopts."[7]

Herbert A. Thelen and his associates have formalized Bion's ideas into a set of categories for recording group behavior.[8] In their version, the group mentality is differentiated into three emotional *modalities*, or recurring patterns of expressive behavior. These are "fight-flight," "pairing," and "dependency." Fight-flight represents the desires of the group to escape the task that faces the group, either by fighting it (or one another) or by running away from the task. Pairing represents the desire of the group to see security by establishing pair relationships between members of the group. This is manifested in a number of ways: friendly smiles and winks, mutually supportive statements, and so on. Dependency represents the group's need to remain dependent on the leader, to retain him as protector, judge, and commander.

A fourth category of the group mentality, called, of all things, work, represents the desire of the group to engage in problem solving activity. The work needs are frequently in conflict with the other needs of the group, and every member is caught in this struggle.

For purposes of categorizing, the work modality can be differentiated into four classes. One-level work is personally need-oriented. An observer watching one-level work feels that it interrupts the flow of the group, and is an expression of purely personal need. Two-level work involves maintaining or following through on the task the group is working on. An observer watching two-level work feels that it is group-oriented and necessary, but routine. Three-level work is group-focused work that usually has some new ingredient. An observer watching three-level work feels that it is group-oriented, focused, and energetic, and that it has direction and meaning for the group. Four-level work is creative, insightful, and integrative. It usually involves an appropriate and insightful interpretation that brings together for the group a whole series of experiences and infuses meaning into them, and at the same time has immediate relevance to present problems. An observer watching four-level work feels that it is creative and exciting.

The relations between work achievement and activity in the other modalities of group mentality is an important matter for students of group dynamics. The definition of work levels helps in reaching an assessment of the achievement of discussion groups.

IV. Role Analysis

In formally organized clubs and associations, some of the members hold special "offices" — chairman, secretary, etc. In connection with their offices, the chairman and secretary have certain duties — they have special roles in the organization.

In any group, whether formally organized or not, there are a number of roles played that are not dignified by a title, but that affect the way the group as a whole operates. If there is one member who habitually opposes all suggestions made by other group members, one cannot assume that he has recently been elected to the office of Group Opposer — it is simply the role that he characteristically takes in the group. Some persons are skilled in playing a number of group roles, but most of us have only a few at our disposal and can be pigeonholed more easily.

Membership roles have received a good deal of study. There are four main questions that can be asked about a membership role. *First,* what are its consequences for the person playing the role —

[7] W. R. Bion. Experiences in groups: II. *Human Relations,* 1948, 5(1-4).

[8] H. Thelen, et al. *Methods for studying work and emotionality in group operation.* University of Chicago Press, 1954.

what needs of his does it satisfy and what problems does it create for him? *Second,* what are its consequences for the other members of the group — what needs of theirs does it satisfy, what needs does it arouse? *Third,* what are its consequences for the integration of the group — does it increase or decrease cohesiveness, solidarity, mutual respect, etc.? *Fourth,* what are its consequences for the performance of the group's task — does it contribute toward the solution of the group's problem, or does it interfere with solving the problem?

A number of systems have been worked out to describe the variety of roles that occur in a group. Any one of these systems may be useful for assessing the potentialities of a group or understanding some of the difficulties the group has in working together.

Perhaps the most common of such role analysis systems is that developed by Benne and Sheats.[9] *

NOTE ON GROUP OBSERVATION METHODS

While each of the four approaches reviewed in the paper reprinted above has certain advantages and disadvantages, the combination of Bales's work with the functional role analysis framework developed by Benne and Sheats seems to be the most generally useful of the more rigorously based observational methods that have been developed to date. This is probably because these two frameworks have been "translated" into formats that make them fairly easy to understand and to *use* in real situations. As you will have noticed by now, these two frameworks have served as the primary conceptual and applied approaches we have developed in this and the preceding chapters. In the discussion below, we present a way of integrating observation into the ongoing participative work of a real group.

COMBINING OBSERVATION AND PARTICIPATION
IN A PROBLEM SOLVING GROUP

Some members of small problem solving groups participate more freely in the task work of the group than others. They talk more, they provide more ideas for action, and they are generally more visible. Other group members do not participate as openly in the work of the group. They are quieter, they are less visible, and because of this they have a greater opportunity to observe how the group is working than do the more vocal members. Whether or not they use this opportunity, however, is another question. Figure 5-6 is a continuum indicating the levels of participation in a problem solving group.

FIGURE 5-6 Participation in Problem Solving

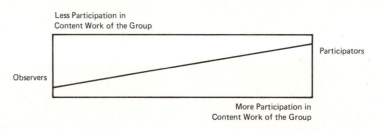

Less Participation in
Content Work of the Group

Participators

Observers

More Participation in
Content Work of the Group

[9]K. D. Benne & P. Sheats. Functional roles of group members. *Journal of Social Issues,* 1948, 2, 42-47.

*Specific details of Benne and Sheats's approach were reviewed in some depth earlier in this chapter (see page 107). See also the following discussion in this section.

There are two dimensions of group activity that need to be considered in the life of a problem solving group. The first of these, the *task* dimension, requires that all job-relevant leadership functions be fulfilled by the group members. The purpose of these functions is to facilitate and coordinate group effort toward defining the problem, developing alternative solutions to the problem, evaluating these solutions, choosing a testable solution, and developing action steps to implement the chosen solution.

High-activity people who participate more freely in the group often provide most task functions quite naturally. However, they are also often unaware of some necessary task functions that need to be fulfilled in order to have the group perform effectively. They are only aware that the problem has to be solved, that the job has to be completed. They do not pause to consider either what functions are necessary for increasing group problem solving effectiveness or whether they or other members are fulfilling these necessary functions.

The second level of group activity needing consideration is the group *building* and *maintenance* dimension. These functions are related to group-centered attitudes and behaviors. Their purpose is to build group cohesiveness and maintain group solidarity as the group goes about working on its task of problem solving. Here it is important not only to "get the job done" but also to be concerned with HOW it gets done by considering the feelings and satisfactions of group members.

Low-activity people who more often observe the process of group interactions also probably more naturally provide the group with its relevant group building and maintenance functions than do the high-activity people who are concerned with the "job." However, also like the high-activity people who may be unaware of some important task functions, low-activity group members are often unaware of some necessary maintenance functions that need fulfillment to insure effectiveness. Unlike the high-activity people, they may be aware that "something is wrong," that the group is not working well together; but they often don't know how to help or what to do about it.

Finally, neither the observer nor the participator is completely aware of the functions being performed by the other, although the observer may be subjectively aware that a distinction between task and maintenance functions is somehow being made from time to time. Providing a framework for the group may help all members become more aware of the process of interaction both in the building and maintenance and in the task dimensions of group life.

Ideally, the high-activity person should learn to be a better observer and the low-activity person should learn to participate more often, using his observational skills. This *can* happen if each learns more clearly *what* to observe. Figure 5-7 indicates this more ideal group participation pattern.

FIGURE 5-7 Combining Observation and Participation in Group Problem Solving

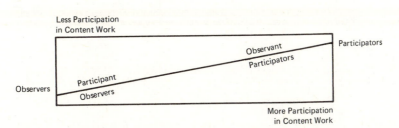

REFERENCES

Bales, R. F. (1950) *Interaction process analysis.* Cambridge, Mass.: Addison-Wesley. · *in social psychology.* 3rd ed.,

Bales, R. F. (1958) Task roles and social roles in problem solving groups. In *Readings in social psychology.* 3rd ed., eds. E. E. Maccoby, T. M. Newcomb, and E. L. Hartley. New York: Holt, Rinehart, & Winston.

Berkowitz, L. (1953) Sharing leadership in small, decision-making groups. *Journal of Abnormal and Social Psychology* **48**: 231-238.

Bion, W. R. (1974) *Experiences in groups.* New York: Ballantine.

Borgatta, E. F.; Couch, A. S.; and Bales, R. F. (1954) Some findings relevant to the great man theory of leadership. *American Sociological Review* **19**: 755-759.

Bradford, L. P. (1961) *Group development.* Washington, D.C.: National Training Laboratories.

Bradford, L. P.; Gibb, J. R.; and Benne, K. D. (1964) *T-group theory and laboratory method.* New York: Wiley.

Burke, R. J. (1967) The development of task and socio-emotional role differentiation. *Sociometry* **30**: 379-392.

**Cartwright, D., and Zander, A. (1968) *Group dynamics.* 3rd ed. New York: Holt, Rinehart, & Winston.

Fiedler, F. E., and Chemers, M. M. (1974) *Leadership and effective management.* Glenview, Ill.: Scott, Foresman.

French, J. R. P., Jr., and Raven, B. (1959) The bases of social power. In *Studies in social power.* Ed. D. Cartwright. Ann Arbor, Mich.: Institute for Social Research, The University of Michigan.

Gorden, T. (1955) *Group-centered leadership: A way of releasing the creative power of groups.* Boston: Houghton Mifflin.

Homans, G. C. (1950) *The human group.* New York: Harcourt, Brace.

Luft, J. (1973) *Group processes.* 2nd ed. Palo Alto, Calif.: National Press.

Maccoby, E. E.; Newcomb, T. M.; and Hartley, E. L. (1958) *Readings in social psychology.* 3rd ed. New York: Holt, Rinehart, & Winston.

Maier, N. R. F. (1953) An experimental test of the effect of training on discussion leadership. *Human Relations* **6**: 161-173.

**Maier, N. R. F. (1963) *Problem-solving discussions and conferences.* New York: McGraw-Hill.

Maier, N. R. F. (1950) The quality of group decisions as influenced by the discussion leader. *Human Relations* **3**: 155-174.

**Miles, M. B. (1959) *Learning to work in groups.* New York: Teachers College, Columbia University.

Olmstead, M. S. (1959) *The small group.* New York: Random House.

Petrullo, L., and Bass, B. M., eds. (1961) *Leadership and interpersonal behavior.* New York: Holt, Rinehart, & Winston.

Shaw, M. E. (1971) *Group dynamics: The psychology of small group behavior.* New York: McGraw-Hill, (2nd ed., 1975).

**Shepherd, C. R. (1964) *Small groups.* San Francisco, Calif.: Chandler.

Tannenbaum, A. S., ed. (1968) *Control in organizations.* New York: McGraw-Hill.

**Thelen, H. (1954) *Dynamics of groups at work.* Chicago: University of Chicago Press.

Thibant, J. W., and Kelley, H. H. (1959) *The social psychology of groups.* New York: Wiley.

White, R. K., and Lippitt, R. (1960) *Autocracy and democracy.* New York: Harper.

**References preceded by a double asterisk are those judged most basic or important.

CHAPTER SIX

Diagnosing Problems: Helping People Learn to Understand Problems and Develop Action Alternatives

"Let's run it up the flagpole . . ."
                    Anon.

INTRODUCTION

As we have noted earlier, people tend to be far more solution-minded than problem-oriented. Perhaps the major benefit for a problem-solving framework — a set of steps to follow — is that it forces people to concentrate on defining the problem and considering a variety of alternatives *before* jumping to solutions. Diagnosis is a critical step in this process, because a full understanding of the problem and its various elements is necessary for the development of good solution alternatives.

The learning designs in this chapter have two aims. First, we want to show that there is more than one way to go about understanding a problem. It is possible for people to be familiar with several diagnostic approaches, and this is important for two reasons: (1) to some extent, what you look for is what you see, thus one must be aware that different diagnostic approaches may define the *same* problem situation — using the same information — in *different* ways; and (2) certain approaches are both easier to use and more appropriate for certain types of problem situations.

Second, we want to provide some basic skill in using one rather general diagnostic approach. No single approach to diagnosis is appropriate for any problem situation, but there is one approach we believe to be more generally useful than any other.

Our goals for this chapter are, then, development of understanding of several diagnostic approaches, awareness of their emphases and the kinds of situations for which each is best suited, and development of skill in using one particular diagnostic technique we find most suited to a problem-solving approach.

I. SPECIFIC SKILL-DEVELOPMENT AND LEARNING DESIGNS

A. Design for Learning the Effects of Different Diagnostic Approaches

1. *Purpose.* The aim of this learning design is actually quite simple: to show the participants, in a graphic and experiential manner, that how one looks at a problem can determine what one sees and does. The frameworks or approaches in part 5 are described in simplified form. The aim is *not* to develop expertise in the use of these approaches but rather to develop *awareness* that a variety of diagnostic approaches does exist and that the use of any one approach does,

to some extent, determine how problems will be defined and the nature of action plans that may be developed to solve those problems.

2. *Materials needed.* Case materials are in part 5 of this design. Also included is a "summary" sheet for use in a variation described in the Instructor's Guide. Newsprint and markers will also be needed.

3. *Steps in using the design.*

    a. Review the diagnostic approaches with the entire group.

    b. Form three subgroups.

    c. Have each subgroup discuss the diagnostic approach assigned.

    d. Have the subgroups read and discuss the case.

    e. Have the subgroups prepare a written diagnosis.

    f. Provide assistance as needed.

    g. Post diagnoses; have each subgroup explain its results to the class.

    h. List similarities and differences among diagnoses.

    i. Summarize and integrate results.

4. *Deriving learnings.* As part of step 3i, the group will probably want to consider the following questions:

    — Which of the three diagnostic approaches seemed to provide the best diagnostic problem statement?

    — Which approach was easiest to use? Which was the most difficult to apply? Why?

    — How should a helper, consultant, or change agent choose which diagnostic approach to use? Can the consultant actually be familiar enough with more than one approach so that a choice is possible?

5. *Support materials.*

DIAGNOSTIC APPROACHES

In describing the "dimensions of the consultant's job," Lippitt (1959) noted that every consultant should have an explicit, systematic "descriptive-analytic theory" to provide diagnostic guidelines. Any useful diagnostic orientation must deal with three major issues. *First,* there must be some basic framework of concepts about the nature of organized social systems. This means, in terms of useful application, that a diagnostic approach must contain some notions of cause-and-effect relationships, in order to be used to predict, as well as to explain, events.

Second, there must be some particular attention to organizational processes — the *way* social systems operate — particularly those processes that lead to or cause problems. To make this diagnostic focus useful, however, there must also be a set of specified diagnostic procedures to measure and define the processes and problems.

Third, a diagnostic approach should include some ideas about the nature of problems in organized social systems. Thus, an approach should be directed toward certain general goals or intentions for the change process. That is, a diagnostic approach should contain a definition or model of what effective organizations "look like" — how they work — as well as definitions of problem areas. Using this element, the diagnostic approach can point out directions for change in terms of the difference between "present" and "effective ideal" images.

We will briefly review three major diagnostic approaches. Each is an example of a more general set of approaches. The three presented here were chosen because they are particularly clear and reasonably easy to understand. While effective use of any of these approaches would certainly require more detailed study, it seems important for a consultant or helper to at the very least have some understanding of a variety of diagnostic approaches. While it would be desirable to be able actually to apply more than one (perhaps several) of the diagnostic approaches that have been developed, it is really *necessary* that such persons be able to have some basic knowledge of more than one approach.

Diagnostic Approach: A Systems Model (French and Bell)

Several writers have proposed "systems" models of organizations. These models are all basically similar in that they define an organization as a set of interrelated groups of subsystems, the organization being the total system. Some models define the subsystems in terms of traditional functional labels (production, managerial, etc.) while others are broader, including organizational processes as well as identifiable structural or functional units.

All of these models are essentially "category lists," into which diagnostic information can be fitted according to the most appropriate category. When this is done, a descriptive picture of the organization emerges that should highlight organizational or subsystem problem areas. One of the most useful systems models was developed by French and Bell (1973). Their text, *Organization Development,* is oriented toward change, and their model is more diagnostically and practically oriented than most other systems models.

The model consists of six subsystem elements: goals subsystem, task subsystem, technology subsystem, structural subsystem, human-social subsystem, and boundary subsystem. Any organized social system can be described in terms of these six subsystems. By fitting descriptive information into these six categories, one should end up with a comprehensive picture of the overall system that, upon careful inspection, clearly identifies problem areas. These problem areas could be within a specific subsystem or could involve relationships between two (or more) subsystems. Let us identify the six subsystems a bit more clearly.*

Goals subsystem. This subsystem consists of the various levels of goals in the organization and its parts, as well as the organizational processes by which goals are determined. The term "levels" refers to the fact that goals exist over a range from broad-organizational (e.g., survival, profit, community impact, etc.) through subunit (e.g., the sales force may have a goal for each product line and the production department may also have specified product-line production goals — and these two sets of goals may be in conflict), down to small-group and even individual-level goals (e.g., a small-group goal of developing weekly team reports that provide accurate predictions for use by top-level decision makers, or an individual-level goal of advancement to a higher job grade). As significant as the specific goals, at whatever level, are the organizational, group, and individual goal-setting processes — the *way* goals are developed.

Technology subsystem. The "content" elements of this subsystem are tools, machines, and knowledge, while the "process" factors are procedures and methods involved in using tools, machines, and knowledge as well as the work-flow process — the way the technology used requires the work to be done from start to finish.

Task subsystem. The specific task or job definitions comprise the content side of the task subsystem. Obviously, the more complex the organization and the more sophisticated the technolo-

*The following material is based on French and Bell's discussion (pp. 77-79).

gical subsystem is, the more task specialization is likely and the more specific and complex will be the task subsystem. The process side of this subsystem is, of course, working — the task actions and activities that are engaged in and accomplished by members of the organization.

Structural subsystem. The content of the structural subsystem consists of formal organizational groups (as indicated on an organization chart), the specified set of hierarchical and reporting relationships. Also included are the various organizational rules and regulations (working hours, office assignments, etc.). The processes involved in the structural subsystem are the work-flow design and the various procedures and practices that are carried out within set rules and policies (such as communication, planning, coordination, control, and decision making).

Human-social subsystem. As one might expect from a behavioral science-based approach, this subsystem is viewed by French and Bell as the most complex and differentiated, certainly in terms of their description if not in terms of their conceptual framework. Although the process element can be very simply stated as "interpersonal interaction," this term covers such a complex variety of more specific processes that it is not terribly helpful in terms of organizing diagnostic data. The content factors are more precisely spelled out. One factor consists of the skills and abilities of organization members. A second content factor is the leadership climate of the system — the basic philosophy and style of leadership — which may be classified in any of a variety of ways (e.g., Likert's [1967] approach defines four basic leadership climates ranging from "exploitative-authoritarian" through "benevolent-authoritarian" and "consultative" to "participative"; Blake and Mouton [1967] define five basic leadership-style combinations that integrate elements of "concern for task" and "concern for people"; Bowers and Seashore [1966] created a "four-factor" theory, which included measures of the leader's efforts to facilitate task achievement, to facilitate interactions, to provide personal support, and to emphasize goal attainment; Lewin, Lippitt, and White [1938] identified three basic styles: authoritarian, democratic, and laissez-faire; several other, more simplistic, approaches focus on two dimensions that are generally defined as interpersonal relationship-orientation or consideration and task achievement-orientation or structuring of work by the leader). The third content factor in the human-social subsystem is the formal aspect — personnel policies, reward policies, and collective bargaining agreements, for example. The fourth and final factor consists of the informal aspect — norms, values, feelings, and the informal power and status structure.

Boundary subsystem. French and Bell actually call this the "external interface subsystem," but boundary subsystem is far more descriptive. The boundary subsystem obviously is what separates any social system from its environment; a system *must* be separated, in order to maintain its identity as an organized system. But, a system must also deal with its environment in many ways; too much separation becomes isolation, which, in an environment containing many other organized social systems, will inevitably lead to the demise of the isolated system. Survival requires obtaining considerable information from outside the system; the addition, from time to time, of more material resources from the environment (people, money, supplies, etc.), as well as attention to demands from the environment (such as government regulations); attempts to influence important parts of the environment; and, output of some organizational product (or service) into the environment (which, for many organizations, is a significant way of getting resources, meeting demands, and influencing other systems in the environment). These are the "content" elements of the boundary subsystem. The process consists, basically, of obtaining data from the environment and formulating appropriate and effective actions or responses on the basis of these data. While the other five subsystems deal with what happens *within* the system and how it happens, an activity that might be called "throughput," the boundary subsystem is involved with the interchange between the system and its environment, which can be labeled "input" and "output" activities.

Summary. Obviously, a familiarity with systems theory and modern organization theory would be very helpful in applying this diagnostic approach. Still, given a careful reading of the above summary description, and a bit of trial and practice, one could make use of this approach at an elementary level, which might still prove useful. The table below summarizes the above discussion.

TABLE 6-1   Diagnosis Using a Systems Approach

Subsystem	Content	Process
Goals	— specific goals at various levels	— goal setting
Technological	— tools, machines, knowledge	— procedures, methods, sequence of work flow
Task	— job definitions	— working
Structural	— organizational chart, — groupings, — defined hierarchy	— work flow design, — procedures involving communication, planning, coordination, control, decision making
Human-Social	— skills and abilities, — leadership climate, — formal aspects (personnel policies, reward policies, collective bargaining agreements), — informal aspects (norms, values, feelings, informal power and status structure)	— interpersonal interaction
Boundary	— information input mechanisms, — resource procurement (materials, people), — environmental impact (affecting the environment in ways favorable for the system), — methods for exporting products or services into the environment	— data sensing and response

Conclusion. As we noted earlier, a variety of other diagnostic approaches based on systems analysis do exist. Three that are particularly relevant for organizational diagnosis are: (1) Leavitt's (1965) model, which can be used to look at an organized social system in terms of four interacting variables: task, structural, technological, and human; (2) the perspective developed by Katz and Kahn (1966), which uses a six-subsystem framework (technical, maintenance, supportive, institutional, adaptive, and managerial); and (3) Seiler's (1967) "sociotechnical systems" approach, which contains four major subsystem variables: human, technological, organizational, and social.

For a deeper understanding of this general approach to diagnosis, we suggest that you read Leavitt's paper.

Diagnostic Approach: A Contingency Model (Lawrence and Lorsch)

Modern organization theory can probably be best characterized as based on a "contingency" approach. Most such approaches attempt to define the circumstances under which one or another organizational structure, form, or design will be most effective or more effective than alternative structures.*

The approach developed by Lawrence and Lorsch (1969) has been used as a *diagnostic* approach for organizational change, and is therefore much more suited to our interests than any other contingency model. The model also has an advantage in being fairly clear and understandable as well as reasonably easy to apply. Let us examine first the primary concepts in the model, differentiation and integration.

Differentiation and integration. These concepts are certainly not new; organized social systems are composed of a variety of differentiated (or specialized) parts, and the activities of these differentiated parts (departments, work groups, etc.) must be integrated or coordinated so that they fit together and accomplish major organizational functions and goals.

While the concepts of differentiation and integration are not new they are more important now than in the past because of the very great degree of specialization, or differentiation, in modern organizations and because of the increasing rapidity of environmental change, which has become quite relevant for most, if not all, organizations. Within the organization, Lawrence and Lorsch see the problem of integration of the various specialized parts as a critical issue. There are a variety of approaches, methods, and techniques for achieving the required degree of integration, but the most effective way is contingent (depends) on two things: (1) the nature of the differentiated units; and (2) the organization's environment. We will review Lawrence and Lorsch's descriptions of each of these factors.

Nature of the differentiated units. An organizational unit (work group, department, division, etc.) could, of course, be described in many different ways, using any number of descriptive variables or measurements. Lawrence and Lorsch see four particular variables or dimensions as being most important. These are: (1) the time orientation of people in the unit; (2) the goal orientation of people in the unit; (3) the interpersonal orientation; and (4) the unit's internal formal structure. In highly differentiated organizations, different units will look very dissimilar in terms of these four characteristics. The four variables should be explained in a little more detail, however.

(1) *Time orientation:* This variable focuses on whether people in the unit look at their work in terms of long-range ends, say years (as would be the case in a basic research group), or in relatively short-term time periods, days or weeks. People who tend to look at their work in terms of a deadline two weeks away are likely to have difficulty in cooperating and coordinating with people who typically view their work goals in terms of years.

(2) *Goal orientation.* Obviously, different units in an organization will have different goals. The goals of a marketing department may involve the development of accurate consumer surveys, audience identification, and marketing strategies; the goals of a sales force could include meeting monthly quotas for certain product lines; those of the production department might emphasize

---

*For a variety of readings on such approaches, see Kast and Rosenzweig (1973).

quality control; and, the aim of a research unit could be the development of new, basic knowledge in a certain scientific area. To some extent all of these goals are in harmony — and in discord. They must, however, fit together — be integrated — within the overall aims of the organization, and the degree of difficulty in doing this will depend on the extent of differentiation of units (in terms of this and the other three characteristics) as well as on the nature of the environment (which will be discussed shortly).

(3) *Interpersonal orientation.* Most organizational units can be characterized as having members who either tend toward interpersonal styles that emphasize relationships — how well the members like and get along with one another — or that emphasize the job or task they are concerned with. Of course, the situation will rarely be extreme toward either style, or orientation, but would, probably, be describable as tending toward one or the other.

(4) *Internal formal structure.* This factor would be measured by such things as the number of hierarchical levels in the unit, the span of control of managers or supervisors (that is, the number of subordinates the average manager or supervisor has), the extent to which rules, policies, and procedures are detailed and enforced, and the degree of control maintained by upper levels (by performance reviews and evaluation or measures of productivity, for example). A research unit would probably be low on formal structure, a sales unit moderate, and a production unit quite high. Thus, to some extent formal structure depends on the task of the unit. On the other hand, however, any of the above-mentioned units *could* be either very high on formal structure or very low. So, while the degree of formal structure may, logically, be related to the task, the actual formal structure may be almost arbitrary, depending most on the desires of those at the top of the hierarchy.

While an appropriate goal orientation obviously depends on the task of a particular unit, an effective, high-performing organization will consist of units whose characteristics match well with the environmental situation. The state of the environment is, then, one of the most important factors in the whole approach, because this environmental state will determine the needed degree and type of differentiation and integration as well as the most appropriate type of characteristics of units (in terms of formality, interpersonal orientation, and time orientation).

Organizational environments. Lawrence and Lorsch found that the type of environment — stable and certain or changing and uncertain — determined the most effective pattern of differentiation and integration. Some organizations exist in environments of high innovation, rapidly changing and developing technology, and strong competition. An example is the plastics industry. Other (and today, fewer) organizations exist in circumstances of rather high stability — stable markets, low innovations, etc. In such cases, a pattern of relatively *low* differentiation is found, while a more dynamic, changing environment requires *high* differentiation for effective performance. While a high degree of integration is needed in both cases, this integration can be achieved more easily when differentiation is low. Furthermore, integration is best achieved in different ways for organizations in stable versus uncertain environments.

We also mentioned that the environment determines the most effective pattern of characteristics of organizational units. When stability is high, units should have more formal structures and long time orientations, while in an uncertain, changing environment the opposite characteristics seem desirable (less formal structure, shorter time orientations). In environments that are either very stable or very uncertain a task orientation is more appropriate as a general interpersonal orientation, while more moderate environmental conditions — some uncertainty or some stability — seem to require more of a relationship orientation in the unit.

Patterns of integration. Two principles stand out in determining the most effective pattern of integration for an organization: (1) the pattern of integration must fit the organization-environment situation; and (2) more complex, highly differentiated organizations, in uncertain environments, require more complex ways or devices for integration. Lawrence and Lorsch found several different devices and combinations of devices: (1) an integrative department with the explicit function of integrating the efforts of various departments or units; (2) permanent or temporary integrating teams (composed of members of different units); (3) formal integrating roles, assigned to certain managers; (4) informal direct contact among managers of different units at various levels; (5) the managerial hierarchy – the formal "chain of command"; and (6) paperwork – memos, written communication, etc.

An organization in a very stable environment might use only the last three of these devices for integration, and could perform quite effectively. In fact, if such an organization tried to install permanent integrating teams, the results would probably be negative, because such an integrative device does not fit the stable environmental situation and is far more complex than is really needed. On the other hand, an organization in a very uncertain, rapidly changing environment might need to use most or all of these devices in order to attain a high degree of integration.

In environments of uncertainty and change, we might say that integration can only be achieved by a combination of structural or procedural mechanisms with interpersonal-process integrative devices (role definitions, personal informal contacts, etc.).

Common patterns. One important factor that Lawrence and Lorsch identified did *not* vary with the organization or the environment. Effective, high-performing organizations tend to handle the conflicts that are created by differentiation (and that form the essence of the problem of integration) by openly confronting these conflicts as problems to be solved rather than by smoothing over the conflict, fighting a win-lose game between the parties to the conflict, or compromising. Confrontation of conflict and problem solving to resolve conflicts is a typical pattern in effective organizations regardless of the environment.

Conclusion: using the approach. This diagnostic approach is most useful in identifying interdepartmental sources of conflict in organizations and suggesting appropriate integrative devices for resolving such conflicts. First, one would determine the nature of the organization's environment. One would then look at the differentiated units in the organization and determine where each falls on the set of four descriptive characteristics. This also tells the overall extent of differentiation. We would then need to know what integrative devices are being used. Finally, a complete diagnosis of the situation could be made, including ideas or directions for change that can be directly determined from the Lawrence and Lorsch model. Table 6-2 reviews these steps in more detail.

Diagnostic Approach: Force-Field Analysis

Force-field analysis (FFA) is a method for identifying the psychological and social forces that affect people's behavior. If in a specific situation we define behavior that would be ideal or most desirable and behavior that would be extremely undesirable – much worse than it is now – we have the two extreme end points of the force field. Actual behavior is somewhere in between these extremes, and usually does not vary much toward one or the other extreme, although there is some variability. That is, behavior is fairly stable within a much more narrow range than the possible extremes, as shown in Figure 6-1.

The reason behavior is fairly stable and does not vary from one end point to the other is that there are forces acting to drive the level upward and forces acting to restrain the level or even move it downward. These can be forces in individuals, such as ambition to attain a goal or fear of failure, or forces in the social environment, such as peer pressure or threat of punishment. If the forces can be identified, there is then the possibility of manipulating or changing some of them — removing or weakening some of the restraining forces and adding or strengthening some of the driving forces.

But how can these forces be identified or changed? One might ask if the forces are more imaginary than real. Well, they seem real enough to be useful, as real as any physical forces. Who, for example, has ever seen or touched gravity or magnetism? Yet, practically everyone would agree that these are "real" forces. Airplanes fly because air pressure pushes on the wings' undersurfaces, but have you ever seen this force? We find such physical forces very useful because we can deal with

TABLE 6-2 Steps in Using Lawrence and Lorsch's Diagnostic Approach

Diagnostic Step	Result
1. Determining the nature of the environment: — is the technology changing rapidly (or at all)? — is there much competition? — is information from the environment easily obtainable?	1. Classify as uncertain (changing); moderate; or certain (stable). Determine "best" pattern of differentiation and integration.
2. Examine at least several of the differentiated units in the organization and describe each in terms of the four characteristics: — formality — time orientation — interpersonal orientation — goal orientation	2. Compare actual pattern of differentiation with environmentally influenced "best" pattern.
3. Describe integrative devices being used at present with particular attention to units that are required to integrate activities.	3. Compare actual state with environmentally determined need for integration. Is the actual pattern over-complex, adequate, or inadequate?
4. Identify typical pattern of conflict management: — is conflict hidden, smoothed over? — do conflicting parties battle it out? — is conflict openly confronted as a problem to be mutually resolved?	4. Collaborate with client in determining how to develop the skills needed for effective confrontation processes for conflict resolution.
5. Determine what new integrative devices are needed, if any.	5. Collaborate with client in developing new integrative devices, if needed.

FIGURE 6-1

Ideal, most desirable behavior

ACTUAL BEHAVIOR

Worst, least desirable behavior

or control their effects, even though the forces themselves are no more concrete than social or psychological forces. Similarly, if we can identify the nature of these latter forces, we may be able to better control or manage them.

Figure 6-2 is a general diagram, like Figure 6-1, but with the forces illustrated. To make practical use of the force field, we must first be fairly specific in defining the actual behavior and the positive and negative end points of the force field. Generally, it is most useful to define specific, realistic positive and negative end points. This effort makes the positive side more usable as a goal, instead of a dream-fantasy.

Let us review one example of an application of the force-field analysis technique to a real situation to give a clearer understanding of the kind of forces we are concerned with.

This example is old, but a classic of sorts. Back in the mid-forties Dr. Alfred Marrow, a social psychologist who happened also to be owner and president of a small pajama manufacturing company, was faced with serious problems concerning the improvement of the technology of the work process in the interests of greater productivity. Such changes, of course, became necessary as new and improved machines and methods were developed. Workers, however, resisted making such changes, even though transfer and pay bonuses and special retraining job rates were used to insure that no worker would be penalized by a change (pay was on a piece-rate basis). In fact, many workers quit rather than change their work procedures. Even among those who did not quit, many became chronic substandard performers.

Using a team of researchers from the Research Center for Group Dynamics (then at MIT, now at the Institute for Social Research of the University of Michigan), who worked in collaboration with managers, a careful attempt was made to gather data about this problem of changes in working procedures. The "researcher-change agent" team carefully gathered a large variety of data: relearning time for new jobs; turnover, during the adjustment period and compared to workers whose

FIGURE 6-2

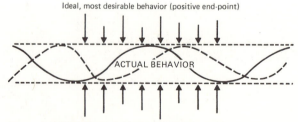

Ideal, most desirable behavior (positive end-point)

ACTUAL BEHAVIOR

Worst, least desirable behavior (negative end-point)

jobs had not been changed; work-group factors (group cohesiveness, attitudes toward management, production norms), etc. They interpreted these data in terms of their understanding of individual personality and small-group dynamics. We need not review the rather complex initial theory they proposed to account for the problem, but the essence of their analysis can easily be seen in Figure 6-3. There we see five major forces that affected the behavior of the individual workers and can see the forces behind the problem of resistance to change in the pajama factory.

FIGURE 6-3 Force Field before Action

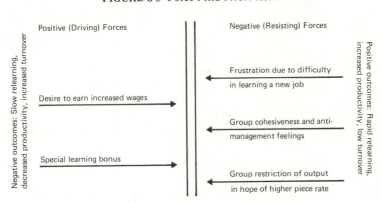

Note that the resisting forces are much stronger, as well as more numerous, than the driving forces. Thus, over time, we would expect continued poor production and increased turnover for workers whose jobs had been changed. This, of course, was precisely the problem that the researcher-change agent team faced. Two general action alternatives are possible for moving this balance of forces in the positive direction: driving forces might be strengthened (or new ones added), or restraining forces might be weakened (or removed). Since, however, for every action there is a reaction, strengthening (or adding to) the driving forces is likely also to strengthen (or produce new) restraining forces. Thus, the most generally productive approach to moving the level of behavior in the positive direction is by *reducing* (or removing) the restraining forces.

In this particular case, the researcher-change agents concluded, based on the force-field analysis, that resistance to change was a combination of an individual psychological force — frustration in learning a new job — and group-induced forces — opposition to management and a group norm of low production. They believed that these negative forces could be reduced or eliminated by using group participative methods to develop and initiate change.

Two somewhat different alternatives were selected for trial. The first involved group participation in planning the changes by representatives of the workers, who were presented with the problem of cost reduction and who informally approved management's plans. The second alternative involved the full participation of a group of affected workers in the actual design of job changes. A third group of workers was subjected to a change under the usual procedure. The results were dramatic. The group treated according to the old procedure performed so poorly that it had to be broken up and scattered throughout the factory. After two and one-half months, five (of the eighteen) had quit. The representative group suffered a sharp drop in performance but, after a month, had slowly reached its old level. The full-participation group, however, recovered to its old production level after *one day* and improved thereafter. Figure 6-4 shows the new force field for the full-participation group.

FIGURE 6-4 Force Field after Action

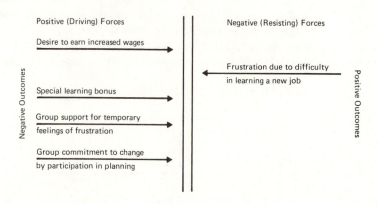

In presenting this example, we have oversimplified a bit and glossed over some of the practical details in using force-field analysis. First, note that the positive and negative end points were clearly defined. Second, a great deal of information was gathered about the situation. We listed only the major forces in Figure 6-3, but there were others. In using the force-field analysis method, one would at this point list as many positive (driving) and negative (restraining) forces as can be thought of. Then, each force would be examined, first for clarity of statement to determine whether the force is real and clearly describable; second to determine the importance or strength of the force; and finally to estimate how difficult or easy it would be to change or eliminate the force.

The third major step would be to find those negative forces that are important (strong) but changeable. Specific plans would then be made to reduce or eliminate these forces, just as in the example given here. Note that this also resulted in some new positive forces (in Figure 6-4). These forces were one by-product of the elimination of some of the negative forces shown in Figure 6-3.

Generally, the first force field is only a rough approximation – it produces leads for further exploration. A second, third, or fourth revised analysis would be the basis for action planning. Later, a new force field can be constructed to evaluate the effects of actions and determine whether or not the goal state has been reached (or is being approached) and what further actions might be necessary. At any point important new forces might be discovered that must be taken into account.

It is also very useful to consider whether any neutral forces are present – forces that, while not active, could enter the situation on either the positive or the negative side. Plans could then include ways to tap potential positive forces while keeping potential negative forces out of the situation.

Conclusion. Table 6-3 summarizes the steps in constructing a force-field analysis. Many problems are susceptible to force-field analysis, particularly problems involving human behavior, for the assumption behind this tool is that human behavior is determined by forces that exist both within the person and in his or her environment. Of course, analysis and understanding alone do not solve a problem. The next step is to examine the forces that can be controlled, that is, negative (restraining) forces that can be reduced or eliminated and positive (driving) forces that can be increased or introduced, and to use this information in the context of a problem-solving model. Given such an analysis, alternative actions – problem solutions – can be generated, and a particular solution can be developed and implemented, with reasonable probability of success.

TABLE 6-3   Steps in Constructing a Force-Field Analysis

1. Define as clearly as possible the *present* behavior, the *positive* end point (desired behavior change) and the *negative* end point (undesired change that could occur).

2. Assemble as much information as possible about the situation. List all possible positive (driving) and negative (restraining) forces. List any major uncommitted (neutral) forces that might possibly become active.

3. Examine each force and determine:
   a. How clearly the force is stated; is it really a force? How certain are you? Should more information be collected about this force?
   b. How important or strong the force is; strong, moderate, or weak?
   c. How manipulable or changeable the force is; would it be easy, moderately difficult, or very difficult to change?

4. Focus on the negative forces that are most clear, most important, and easiest to alter; what specific actions can be taken to reduce or eliminate these forces? Consider also how positive forces can be retained or enhanced, how potentially positive neutral forces can be activated, and how potentially negative neutral forces can be kept neutral.

DRAKE'S READY SANDWICH COMPANY

Summary

Joe Drake is founder and president of a small company that produces a variety of sandwiches. The sandwiches are sold to small markets and lunchrooms of small firms and factories. Customers lease ovens, used to heat the sandwiches on the premises. A staff of salesmen solicits accounts and makes rounds taking orders from regular customers. Deliveries are scheduled daily by Bill Phillips and made by a crew of driver-deliverymen.

Various problems have become worse over the past year. Occasionally production of the various types of sandwiches does not match orders. More frequent are drivers' complaints of overload and impossible schedules.

Drake works hard to keep on top of things – in fact, he's been overworking lately and his health is suffering. Even so, the problems have not improved and he's considering selling out.

DRAKE'S READY SANDWICH COMPANY

Joe Drake is president and owner of a small company (about a hundred and seventy-five employees in all) producing prepared sandwiches of all kinds, which are sold to small markets and business firms large enough to need luncheon facilities but too small to run a full-scale lunchroom. Most customers lease small ovens, which are used to heat sandwiches on the spot. Drake started out running a small sandwich shop; his business did very well. In fact, his sandwiches became so popular that he was about to expand when a friend suggested the idea that became the basis for his present business. So, Joe closed the shop, hired a salesman to solicit accounts with local markets, and hired his nephew to make deliveries. Drake continued to prepare sandwiches.

The idea worked; slowly his business grew, especially after he thought of leasing the ovens to customers. Workers were hired and taught how to prepare the sandwiches; more salesmen as well as professional drivers were hired to get new accounts and expand deliveries. An office staff became necessary, along with a couple of men to install and service the ovens. Then the company started servicing the small factories and firms mentioned above. (Joe was careful to avoid moving in on larger factory lunch services, some of which were controlled by "the mob." In any case, he didn't want to try setting up complete lunch concessions since he knew the problems of running restaurant-type facilities would outweigh by far the potential profit.)

After ten years, Drake's employs a hundred and twenty workers who produce and package the sandwiches (which are distributed in a fifty-mile radius around Chicago), fifteen driver-delivery men, eight loaders (supervised by Bill Phillips, who is head scheduler), an office staff of ten (including Drake), a customer maintenance crew of four men who install and repair the ovens, seven salesmen, and various miscellaneous personnel (janitors, nightwatchman, factory maintenance crew, a couple of mechanics who keep the trucks in good repair, etc.).

The salesmen solicit accounts and take orders from regular customers. These orders are written up and delivered to Drake, who passes them on to Phillips. Sometimes the office will send Phillips instructions to discontinue delivery, or accept only cash on delivery for accounts that are overdue, in which case the salesmen's orders are canceled or corrected. Phillips passes on these orders to the drivers, adding new accounts to those of the driver whose route is closest to the new customer's location.

Based on the type of orders the salesmen report to Drake, he provides the chief of production, Irene Reynolds, with a weekly schedule. Both overall and specific variety demands change on a seasonal basis. Variety demands also change over time, based on food preferences of the public.

The system has gradually developed a number of problems. The drivers complain that the allocation of new orders, as well as fluctuations in customer orders, often make complete deliveries impossible — the trucks are full. (The trucks are, of course, refrigerated and have a fairly large, but still limited, load capacity.) Phillips responds that he's just passing on the orders. Actually, he's often not around when orders come in, since he also takes care of customer calls about defective ovens or installation of new ovens. (Things were particularly bad for quite a while, after they started using microwave ovens, which broke down because customers were unfamiliar with their operation. Such problems have been decreasing, though.) Salesmen are not around when the drivers are, either. Drake has talked with some of the drivers, and this seems to calm them down for a while. Drake is slow to hire new drivers because of the seasonal variations in demand; only when it is clear that all drivers will be needed year-round will he consider hiring a new one.

Still another type of problem occurs when the varieties of sandwiches produced do not match up with orders. This happens when, for example, a customer changes an order through Phillips but Drake is not informed and the week's production schedule is unchanged. Or, a cancellation due to an overdue unpaid account may be ordered without a change in the production schedule.

Drake tries to keep up with everything but has become increasingly frustrated. He's a strong-minded individual, and a good leader, but the situation seems to keep getting out from under him. His doctor recently told him that if he didn't ease up he'd be dead of a heart attack in a few years. Drake is giving serious thought to selling out now.

B.   Designs for Learning to Use Force-Field Analysis as a Diagnostic Tool

1.   *Purpose.*   Once a specific problem is defined and positive (improved) and negative (worsened) outcomes stated, the force-field approach can be extremely helpful in making a detailed diagnosis and developing action plans. The objective of this design is to provide some detailed skill practice in using force-field analysis (FFA), which was described at length in part 5 of Design A, above. The present design is given in two parts. The first part (3A) uses a role-play simulation as material for a demonstration of FFA. The second part (3B) involves the use of FFA with real problems.

Force-field analysis has become such a common tool* that a word of caution may be appropriate: FFA does *not* solve problems. It is a diagnostic and action-planning tool. The immediate outcome of a good force-field analysis is likely to be better understanding of the dynamics of the problem situation − the forces within the situation that are producing the problem − but unless this understanding is turned into action plans the problem will remain, as the situation will not be changed.

2.   *Materials needed.*   Role instructions in part 5, newsprint and markers.

3A. *Steps in using the design: Classroom or preparatory practice.*

    a.   Select the role players.

    b.   Set up and begin the role play.

    c.   Conclude the role play.

    d.   Review the description of FFA.

    e.   Brainstorm driving, restraining, and neutral forces.

    f.   Evaluate forces.

    g.   Examine negative forces.

    h.   Develop a plan of action for improvement.

    i.   Summarize results (if the entire class participated in role play, compare group solutions); derive learnings.

3B. *Steps in using the design: Real groups.*

    a.   Introduce the concepts of FFA.

    b.   Brainstorm a list of problems.

    c.   Define the extremes of the force field.

    d.   Brainstorm all possible forces.

    e.   Evaluate forces (step 3 of Table 6-3).

    f.   Look for unclear forces.

    g.   Decide which forces to work on.

    h.   Have subgroups work on specific forces.

*Additional descriptive material can be found in Jones and Pfeiffer (1973). Advanced students may find helpful the classic paper on FFA, "Overcoming Resistance to Change," by Coch and French (1948). Graduate students may also want to refer to some of Kurt Lewin's writing. Particularly useful is his paper "Group Decision and Social Change" in Maccoby, Newcomb, and Hartley (1958).

    i.   Have subgroups report to full group on action plans developed.

    j.   Have subgroups meet to plan implementation of approved actions.

4.   *Deriving learnings.* The relevant derivation questions for designs 3A and 3B will differ somewhat. For the first design, the primary focus must be on the FFA technique itself. Questions that might be useful in discussion include:

- Could the imaginary subjects of the role play have enough objectivity to use FFA themselves?

- What general categories of situations is the FFA technique best suited for? Are there any types of problems that FFA is not particularly suited for?

- Can the FFA technique be expected to result in the "best" possible solution? This question is particularly relevant for classes that have used the role play as a multiple group exercise and have produced a variety of solutions with which to compare the FFA outcome.

The real group, or organizational, design (3B) makes the action portion of problem solving, which follows the FFA, of major relevance. Some significant questions are:

- What other information do we need to complete the force field? How can we get it?

- Do our plans take into consideration all those persons affected by them and by the problem?

- How will we know if the problem is solved? How do we evaluate the effects of our actions?

- What is our time frame? How long will it take to implement these actions and evaluate the results?

- What sort of solutions did we have in mind before trying FFA? Is the FFA-derived action plan similar to any of these?

5.   *Support materials.*

NOTES ON FORCE-FIELD ANALYSIS

The force-field analysis technique is most useful for problems involving the behavior of a group of people. The major virtue of FFA is that when a good force field is constructed this leads naturally and almost automatically to specific action steps. By feeding the results of action into a *new* force field analysis, the information generated is used to improve on action plans and thus move closer to a final solution of the problem. When used in this way, FFA is an important tool for action research, a change process that is similar in nature to the problem solving model proposed in this book.

FFA can also be used by individuals; it is a structured, rational technique that is far easier to use than many of the complex procedures that have been created for such purposes (such as the Kepner-Tregoe method) and is also generally more productive.

One twist that is often helpful is the identification of uncommitted or neutral forces — forces that *could* come into play on one side of the force field or the other but that are presently inactive or dormant. Often such forces become activated as a result of changes involving the presently active forces (e.g., increasing one or more positive forces or removing some of the negative forces). By identifying these neutral forces *before* any actions are attempted, it becomes possible to anticipate activation of potentially negative forces and plan to prevent this, and to anticipate activation of potentially positive forces and plan the best ways to accommodate and use them.

In summary, one can think of a variety of strategies for using the results of an FFA:

1. Increase the strength of positive forces.

2. Add new positive forces.

3. Decrease the strength of negative forces.

4. Remove some negative forces.

5. Determine how to switch some of the negative forces to the positive side.

6. Ensure that potential negative forces that are presently neutral do not become active.

7. Determine how to activate potentially positive forces that are presently neutral.

It is important to realize that some of these strategies are likely to be unproductive or even counterproductive. Adding positive forces or strengthening them is generally counterproductive because, in reaction, new negative forces are very likely to form or old negative forces are likely to increase. Nothing changes, except that a much higher level of tension is generated — which can eventually make the situation "explode." The next three strategies — decreasing negative strength, removing negative forces entirely, or forming negatives into positives — all operate on existing negative forces. These strategies are likely to be very productive. Often the reduction in tension that results from removal of negative forces allows neutral but potentially positive forces to become active, or leads to the addition of new positive forces. The final two strategic points concern forces that are presently neutral but that could become active on one side or the other. It is important to identify potentially negative forces and plan to avoid their activation, but this is a secondary strategy. It is useful to plan for the fit of new positive forces that are now uncommitted but can (or might) be activated, but again this should be a secondary concern. The primary strategic concern in using FFA is twofold: work to remove or reduce in strength the negative forces while avoiding any immediate, overt increase on the positive side.

THE ASSEMBLY JOB

Background*

This situation takes place in a plant that does a large number of subassembly jobs, such as assembling fuel pumps, carburetors, and starters. Gus/Gussie Thompson is foreman over several work groups, including one in particular that we're concerned with. This group has three persons, Jack/Jackie, Walt/Wilma, and Steve/Stephanie, who work together in assembling fuel pumps. The assembly operation is divided into three job positions; all three are rather simple. The job is set up so that the first worker gets a casting, adds the appropriate parts, and passes it on to the next worker. This person adds more parts, and, again, passes the partly-assembled fuel pump on to the third worker who finishes the job by adding the final set of parts. Quite some time ago, the group worked out a method of rotation; after a period of time they switch positions. Since each worker is familiar with all three jobs, and all are simple, they've found this procedure to be desirable. The workers are paid on a team piece-rate basis. This means that all three workers get the same pay, based on the total number of acceptable fuel pumps they have produced. Today Gus/Gussie asked these workers to meet with him/her in his/her office. (S)he just said that (s)he "wanted to talk about something."

*The background and roles for this case derive from a case which originally appeared in *Principles of human relations* by N. R. F. Maier (New York: Wiley, 1952). Used by permission of Norman R. F. Maier. The most current (and somewhat different) version of this case appears in *The role-play technique*, by N. R. F. Maier, A. R. Solem, and A. A. Maier (La Jolla, Calif.: University Associates, 1975). This other version is copyrighted by University Associates, Inc., and the modified version given here is used with permission.

THE ASSEMBLY JOB

Role for Gus/Gussie Thompson, Foreman

You are the foreman in a shop and supervise the work of about twenty workers. Most of the jobs are piece-rate jobs and some of the workers work in teams and are paid on a team piece-rate basis. In one of the teams, Jack/Jackie, Walt/Wilma, and Steve/Stephanie work together. Each one of them does one of the operations for an hour or so and then they exchange positions, so that all the workers perform each of the operations at different times during the day. The workers themselves decided to operate that way and you have never given the plan any thought.

Lately, Jim Clark, the methods man, has been around and studied conditions in your shop. He timed Jack/Jackie, Walt/Wilma, and Steve/Stephanie on each of the operations and came up with the following facts:

	Time per Operation			
	Position 1	Position 2	Position 3	Total Time
Jack/Jackie	3 min.	4 min.	4½ min.	11½ min.
Walt/Wilma	3½ min.	3½ min.	3 min.	10 min.
Steve/Stephanie	5 min.	3½ min.	4½ min.	13 min.
				34½ min.

He observed that with the workers rotating, the average time for all three operations would be 1/3 of the total time or 11½ minutes per complete unit. If, however, Jack/Jackie worked in the number 1 spot, Steve/Stephanie in the number 2 spot, and Walt/Wilma in the number 3 spot, the time would be 9½ minutes, a reduction of over 17 percent. Such a reduction in time would amount to a saving of more than 80 minutes. In other words, the lost production is about the same as that which would occur if the workers loafed for 80 minutes in a 8-hour day. If the time were used for productive effort, production would be increased more than 20 percent.

This makes good sense to you, so you have decided to take up the problem with the workers. You feel that they should go along with any change in operation that is made. You therefore have called them in for a meeting.

THE ASSEMBLY JOB

Role for Jack/Jackie

You are one of three workers on an assembly operation. Walt/Wilma and Steve/Stephanie are your teammates and you enjoy working with them. You get paid on a team basis and you are making wages that are entirely satisfactory. Steve/Stephanie isn't quite as fast as Walt/Wilma and you, but when you feel (s)he is holding things up too much each of you can help out.

The work is monotonous. The saving thing about it is that every hour you all change positions. In this way you get to do all three operations. You are best on the number 1 position so when you get in that spot you turn out some extra work and so make the job easier for Steve/Stephanie, who follows you in that position.

You have been on this job for two years and have never run out of work. Apparently your group can make pretty good pay without running yourselves out of a job. Lately, however, the company has had some of its experts hanging around. It looks like the company is trying to work out some speedup methods. If they make these jobs any more simple you won't be able to stand the monotony. Gus/Gussie Thompson, your foreman, is a decent person and has never criticized your team's work.

THE ASSEMBLY JOB

Role for Walt/Wilma

You work with Jack/Jackie and Steve/Stephanie on a job that requires three separate operations. Each of you works on each of the three operations by rotating positions once very hour. This makes the work more interesting and you can always help out the others by running the job ahead in case one of you doesn't feel so good. It's all right to help out became you get paid on a team piece-rate basis. You could actually earn more if Steve/Stephanie were a faster worker, but (s)he is a swell person and you would rather have him/her in the group than someone else who might do a little bit more.

You find all three positions about equally desirable. They are all simple and purely routine. The monotony doesn't bother you much because you can talk, daydream, and change your pace. By working slow for a while and then fast you can sort of set your pace to music you hum to yourself. Jack/Jackie and Steve/Stephanie like the idea of changing jobs and even though Steve/Stephanie is slow on some positions, the changing around has its good points. You feel you get to a stopping place every time you change positions and this kind of takes the place of a rest pause.

Lately some kind of efficiency expert has been hanging around. He stands some distance away with a stopwatch in his hand. The company could get more for its money if it put some of those guys to work. You say to yourself, "I'd like to see one of these guys try and tell me how to do this job. I'd sure give him an earful."

If Gus/Gussie Thompson, your foreman, doesn't get him out of the shop pretty soon, you're going to tell him/her what you think of his/her dragging in company spies.

THE ASSEMBLY JOB

Role for Steve/Stephanie

You work with Jack/Jackie and Walt/Wilma on an assembly job and get paid on a team piece-rate basis. The three of you work very well together and make a pretty good wage. Jack/Jackie and Walt/Wilma like to make a little more than you think is necessary but you go along with them and work as hard as you can so as to keep the production up where they want it. They are good people and often help you out if you fall behind and so you feel it is only fair to try and go along with the pace they set.

The three of you exchange positions every hour. In this way you get to work all positions. You like the number 2 position the best because it is easier. When you get in the number 3 position you can't keep up and then you feel Gus/Gussie Thompson, the foreman, watching you. Sometimes Walt/Wilma and Jack/Jackie slow down when you are on the number 3 spot and then the foreman seems satisfied.

Lately the methods man has been hanging around watching the job. You wonder what he is up to. Can't they leave people alone who are doing all right?

THE ASSEMBLY JOB

Instructions for Observers

Basically, you are to observe and take notes on the methods Gus/Gussie uses in handling a problem with the workers. Pay particular attention to the following questions:

1. How did Gus/Gussie approach the workers? How did (s)he present the problem? Did (s)he criticize, suggest a solution, ask for their help with a problem, at the beginning of this meeting?
2. How did the group members react?
3. Did Gus/Gussie listen or did (s)he argue? Did (s)he try to persuade the workers? Did (s)he use threats? Did the workers have any meaningful say or participation in creating a solution?
4. What resistance did group members make, if any? Did they express fear, hostility, etc.?
5. Was Gus/Gussie open with the group, sharing all of his/her information with them, or did (s)he withhold relevant data? (look over Gus/Gussie's role on page 143.)

THE ASSEMBLY JOB

Role Play Result Questionnaire

1.   Name of the role you played: (circle one)   Jack/Jackie   Walt/Wilma   Steve/Stephanie

2.   Briefly state the final outcome of your discussion, the solution agreed to:

3.   If this solution is put into effect, what will be the result in terms of the productivity or effectiveness of your group? (check one)

Productivity will: [ ] go up   [ ] go down   [ ] stay the same

4.   How did the supervisor initially approach the group? (check one)

[ ] stated or posed a problem regarding productivity/effectiveness and present work arrangements

[ ] offered a choice of leaving things as they are or changing things as (s)he suggested

[ ] tried to convince us to change or ordered the group to adopt a certain change in work procedures

5.   Did the supervisor share the time-study data with the group? (check one)

[ ] showed us the time-study data

[ ] read or told us about the time-study data

[ ] did not share the time-study data

6. . How satisfied are you, as the person whose role you played, with the solution? (check one)

[ ] fully satisfied

[ ] mostly satisfied

[ ] somewhat satisfied

[ ] slightly satisfied

[ ] not at all satisfied

FORCE FIELD WORKSHEET (1)

"Where I (We) Want To Be": _____ (<u>More</u> Desirable Behavior)

orces within the person (s) in this situation toward
ss desirable behavior

Forces in the environment (the situation itself)
toward less desirable behavior

ist "Neutral" forces here:

"Where I (We) Am (Are) Now:

(Present Behavior/Activity Level)

orces within the person(s) in this situation toward
ore desirable behavior

Forces in the environment (the situation itself)
pushing toward more desirable behavior

"Where I (We) Want to Avoid Being": _____ (<u>Less</u> Desirable Behavior)

FORCE FIELD WORKSHEET (2)

How might the forces identified on sheet 1 be changed (strengthened or weakened) to result in a new activity level closer to the "more desirable" end?

Positive Forces (forces pushing toward *more* desirable behavior):

A.   In the person:

B.   In the environment:

Negative Forces (forces pushing toward *less* desirable behavior):

A.   In the person:

B.   In the environment:

Neutral Forces:

Which can be activated as positive forces? How?

Which must be kept neutral or eliminated? How?

II. CONCEPTUAL SUPPORT MATERIALS: DIAGNOSING PROBLEMS

The preceding chapters provide the basic skills needed as the groundwork for diagnosis. Those skills, however, are not adequate for the accurate diagnosis of problems. That requires two things: (1) an explicit theory or conceptual framework; and (2) specific procedures for using it. This is the "descriptive-analytic theory" Lippitt (1959) speaks of. We all have some such theory, but it's usually not explicit; more often, it's a somewhat disorganized and unspoken set of assumptions about what makes people, groups, and organizations tick. Whether you particularly like one of the three diagnostic approaches covered in this chapter, some other approach (e.g., Levinson, 1972), or prefer your own unique approach, it is important that in a helping relationship the approach you use be clear and explicit to you and communicable (ideally, teachable) to the other party. Even better would be having a variety of approaches at your disposal; at least, you should understand how different approaches work and lead to different diagnoses and actions. This was the aim of the first design in this chapter.

Probably the clearest, most explicit, and easiest to use set of procedures for applying a diagnostic approach is force-field analysis. The theory behind it is quite complex, but can be simplified; in any case, the procedures for application are so clear that full understanding of the theory is not really necessary. For these reasons, we have concentrated in this chapter on FFA as a diagnostic approach.

The concepts and procedures that are the basis of this chapter will not be as effective in use as is possible unless the user has as background the skills we have worked on in earlier chapters. We refer the reader back to our discussion in Chapter One about the difference between skills and procedures. In terms of our problem-solving model we are trying, at this point, to integrate helpful diagnostic procedures with the set of skills that will result in a high degree of effective problem solving.

REFERENCES

Beckhard, R. (1967) The confrontation meeting. *Harvard Business Review* **45** (2): 149-153.

**Blake, R. R., and Mouton, J. S. (1968) *Corporate excellence diagnosis.* Houston, Texas: Gulf.

Blake, R. R., and Mouton, J. S. (1964) *The managerial grid.* Houston, Texas: Gulf.

Bowers, D. G., and Franklin, J. L. (1972) Survey guided development. *Journal of Contemporary Business* 1: 43-55.

Bowers, D. G., and Seashore, S. E. (1966) Predicting organizational effectiveness with a four-factor theory of leadership. *Administrative Science Quarterly* 11: 238-263.

Coch, L., and French, J. R. P., Jr. (1948) Overcoming resistance to change. *Human Relations* 1: 512-532.

**French, W. L., and Bell, C. H., Jr. (1973) *Organization development.* (Chapters 4 and 7). Englewood Cliffs, N.J.: Prentice-Hall.

Jones, J. E., and Pfeiffer, J. W. (1973). *The 1973 annual handbook for group facilitators.* Iowa City, Iowa: University Associates.

Kast, F. E., and Rosenzweig, J. E., eds. (1973) *Contingency views of organization and management.* Chicago: Science Research Associates.

Katz, D., and Kahn, R. L. (1966) *The social psychology of organizations.* New York: Wiley.

**Lawrence, P. R., and Lorsch, J. W. (1969) *Organization development: Diagnosis and action.* Reading, Mass.: Addison-Wesley.

Lawrence, P. R., and Lorsch, J. W. (1969) *Organization and environment: Managing differentiation and integration.* Homewood, Ill.: Irwin.

Leavitt, H. J. (1965) Applied organizational change in industry. In *Handbook of organizations,* ed. J. G. March. Chicago: Rand-McNally.

**Levinson, H.; Molinari, J.; and Spohn, A. G. (1972) *Organizational diagnosis.* Cambridge, Mass.: Harvard University Press.

Lewin, K. (1958) Group decision and social change. In *Readings in social psychology.* 3rd ed., eds. E. E. Maccoby, T. M. Newcomb, and E. L. Hartley. New York: Holt, Rinehart, & Winston.

Lewin, K.; Lippitt, R.; and White, R. K. (1939) Patterns of aggressive behavior in experimentally created social climates. *Journal of Social Psychology* **10**: 271-301.

Likert, R. (1967) *The human organization.* New York: McGraw-Hill.

Lippitt, R. (1959) Dimensions of the consultant's job. *Journal of Social Issues* **15**(2): 5-12.

**Lorsch, J. W., and Lawrence, R. R. (1969) The diagnosis of organizational problems. In *The planning of change.* Rev. ed., eds. W. G. Bennis, K. D. Benne, and R. Chin. New York: Holt, Rinehart, & Winston.

Maier, N. R. F. (1973). *Psychology in industrial organizations.* 4th ed. Boston: Houghton Mifflin.

Maier, N. R. F., and Solem, A. (1962) Improving solutions by turning choice situations into problems. *Personnel Psychology* **15**: 151-157.

**Pounds, W. F. (1974) The process of problem finding. In *Organizational psychology: A book of readings.* 2nd ed., eds. D. A. Kolb, I. M. Rubin, and J. M. McIntyre, Englewood Cliffs, N.J.: Prentice-Hall.

Seiler, J. A. (1967) *Systems analysis in organization behavior.* Homewood, Ill.: Irwin.

Winn, A. (1966) Social change in industry: From insight to implementation. *Journal of Applied Behavioral Science* **2**: 170-183.

**References preceded by a double asterisk are those judged to be most basic or important.

CHAPTER SEVEN

Goal Setting: Helping People Learn How to Determine Where They Want to Go

"What'cha want ta do, Marty?"
"I dunno, wadda you want ta do?"

Line from the movie Marty.

INTRODUCTION

Setting goals is a major issue for most groups. There are two parts to this problem. First, most people do not go about developing their goals in any logical, structured way. Often ideals or fantasies become confused with real, possible goals that *could* be achieved. Much research* has shown that the goals most likely to be attained are those that the individual has a strong commitment to or desire for *and* that are neither too easy nor too difficult to reach. Goals, then, should be moderately difficult; they must be hard enough to pose a challenge, but not so hard as to give an automatic excuse for failure. In this chapter we present some goal-setting procedures that provide a step-by-step logical approach to goal definition, that foster commitment to the goals, and that push the goal-setter(s) toward realistic goals.

Second, there is the problem of developing shared goals in a small or large group. Here, the procedures we offer become even more important. It is possible but not "natural" for a group of people to agree on shared goals. Attaining such consensus requires considerable attention to group process, applying the problem solving approach in a particular way such that the *quality* of the goal is preserved *and* consensus is developed.

Like Chapter Five, this chapter is tightly sequenced, going from individual, through small-group, to organizational goals and, finally, looking at ways of integrating these goals. An effective group or organization is not necessarily one in which individual, group, and organizational goals are identical, but is a system in which they are all compatible *and* mutually facilitative. Thus, through the attainment of group goals, the individual's goals are furthered; through the achievement of organizational goals, the group's goals are reached. To design a social system process that works this way is not easy. The first learning design emphasizes the logical format for setting goals, at individual, group, or organizational levels. The following designs use this format in the context of group processes that facilitate the development of compatible (not necessarily identical) goals, moving from individual to group to intergroups to organization, and finally integrating across levels.

This chapter, we must point out, could fit well much earlier in the book. Looking back to Table 1-1 and the discussion of it, you will notice that defining goals should be an integral part of prob-

*E.g., Atkinson (1957), Lewin (1935), Starbuck (1963).

lem definition: "where do we want to go?" In fact, in both classes and organizations we have often used parts of this chapter at the very start of the problem solving process. However, this is also *very* difficult, because to set goals most effectively people have the skills or the "hows," prior to working on the "whats." Chapters Two through Six are designed to help you learn the "hows," so that you will find it far easier to determine the "whats" in setting goals.

I. SPECIFIC SKILL-DEVELOPMENT AND LEARNING DESIGNS

A.   Design for Learning to Set Individual Goals

1.   *Purpose.* Individuals as members of groups and organizations are often unaware of what they can accomplish or achieve as participants in the work of these larger goal-oriented systems. This relatively simple learning design is offered as a tool for individuals to use in this process of linkage and association with their membership groups.

2.   *Materials needed.* Paper and pencils, appropriate meeting space.

3.   *Steps in using the design.*

    a.   Make distinction between actual and ideal goals and hold short discussion.

    b.   Have each individual list personal goal statements.

    c.   Form trios to share goal statements.

    d.   Have group derive learnings.

4.   *Deriving learnings.* It is obvious that just thinking about and then writing down one's goals does not necessarily mean that anything will happen as a result. Further planning and then specific individual actions have to take place before goals can be attained. It is important to make the point, however, that most individuals never take the time adequately to start this process for themselves by clearly conceptualizing what they want to accomplish and then talking it over with others to do "reality testing." As this "first-level" kind of session ends, we should encourage ourselves to continue our personal planning processes by asking ourselves questions such as:

   — Now that I have stated some particularly realistic goals for myself, what are the very first things I must do to insure that what I say I want for myself will actually come about?

   — What specific resources both within and outside of myself can I use to best advantage?

   — When in the next couple of weeks will I sit down with myself and actually take stock of how I'm doing?

   — Is there someone in my group that I could make a contract with to sit down once in a while and share accomplishments and frustrations?

B.   Design for Learning to Set Group Goals

1.   *Purpose.* The aim here is to illustrate, experientially, the goal-setting process of groups, rather than to develop actual goals of the groups.

2.   *Materials needed.* Leader instruction/recording forms, post-discussion questionnaires, newsprint and markers, pocket-size calculator.

3. *Steps in using the design.*

   a. Give instructions on developing group goals.

   b. Form even number of small groups.

   c. Select leader for each small group.

   d. Have group leaders begin discussions.

   e. End discussion and have participants fill out questionnaires.

   f. Summarize each subgroup's goal list.

   g. Review and categorize goals for whole group.

   h. Have groups form group-pairs; have new groups create goals.

   i. Calculate group means during group meeting period.

   j. Post and review group-pair goals.

   k. Conduct group process and derivation session.

4. *Deriving learnings.* When used with classroom groups, the primary focus for learning should be on the goal-setting process. In such cases, we strongly recommend the use of both leader/recorder instruction formats. Some questions for the postexercise discussion are:

   — Why did the more structured discussion format make group members feel freer than the less structured format?

   — Which groups were more satisfied with and more committed to their goals? Why?

   — Is the more structured format always best for goal setting? For group discussions in general? How could it be altered to fit the requirements of other types of group discussion?

   For real organizational groups, the primary (or an equally important) focus is on the specific goals developed. Relevant questions for discussion include:

   — Can this approach (the problem solving structured format) be usefully applied to other groups we are members of? Which groups? How?

   — What are the next steps in reaching the goals we've defined today? How can we best organize to achieve these goals?

   — Can we really work toward these goals now, or have we left out some significant person(s) or group(s) whose support and collaboration will be necessary?

   In both cases the merger of two small groups into one large group of ten raises certain issues (note:

   Learning Design B in Chapter Eight is focused on this problem) such as:

   — What was the effect of the different small-group instructions on the larger-group process?

   — When the small groups have developed goals that they are really committed to, how can two such groups best collaborate on a shared goal list?

   — How can a win-lose situation be avoided even though the subgroups each identify strongly with their own goals?

   — How can the two groups really merge into one group that the members see as one entity, not two?

5. *Support materials.* On the following pages are leader instruction forms and a post-discussion questionnaire form.

SETTING GROUP GOALS

FORM D

Leader/Recorder Instruction Sheet

Your task is to arrive at a list of the three most important aims or goals for the entire group that all of you in this small subgroup can agree on. You have been selected as leader/recorder for this subgroup. Follow the procedure below as closely as possible:

1. Ask the persons in your group to suggest as many goals as possible. List these below as they are offered.

    Goals:

2. Ask the group to vote for the three most important goals and keep a tally. Each person has five votes. Suggest that each person vote for those goals he or she really feels are the best, *not* just those he or she suggested or those that are similar to the person's suggestions.

3. Briefly discuss those goals that received the most votes. Can any be modified or combined with others? Are they stated as clearly and concisely as possible?

4. Write a final statement of the three most important goals:

    Goals:

    1.

    2.

    3.

SETTING GROUP GOALS

FORM F

Leader/Recorder Instruction Sheet

Your task is to arrive at a list of the three most important aims or goals for the entire group that all of you in this small subgroup can agree on. You have been selected as leader/recorder for this subgroup. You may conduct the discussion in any manner you choose. List the three most important goals below:

Goals:

1.

2.

3.

SETTING GROUP GOALS

Post-Discussion Questionnaire

1. Indicate how you are now feeling about this group discussion by drawing a circle around the number that best represents your feelings:

    a. Objectives of the discussion not clearly understood by me . . . .   1 2 3 4 5 6 7 . . . . .   Objectives of the discussion clearly understood by me

    b. My own feeling about these objectives was very negative . . . .   1 2 3 4 5 6 7 . . . . .   My own feeling about these objectives was very positive

    c. Abilities, knowledge, and experience of the persons in this group were not used well . . . .   1 2 3 4 5 6 7 . . . . .   Abilities, knowledge, and experience of the persons in this group were fully used

    d. Little or no involvement of group members in the discussion . . . .   1 2 3 4 5 6 7 . . . . .   A very high degree of involvement of group members in the discussion

    e. Control and influence over the direction taken in the discussion were imposed on the group . . . .   1 2 3 4 5 6 7 . . . . .   Control and influence over the direction taken in the discussion were shared by group members

    f. Leadership functions were concentrated in one or two members . . . .   1 2 3 4 5 6 7 . . . . .   Leadership functions were shared and distributed among all members

    g. Little or no learning for myself from this experience . . . .   1 2 3 4 5 6 7 . . . . .   A great deal of personal learning for myself from this experience

2. Taking all things into consideration, how satisfied are you with the discussion?
    [ ] very dissatisfied   [ ] somewhat dissatisfied   [ ] neither satisfied nor dissatisfied
            [ ] somewhat satisfied   [ ] very satisfied

3. To what degree do you personally feel committed to the goals arrived at by this group?
    [ ] to a very great degree   [ ] to a considerable degree   [ ] to a moderate degree
            [ ] to a slight degree   [ ] to no degree

4. Why did you answer the way you did on the above questions?

5. Were you the formal leader of this group discussion?   [ ] Yes   [ ] No

C.   **Design for Learning to Set Large-Group or Organizational Goals**

1.   *Purpose.* Organizations and subsystem groups in organizations often arrive at the point where it is desirable and even necessary to refine or redefine goals and to take stock of the degree to which these goals have been or are being attained in relation to where they are at present; where they would like to go and how this might differ from where they are now; and where they could go if they could learn to pool the total creative thinking of all their members.

2.   *Materials needed.* The instructor will furnish all materials for this design. Separate rooms are desirable for the "building" groups. A large meeting area may also be used to separate the groups.

3.   *Steps in using the design.*
   a.   Give brief lecture on long-range planning.
   b.   Divide class or large group into small work teams.
   c.   Start "Future Building" or "Castle Building" activity time.
   d.   End work period. Have groups tour building locations and hear "sales pitches." Have judges caucus to determine "winner." (Classroom groups may now derive learnings from the activity. Real organization groups should continue through the following steps.)
   e.   Have small groups meet to derive central goal statement.
   f.   Post small group goal statements — have all circulate and read.
   g.   Conduct summary discussion on similarities and differences and help make plans for future work.

4.   *Deriving learnings.* Planning for change is easy to think about but difficult to put into action. This learning design is an attempt to help a larger system of interrelated members do just a little more than think about change. It is, in effect, an attempt to help with the *very first step* of an active, doing process — that of putting on their collective creative thinking caps to define just where they really want to be at some point in the future. If organizations and groups know more clearly than they usually do where they *want* to go and, within that domain, where it is *possible* to go, then their chances of planning rationally how to get there and eventually of arriving are considerably enhanced.

   Thus, this learning design may offer help in the first step of that long-range process. The leader, if he helps to begin this process, should be prepared to help the organization deal with questions about next steps, such as:

   — Should there be a pause, say two weeks, while the top leadership of the organization attempts to integrate the work of the "Future Building" session into a position or summary paper?

   — What are other next-step activities? Would one of them be a scheduled time to reconvene the total group?

   — What are some additional resources that need to be included in the next phase of work?

   — Were there specific points surfaced in the session around which smaller groups of people could meet to do some work for the larger group?

— Should the statements of the small groups be collected, typed up, and distributed quickly to all members with instructions to continue thinking about the process of integrating the work done so far?

If the learning design is used in the classroom, a different set of questions should be discussed:

— What do you think made one "castle" "win" over the others?

— How much difference did the "sales pitch" make?

— Is one group organizing structure better than another? Are others more useful in different "Castle Companies" or different situations?

— Was communication influenced by any particular structure?

— What other dynamics of your group seemed to be important and influenced your final product?

5.   *Support materials.* On the following pages are materials needed for this design when used as a classroom simulation.

CASTLE BUILDING

Background

Your group is one of three product-development teams working within the research and development division of the GTM (General Turret and Moat) Corporation. GTM has decided to enter new markets by expanding the product line to include fully designed and produced castles, rather than selling components to other companies, as it has in the past.

Each of the three teams has been asked to design a castle for the company to produce and sell. Given limited resources, the company cannot put more than one design on the market. Therefore, the company will have to decide which of the three designs it will use, discarding the other two designs.

Your task is to develop and build a castle. You will have forty-five minutes to produce a finished product. At the end of this period, several typical consumers, picked by scientific sampling techniques, will judge which is the best design. Before the consumers make their choice, each group will have two minutes to make a sales presentation.

CASTLE BUILDING

MEMORANDUM

TO: PROJECT TEAM #1

FROM: Edward Grimbsy Bullhouse III
         Chief Executive Officer
         General Turret and Moat Corporation

SUBJECT: Development of new castle product

In order to perform effectively and to develop a useful product for our firm, I have decided that _____ will serve as manager of the product development team #1. It is _____ responsibility to see that the team develops a useful and feasible product, and I hope that all of you will cooperate with _____ in this effort.

CASTLE BUILDING

MEMORANDUM

TO: PROJECT TEAM #2

FROM: Edward Grimbsy Bullhouse III
         Chief Executive Officer
         General Turret and Moat Corporation

SUBJECT: Development of new castle product

In order to perform effectively and to develop a useful product for our firm, I am asking that you select one of your team to serve as manager of product development team #2. I trust that you will also determine and select any committees, task forces, subgroups, etc. that are needed in order to perform your job.

CASTLE BUILDING

MEMORANDUM

TO: PROJECT TEAM #3

FROM: Edward Grimbsy Bullhouse III
             Chief Executive Officer
             General Turret and Moat Corporation

SUBJECT: Development of new castle product

In order to perform effectively and to develop a useful product for our firm, I am asking that each of you put forth your maximum effort. I trust that you will provide us with a worthwhile product that can contribute to the profits of the firm.

CASTLE BUILDING

Observer's Guide

During the course of the building period, observe what is happening within your particular group. Specifically, you should look for the following things:

1. What was the reaction of the group to the memorandum?

2. What was the basic structure of the group?

3. To what degree did people specialize and work on the some particular part of the overall task? How did this specialization come about?

4. Who was (were) the leader(s) of the group? How was leadership determined? How effective was the leadership in helping the group to perform its task?

5. Were there any specific patterns of communication among members of the group, or did everyone talk with everyone else?

6. How were important decisions made? Did you see conflicts or were decisions made cooperatively and with compromise?

7. Other general observations:

After the session be prepared to discuss your observation with the entire group.

D.   Design for Learning to Integrate Group and System Goals

1. *Purpose.* This learning design uses a more rational-logical approach than that of the previous design on "castle building" in order to tie together the goals of groups and relate them to an overall organizational goal. It should be used with real-world organizational groups. In order to use this design in a classroom setting there would have to be several natural subgroups in the class, each having the possibility of natural and specific goal setting relevant to that subgroup. Otherwise, the exercise would only be an intellectual one. This, in itself, is not bad, as we believe the framework we propose in this design is an important one for group leaders, consultants, and change agents. Although actual classroom practice of the process might be difficult, we have found it very useful for classes with continuing subgroup teams.

   The purpose, then, of this learning design is to experience an open process of intergroup goal setting within a total organizational setting. Like Design C, this activity helps organization members set goals and objectives. It helps them to begin identifying realistic paths they might follow to attain these objectives. This is, in fact, only the beginning of an organizational problem solving effort. The design should be followed by the generation of alternative solutions to the problems of goal attainment, the identification of helping and hindering forces in this process, and the planning of specific actions that will bring attainment. Other learning designs in this book can be used for these purposes.

2. *Materials needed.* Newsprint, markers, small-group meeting space, and a large seminar room for the whole group.

3. *Steps in using the design.*
   a.   Give conceptual input on goal setting.
   b.   Form small heterogeneous groups.
   c.   Have small groups formulate overall organization goal statements.
   d.   Reconvene large group and post goal statements.
   e.   Summarize and discuss similarities and differences noted in statements.
   f.   Have small groups resume work, attempting to reconcile differences.
   g.   Reconvene large group and post goal statements.
   h.   Help total group integrate subgroup goals with organization goal statements. Have groups plan for next steps in the process.

4. *Deriving learnings and deciding on next steps.* It should be obvious from the learning design we have just outlined that an organizational problem solving process has only just begun. Those who would formally open such a process must be prepared to offer help on its continuation. The "can of worms," if you please, is now ready for inspection. Some questions that need to be faced, either in the goal-setting session or in a special session with the leadership group are:

   — How do we continue the process we have started?

   — Is there a need for skill training on problem solving and action planning for members of our group?

— What kinds of outside resources do we need to help us as we begin moving toward our objectives?

— How can we learn to set individual and small-group short-range targets and define specific behaviors that are necessary for the attainment of these objectives?

— How do we plan to deal with other organizational groups and individuals that need to be brought up to date on what we have done so far? With groups from outside who have a stake in what we're doing?

Classroom groups may wish to discuss and evaluate the various next steps and the potential problems involved in any such attempts.

5.   *Support materials.* The figure and notes that follow may be useful at various times in this learning design as discussion and conceptualization aids.

FIGURE 7-1 Defining and Integrating System and Subsystem Goals

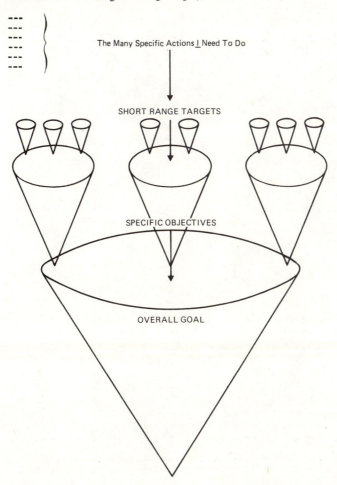

Some Suggestions on Using the Goals Figure

— Maybe you can use the idea of a "funneling" effect as you look at the chart. *Actions* lead to *targets*, which lead to *objectives*, which move toward the attainment of the overall *goals* of the organization.

— Turn the chart upside down and notice the "umbrella" effect. The overall *goal* covers everything. It is your purpose, your mission; and each *objective, target,* and *action* must somehow fit together to move toward its attainment.

— It's particularly significant to be aware of the important interrelationships among individual, group, and organization goals.

— Can you think of other ways to use the chart? Turn it sideways and what do you see?

II. CONCEPTUAL SUPPORT MATERIALS: GOAL SETTING

ACTUAL AND IDEAL GOALS

"Give me a lever long enough and I will move the earth."
"Sorry, we don't stock wood in 10,000,000 foot lengths."

We believe that there are major conceptual differences between *ideal* goals and *actual* goals. In a rational sense, ideal goals may, in fact, not be attainable. Rather, they may often be emotional statements of need and desire to attain ethically and morally nonattainable standards: "Rid the world of war"; "Everyone should have a Communistic type of government"; "Convert everyone to Christianity"; "Stop drug traffic in our city"; "See that every employee is satisfied and productive"; "Treat every group member's ideas with serious consideration"; "Love, honor, and obey your husband/wife"; "Become the greatest inventor that ever lived."

The point is not that ideal goals are bad or should be ignored, but that it is foolish to confuse actual, attainable goals with ideals. Ideal goals are just that; they should not be used to evaluate achievement because they are, by definition, not achievable, or, at least, not directly achievable. If we do confuse the two the inevitable result is one of two undesirable conditions of failure: (1) it becomes clear, eventually, that the goal cannot be reached and it is discarded, along with *parts* of the goal that *could* be attained; or (2) there is continued effort to attain the ideal goal with the recognition, possibly unconscious, that this is impossible but by continuing to try the individual or group has an excuse for not attaining possible, realistic goals related to the ideal (or going on to try for other realistic goals) and, therefore, cannot be blamed for failing to attain the ideal goal, since it is so obviously difficult (really, impossible).

At any level – individual, dyad, group, organization, community, society, or world – specific goals are useful to the extent that they are reality-based, that is, possible to reach. This does *not* mean simple or easy; a specific, realistic goal may be quite difficult to attain. In general, it has been found that people, individually or in groups, can work most effectively toward goals that are realistic and moderately difficult. This provides a meaningful challenge, but not one that is so frustrating as to discourage effort or serve as an excuse for failure.

SUPPORT SYSTEMS

"Support system" is a jargon term referring to some direct or indirect means that will be used or aid in attaining some goal. A support system can be something as simple as a daily calendar or as complex as the life-support system in a space capsule. Once goals have been determined, the means for attaining those goals are of primary importance, and specific actions must be defined that are directed toward goal attainment or toward the development of support systems for goal attainment.

Often we devise elaborate devices or procedures to support goal attainment; sometimes these devices are actually useful. But we generally forget the most significant and powerful support system of all: other people and our relationships with them. The learnings in Chapter One are most relevant here. The helping relationship is a *human* relationship; it is useful not only for a "client" and a "consultant" but for any pair or group of people. The best support systems for attaining goals are systems of relationships between and among people. When considering how to attain the goals one sets, one of the first questions to ask is, "Who can help me, and how?" and even more important, in an organization where one's goals interrelate with the overall goals of the system, one of the first questions to ask is, "How can I help my peers attain *their* goals?"

REFERENCES

Argyris, C. (1964) *Integrating the individual and the organization.* New York: Wiley.

Atkinson, J. W. (1957) Motivational determinants of risk-taking behavior. *Psychological Review* **64**: 359-372.

**Beck, A. C., Jr., and Hillmar, E. D. (1972) *A practical approach to organization development through MBO.* Reading, Mass.: Addison-Wesley.

Beckhard, R. (1967) The confrontation meeting. *Harvard Business Review* **45(2): 149-153.

Clark, J. V. (1970) Task group therapy I: Goals and the client system. *Human Relations* **23**: 263-277.

Forward, J., and Zander, A. (1971) Choice of unattainable group goal and effects on performance. *Organizational Behavior and Human Performance* **6**: 184-199.

Hughes, C. L. (1965) *Goal setting.* New York: American Management Association.

Kolb, D. A., and Boyatzis, R. E. (1974) Goal-setting and self-directed behavior change. In *Organizational psychology: A book of readings.* 2nd ed., eds. D. A. Kolb, I. M. Rubin, and J. M. McIntyre. Englewood Cliffs, N.J.: Prentice-Hall.

Levinson, H. (1970) Management by *whose* objectives? *Harvard Business Review* **48**(4): 125-134.

Lewin, K. (1935) *A dynamic theory of personality.* New York: McGraw-Hill.

Lewin, K. (1958) Group decision and social change. In *Readings in social psychology.* 3rd ed., eds. E. E. Maccoby, T. M. Newcomb, and E. L. Hartley. New York: Holt, Rinehart, & Winston.

Lewin, K.; Dembo, T.; Festinger, L.; and Sears, P. S. (1944) Level of aspiration. In *Personality and the behavior disorders.* Vol. 1, ed. J. McV. Hunt. New York: Ronald Press.

Lippitt, R.; Fox, R. S.; and Schindler-Rainman, E. (1972) *Toward a humane society: Images of potentiality.* Fairfax, Va.: NTL Learning Resources Corporation.

**Mager, R. (1972) *Goal analysis.* Belmont, Calif.: Fearon.

Mager, R. (1962) *Preparing instructional objectives.* Belmont, Calif: Fearon.

Meyer, H. H.; Kay, E.; and French, J. R. P., Jr. (1965) Split roles in performance appraisal. *Harvard Business Review* **43(1): 123-129.

Morrisey, G. L. (1970) *Management by objectives and results.* Reading, Mass.: Addison-Wesley.

Odiorne, G. (1965) *Management by objectives.* New York: Pitman.

Raia, A. P. (1965) Goal setting and self control. *Journal of Management Studies* **2**: 34-53.

Reddin, W. J. (1971) *Effective management by objectives.* New York: McGraw-Hill.

Simon, H. A. (1964) On the concept of organizational goal. *Administrative Science Quarterly* **9**: 1-22.

Starbuck, W. H. (1963) Level of aspiration. *Psychological Review* **70**: 51-60.

Vroom, V. H. (1960) The effects of attitudes on perceptions of organizational goals. *American Sociological Review* **13**: 229-239.

Zander, A. (1971) *Motives and goals in groups.* New York: Academic Press.

Zander, A., and Meadow, H. (1963) Individual and group levels of aspiration. *Human Relations* **16: 89-105.

**References preceded by a double asterisk are those judged to be most basic or important.

CHAPTER EIGHT

Conflict Management: Helping People Learn to Deal with Conflict

"You haven't been listening to a word I've said!"
"I sure have – you're just looking for a fight!"

INTRODUCTION

Conflict is not only a part of life, it is a *necessary* part of life. Imagine how dull the world would be if everyone agreed on everything. This would mean that everyone would look, think, and act exactly alike – differences lead to conflict. In fact, it would mean a world of smoothly running human "machines." Scholars and skillful managers now generally agree that some conflict is (a) unavoidable, (b) necessary, and (c) in and of itself neither good nor bad. Because people are invariably different, to a greater or lesser degree, in their appearance, attitudes, values, and goals, conflict is unavoidable. Because new ideas, practices, and solutions to problems are often the result of conflict (in one form or another), conflict is necessary for the growth and development of individuals, groups, and organizations. And, while the consequences of conflict may be quite negative (ranging from personal unhappiness to worldwide destruction) the outcomes can also be quite positive. Whether outcomes are bad or good often depends on how the conflict is handled; thus, negative outcomes are not usually "inevitable."

Conflict is, perhaps, the most obvious signal that some *problem* exists. The first reading at the end of this chapter describes briefly the various types of conflict that often arise. To yield positive, productive – rather than negative, destructive – outcomes, the problems underlying the conflict must be identified and explored. The second reading gives some very basic ideas about the means by which conflict can be directed toward positive outcomes. This entire chapter is devoted to the procedures and skills needed for the positive management of conflict. Before we sound too idealistic, though, we must add that not all conflicts are, with our present level of knowledge and skill, resolvable. Unfortunately, many of the most serious conflicts facing us today fall into this category. Not too long ago, several leading behavioral scientists, experts in conflict resolution, brought together (on "neutral" ground) representatives of two African nations engaged in a long-standing border dispute. After a two-week workshop, the representatives left with measurably increased understanding of each others' position. The low-level border conflict, however, is still going on.

While we cannot say that all conflicts are resolvable, in light of our present knowledge and skills, we can, at least, increase understanding, which is a necessary first step toward conflict resolution. How to do this is the focus of the first learning design in this chapter.

The remaining learning designs in this chapter provide structured methods for dealing with conflicts between groups. Such conflicts are, of course, common in any organization, formal or informal. These methods tend to be more effective the more the groups are interdependent — the more they really *need* one another.

For many people (and groups) conflict is seen as threatening, dangerous, and to be avoided at any cost. Even when handled using the methods and skills contained in this chapter, conflict may, in fact, have negative consequences. We believe, however, that confrontation of conflict within a problem solving approach can generally (though not invariably) lead to positive outcomes for the parties involved. Facing and dealing with conflict with a problem solving orientation is, in the long run, always a better strategy than trying to avoid the conflict or fighting it out.

I. SPECIFIC SKILL-DEVELOPMENT AND LEARNING DESIGNS

A.   Design for Learning to Listen When in Conflict: The CATSAT Skill*

1.   *Purpose.* Whether they are in a group discussion or just speaking with one other person, most people are quite taken with their own ideas and their personal feelings about those ideas. So much so, in fact, that they often do not listen very effectively to points of view that others in the discussion are attempting to express. Sometimes very little of another's message actually gets through. How often can you see yourself thinking up what you're going to say next while someone else is talking, waiting impatiently for him to put in a comma or catch his breath so you can interrupt and say what you want to say — so you see how important this is to know and understand why you must let me finish this for it *is* important and I feel strongly about it because we all do and I need to say it but others should too in spite of the fact that they won't although I agree that they should and; (whew) — you'd better come in here or I'll go on! Have you ever watched senators being interviewed on TV? They're good at this.

This exercise is designed to help one learn to listen more effectively to another person. Not listening often leads to misunderstandings about what the other person is saying. It also may lead to misunderstandings about the other person himself. Even though one person may believe that a real difference with another exists, it may be discovered, after listening clearly, that there is, in fact, no difference. Of course, it is also quite possible that a real — and serious — difference will be discovered and clarified. A variety of things could then happen: a husband and wife may seek divorce; an employee may quit or be fired by the boss; or the parties may collaborate in trying to resolve their problem. Our point is that real work on problems involving disagreement, differences, and conflict cannot begin until effective communication occurs and any misunderstandings at this basic level of interaction are cleared up.

2.   *Materials needed.* Movable chairs, newsprint and markers, role-play instructions.

---

*The original design for the "Effective Listening Skills" exercise — expanded and renamed the "CATSAT Skill" — was prepared by Floyd C. Mann, with the assistance of William C. Morris, during the period when Dr. Mann was director of the Center for Research on Utilization of Scientific Knowledge at the Institute for Social Research.

3. *Steps in using the design.*

    a.   State the purpose of the exercise.

    b.   Choose volunteers for role play.

    c.   Choose the setting and the problem to be worked on.

    d.   Create roles for the two points of view.

    e.   Choose which role players play which points of view.

    f.   Set up the first role play.

    g.   Conduct the first short role play.

    h.   Discuss and debrief the role play.

    i.   Conduct the second role play.

    j.   Discuss and debrief the role play.

    k.   Divide into trios to practice the CATSAT skill.

    l.   Stop action and post observations.

    m.   Derive learnings from the experience.

4. *Deriving learnings.* After completing this exercise, it might be helpful to review Jack Gibb's paper on "Defensive Communication" in Section II of Chapter Four. Consider how the CATSAT skill fits in with Gibb's suggestions and with the "Rules for Helpful Feedback." In part 5 of this design we have included a summary paper that should help in reviewing and understanding the CATSAT skill and approach. Some specific questions the class may wish to discuss are:

    — In what kinds of situations would you be prepared to act as a third party in an obvious misunderstanding?

    — When might you use the CATSAT skill on yourself?

    — What makes using this skill slightly "nonnormal"?

    — Why is it difficult to make a verbal intervention in someone else's argument and not appear to be taking sides?

    — How can you use your body to indicate both interest and impartiality as you try to give help?

    — If emotions are too high for one to talk directly to the other, can you use *yourself* as the channel through which one gives feedback to the other? How would your instructions to the pair differ in this case?

    — What would be the very first step you would take if you found that each individual really understood the other and that there were no longer any misunderstandings, but that there was really a basic value difference present?

5. *Support materials.* On the following pages are instructions and role-orientation sheets for the demonstration role play and for two practice role plays that may be used instead of developing a role play in class.

USING THE CATSAT SKILL IN REAL-LIFE SETTINGS

After completing the CATSAT design, people often ask two very significant questions. The first is, "Shouldn't you be able to use the CATSAT skill *yourself*, when you're in a conflict with another person — when there's no third person around to help?" The answer is, *certainly!* It's often helpful to extend the learning design by repracticing in *pairs* (instead of trios), and then collecting data about that experience.

The second question that comes up is: "But what if we've done this and it doesn't do any good — we really do have a basic disagreement, a problem with each other?" Our answer is, of course that happens. You may find that when you listen to each other effectively and are able to understand each other's point of view, you really don't have a problem of central importance to work on — and in fact, many of the problems we have in organizations stem from the fact that we don't communicate well to start with. This has been the purpose of the CATSAT design, to learn a skill useful in clearing up such misunderstandings. The subject of another learning design would be actually to go to work on solving *real* conflict problems. At this point we would refer you to the first of the brief readings in Section II of this chapter, reviewing the types of conflict.

We have not, however, proposed a specific learning design in this book on working through value differences.* We find this process difficult to learn in other than a real situation with a real value difference between two people. Although we have simulated the experience, we find only minimal learnings. The only way we have found to learn to deal with these more serious differences is to prepare ourselves well with the basic learnings and skills, and then to work up to the point in real-life practice where we can be helpful in working through such problems.

DEMONSTRATION ROLE PLAY

Role for George/Georgia Miller

You are a unit head in the Production Supply Department of the Gray Bearing Works Corporation. You've been with the company almost two years now and are quite pleased with your job.

This is the first year you'll be entitled to the standard week's vacation, and you're planning to go to Florida with your spouse, for the last week of the month. You've made arrangements for relatives to take care of the kids and are expecting to have a really good time. You've already made airline reservations and have put a deposit on the hotel room. You're really looking forward to this vacation and you submitted your vacation time request form well in advance of anyone else, so that you'd get first priority, because company policy has been that only one supervisor in a department can take his vacation at a given time. Everything seems set, though, and you're starting to count the days.

You've just stepped out to the coffee room with one of your colleagues, Bill Blake, and have begun to talk about your vacation plans. In fact, he might be able to keep an eye on your unit while you're gone.

---

*Chapter Five does contain a learning design for "surfacing" — becoming aware of — value differences. While the purpose of that design is to promote awareness, not resolution, of value differences, this still represents a very significant learning, since people are often unaware of the nature or existence of value conflict.

DEMONSTRATION ROLE PLAY

Role for Bill Blake

You are a unit head in the Production Supply Department of the Gray Bearing Works Corporation. You've been with the company almost twenty years now, and are generally very happy with your job.

Your usual vacation time is coming up soon. The deer-hunting season will be opening at the end of this month, and you've made plans to go the first week of hunting. You and your brother and nephew have rented a cabin up north, and you're really looking forward to the trip. You've gone hunting every season for the past fifteen years, but this is the first time in several years that you've been able to arrange things so that you and Tom can go together. Your wives and kids have also arranged to stay together while you're gone. Your nephew John is quite excited, since this will be his first real hunting trip.

You already mentioned to your boss that you'd be taking off, as usual, during the hunting season, and turned in the time form, so everything should be set up for the other supervisors to cover for you while you're gone. The company policy has generally been to have only one supervisor in a department off at any one time, if it's at all possible, but there shouldn't be any problems there, since everyone knows your standard vacation time.

One of your colleagues, George/Georgia Miller, and you have just sat down for coffee and begun to talk about vacation plans. In fact, (s)he might be able to keep an eye on your unit, and help out Jim, your senior subordinate, if any unusual problems develop.

DEMONSTRATION ROLE PLAY

Role for John/Jane Crane

You are a unit head in the Production Supply Department of the Gray Bearing Works Corporation. You've been with the company for seven years and are quite happy in your job.

As you walk into the coffee lounge this morning, you notice that the other two unit heads in your department, George/Georgia Miller and Bill Blake, seem to be engaged in an argument of some kind. You decide to sit down with them and see if you can help them work out whatever is bothering them.

DEMONSTRATION ROLE PLAY

Instructions for "Failure" Third Party (Crane)

You are going to demonstrate how one can *fail* in helping two people who are in conflict, which can happen even when one has the best of intentions. It is important for the demonstration that you follow the directions below as closely as possible. In real life, of course, you would not do as badly as in this demonstration. Remember that you're trying to be serious about helping the two parties but are going about it in all the wrong ways.

1.   Listen to the discussion/argument for a short time.

2.   Begin to communicate nonverbally your discomfort with the discussion (e.g., sit back, fidget a bit).

3.   Intervene in the discussion. Some possible actions you might take are:

   a.   Agree with one of the people but not the other one — take sides.

   b.   Say that they shouldn't be talking about this kind of thing at work or where others can hear them.

   c.   Suggest that their discussion would better be held later, when they've cooled off.

   d.   Talk about the fact that they're both wrong.

   e.   Say that you think the boss ought to be handling this, settling the dispute.

   f.   See if you can get both of them to attack you.

   g.   Get up, wash your hands of the whole affair, and leave.

Instructions for "Success" Third Party (Crane)

You are going to demonstrate how one might effectively help two people who are engaged in a heated argument to listen to each other and begin to work together on solving their problem. It is important for the demonstration that you follow the directions below as closely as possible. Even though you might not behave this way in a real-life situation, try your best to act exactly as we suggest below.

1.   Listen to the discussion/argument for a short time.

2.   Begin to lean forward intently to listen to both persons. Show your interest by physical movements.

3.   Intervene in the discussion, attempting to use the following process:

    a.   Say something like: "It may be that we're not really clear about what either of you is saying; I'd like to ask you to try something with me, if you will."

    b.   Then go on quickly, picking one of them and asking him if he will take a few seconds and try to tell the other person (let's say George) what he thinks George has been *saying*, and how he thinks George *feels* about what he has said. Ask him (let's say Bill) to, when he's finished, "check it out with George" to see whether he was right or wrong — whether he really heard George or not. Be sure to check for *both* the ideas or concepts *and* the feelings that have been expressed.

    c.   Quickly, and before Bill starts to do this, turn physically toward George and say to him that after Bill has finished you would like to ask him, George, to try the same thing with Bill. This act should convey to both of them that you are not taking sides, but only trying to help in the communication process.

    d.   If they have trouble during the process, help them, continue to be active, be positive about what you want them to do.

THE ACCOUNTING OFFICE

Role for John/Jane Burns, Director of Accounting

You are a CPA, have a Harvard MBA, and have been with Wilcox Company for ten years. You have been Director of the Accounting Office for the past three years. During this period, conditions have steadily worsened, in terms of managing up-to-date accounts for the organization (which is a moderately large firm, with eight thousand employees). At this point, you are seriously concerned that the upcoming annual audit will be so confused as to create serious problems with the Securities and Exchange Commission.

The major source of the problem is that neither Sales nor Purchasing provides your office with accurate current information. After investigating the situation thoroughly, you have decided that the only way to get this mess cleared up is by instituting greater controls over these divisions. Specifically, you have drawn up a new policy that requires that all sales and all purchase orders pass through your office for recording prior to final authorization.

While this may cause a slight increase in delay time for the two departments, the need is so urgent that this minor disadvantage is entirely justified.

You have asked the heads of the two divisions to meet with you today, so that you can explain the new policy in detail. Although you anticipate some resistance from them, you have no choice but to insist that the policy be followed, beginning tomorrow.

THE ACCOUNTING OFFICE

Role for Tom Turner, Director of Production Division

You have been with the Wilcox Company, a moderately large manufacturing firm (six thousand line workers, eight thousand employees in all) for twenty years. You started fresh out of high school, "on the line," and worked your way up to head the entire Production Division. You feel that your division is doing a good job, and the company as a whole is in sound shape.

For the past three years John/Jane Burns has been Director of the Accounting Office. Ever since (s)he was promoted, Burns has tried to tighten things up — you have a hunch (s)he even counts the paper clips used! Now, there are rumors that Burns is about to drop some new bomb, regarding accounting policies. (S)he's asked for a meeting this afternoon. You're perfectly willing to listen to her/him, but you've had it with her/his petty bureaucratic procedures. It's rough enough going through (or, actually, getting around) the procedures as they're set up now. In fact, this meeting may be a good time to let Burns know exactly what a mess (s)he's been creating for you. How are you supposed to get the materials you need to keep the lines running when it's "fill out this form in quadruplicate" every time you need a part order? Maybe it's time (s)he had an earful!

THE ACCOUNTING OFFICE

Role for Sara Caine, Director of Marketing Division

You have been with the Wilcox Company (a moderately large manufacturing firm, employing eight thousand persons) for five years, having come up through the sales ranks to become Director of the Marketing Division last year. You have an MBA, with a concentration in marketing, from the state university.

Since you took over as director, you've begun to appreciate the difficulties in administering a large division. For example, you can appreciate some of the problems John/Jane Burns, Director of Accounting, must continually face, even though you still get annoyed with all of his/her forms and such. In fact, Burns has seemed more uptight than usual lately. (S)he's called a meeting with you and Tom Turner, Director of Production, for this afternoon. Probably some new policy (s)he wants implemented. Well, you'll try to be helpful, but from the way Tom's been acting lately toward Burns this meeting sounds like it'll be like putting two fighting fish in a small bowl! Well, you just finished going through one of the new sales training courses that involved practice in handling conflicts through active listening: having one party restate the ideas (concepts) and feelings (attitudes) of the other, then checking with the other to see if (s)he's satisfied with the accuracy of the restatement. If a conflict does, as you expect, develop, you figure you'll try out this technique and see if it does help.

THE COLLEGE HIRES

Role for Jim Alfred, Director of the Administrative Services Division

You've had a continuing problem with Nancy Brown, Personnel Director of the company. For the past couple of years, she's been pushing the hiring of new college kids; as far as you're concerned, they're more trouble than they're worth. You'd think that she'd at least be willing to try to find places for them elsewhere, knowing how you feel about the situation; after all, Personnel should be helping you, not making things harder than they are.

In your experience, it's the older, more mature workers who are the backbone of the company. The five department managers under you feel the same way. These college kids come in with a know-it-all attitude and expect everything to be done *their* way, instead of the ways the company has found best over years of practice. They're not even interested in learning the right way; they just criticize. They often are out on Fridays or Mondays — all they really want is to fool around. A couple of times you really worked hard with some of the more promising kids, who were willing to work and learn, and what happened? They quit, wasting all the valuable time and effort you spent in training them! What really gets your goat is the way they act toward their superiors — never outright insubordinate, but just close enough to make you angry. Someday, when one of them greets you with "how goes it, boss-man" (and a not-too-hidden sneer) you just might punch him in the nose!

Yesterday, Brown called and asked if you and she could get together and discuss the "problems" with the college hires. Well, okay, you'll go talk to her — but you're tired of going over the same issues again and again. You'd rather she would do her job and help get you the kind of employees you want, instead of giving you more garbage about how great the college hires really are.

Here are some of the things you have observed and know about the behavior of the college hires, compared to older employees:

- They are able to adapt to new job assignments more quickly.
- They are absent more often.
- They are more energetic.
- They are more likely to quit.
- They are equally productive.
- They are more friendly.
- They are more flippant toward their bosses.
- They are late to work less often.
- They are more willing to take on new assignments.
- They are less familiar with standard company procedures.

(Don't try to memorize these points; just think of them as background information, as you'd be aware of in a real-life situation.)

You are on your way now to Brown's office for the meeting.

THE COLLEGE HIRES

Role for Nancy Brown, Personnel Director

You've had a continuing problem with Jim Alfred, the Director of the Administrative Services Division of the company. He has a hang-up about the new college grads you've been hiring the past couple of years. When they're assigned to units in his division, he tries to get them transferred out, and the managers under him consistently give the college hires poorer ratings than older employees, apparently because of Alfred's biases. He's always bugging you to find places for college hires in other divisions, too. It looks like he's just prejudiced against them.

Personally, you think that the college hires are good employees. They really are the future of the company. They're willing, and eager to do their best when challenged, and they're generally more friendly than older employees. Based on your observations and records, you are aware of the following facts about the college hires, as compared with older employees:

- They are absent more often.
- They are more willing to take on new assignments.
- They are more energetic.
- They are more flippant toward their bosses.
- They are equally productive.
- They are more friendly.
- They are more likely to quit.
- They are able to adapt to new job assignments more quickly.
- They are less familiar with standard company procedures.
- They are late to work less often.

(Don't try to memorize these points; just think of them as background information, as you'd be aware of in a real-life situation.)

You really can't understand Alfred's position, so you've decided to try and talk over the whole problem with him. You asked him to come to your office because it's more comfortable and private than his. Rather than arguing or trying to convince him, you are going to try to listen to Alfred and understand his views, as best you can, by applying the principles of *active listening*: restating, in your own words, the ideas (concepts) and feelings (attitudes) that he expresses, and then checking with him to make certain that you have accurately understood him — that he is satisfied that you understand his ideas and feelings.

THE COLLEGE HIRES

Observer's Instructions

Both parties to the discussion you are going to observe have the same information about the college hires given in their roles. They also have been given quite different attitudes. The attitude of the division manager is negative, while that of the personnel director is positive. In an "ordinary" discussion set up like this, the parties could be expected to select facts favorable to their own viewpoints, and the discussion could easily become a conflict-argument. However, the personnel director has been instructed to use the CATSAT skill, to draw out and listen to the division manager. If this is done well, the division manager will present *all* the facts, negative *and* positive. If the interview is accomplished with unusual skill, the parties may even begin to develop a solution to the problem.

The table below gives the facts about the college hires and is set up so you can conveniently record who *first* brings up each fact, as well as the frequency with which the personnel director uses the CATSAT active listening skill: repeating in one's own words the ideas (*concepts*) and feelings (*attitudes*) of the other person, then checking with the other person to make sure that the restatement is accurate (*sat*isfaction).

| FACTS | FACT WAS FIRST MENTIONED BY | |
Compared to older employees, the college hires are:	Personnel Director	Division Manager
Positive		
More energetic		
Open to try new assignments		
Late to work less often		
Able to adapt to new jobs more quickly		
Negative		
Absent more often		
Less familiar with standard company procedures		
More likely to quit		
More flippant toward their bosses		
Neutral		
As productive		
More friendly		

Tally the number of times the personnel director uses the CATSAT active listening skill:

B.   Designs for Learning to Surface Intergroup Problems

The following two designs and five variations of those designs are concerned with learning how to surface and identify problems that groups in organizational systems may have with each other; we call them intergroup designs.

Organizations are made up of many different groups that must work together toward the accomplishment of common objectives — such as doctors and nurses in a hospital, professional staff and lay committee members in a voluntary organization, vice-presidents and middle managers in a business, and workers of a first and second shift in an organization. The members of these subgroups often differ widely in the ways in which they see things. They may have come from markedly different backgrounds, have been trained quite differently, occupy different levels in the organization, or relate to quite different groups outside of the organization that affect their definitions of the situation. With such differences, it is not uncommon to find problems of communication, misunderstandings, and conflicts, which these people do not handle as effectively as necessary to achieve a high order of coordination.

There are several techniques that have been found to be consistently useful in surfacing and identifying these interface problems — an important step in preparing to begin to work openly toward their solution. The two principal ones are the Merger Group Exercise and the Fishbowl.

THE MERGER GROUP EXERCISE

1.   *Purpose.* This technique facilitates the initiation of a good problem solving discussion. It can be used when two groups recognize that they have not been working together as effectively as they might in doing their jobs and are willing to come together to work on problems they have in common. Before they can begin to make effective use of such problem solving steps as problem definition, alternative solution identification, and the evaluation and selection of specific solutions, it is necessary to get out into the open the problems that the groups have with one another. Thus, this technique has much value with real groups in real organizations. The Merger Group design can also be used in the classroom if a relevant role play is created first, and we have provided an alternate set of steps in using the design for this purpose.

2.   *Materials needed.* Meeting rooms for small groups, newsprint and markers, role-play materials.

3A.   *Steps in using the design: Real groups.*

    a.   Open meeting by restating the objectives of the organization and giving the purpose of the meeting.

    b.   Have each group meet separately to identify cross-group problems.

    c.   Have each group list what it believes the other group will cite as problems.

    d.   Reconvene large group and post problem lists.

    e.   Have each group leader report on work done.

    f.   Have group discuss cross-group problems; merge old lists to develop one new list.

    g.   Establish priorities for new problem list.

    h.   Plan for next steps in problem solving.

3B.   *Steps in using the design: Classroom simulation.*

    a.   Have group read background case material.

    b.   Divide the group into subgroups of six.

    c.   Assign roles and read role-orientation sheets.

    d.   Give initial instructions for the role play and have students begin work on developing lists describing own and other group.

    e.   Review lists together (two trios); record discrepancies.

    f.   Revise lists, in trios, to reduce discrepancies; repeat step e.

    g.   Have subgroups produce final lists, one for each trio.

    h.   Summarize work and derive learnings.

4.   *Deriving learnings and deciding on next steps.* Surfacing intergroup problems within a system often takes a lot of time before a continuing small-group problem solving process can actually begin. At the close of the half-day design the total group should deal with several basic questions.

    — Do we have all of the major intergroup problems surfaced and recorded on our priority list?

    — Now that we know what the problems are, what are the next steps that we plan to take? And when?

    — How will we organize to do work and who will accept leadership responsibility?

    — What kinds of additional resources do we need and where will we find them?

From here the total group can move in several ways: (a) the large group can work together to develop solutions to the one high-priority problem between the groups; (b) new, smaller groups made up of members of each of the original groups can meet to develop tentative solutions to the problems for the whole group; (c) short-term organizational task forces can be appointed to develop solutions to more complicated problems. Whatever the grouping used to continue the problem solving process, any eventual working-through of the problems that demand action steps for implementation must be approved by the total group before actions start. This allows final input by all concerned into the solution to be implemented.

Here we refer the reader and user of this design to Design B in Chapter Ten for a description of a recommended small-group problem solving process, one that will help user groups arrive at realistic action and evaluation plans of their work.

In summary, a Merger Group Exercise allows each group and each person within a group the opportunity and freedom to indicate the problems that they have with the other group or members of that group without being publicly identified with their statement of the problem. This opportunity is often useful — especially if the groups have not had much experience with problem solving.

For groups that have participated in the role-play simulation, the data obtained in step should provide considerable material for discussion. Some relevant questions are:

    — Why did some groups succeed in arriving at final lists that everyone agreed on while others didn't?

    — Is success related to improved understanding of the other group? Respect for the other group? Liking of the other group?

    — Are understanding, respect, and liking levels related?

    — Are changes in understanding, respect, and liking related?

5.   *Support materials.* The background and roles for the classroom simulation follow on the next pages.

CASE OF THE POLLUTED STREAM

Background

The Apex Company is a moderate-sized manufacturing firm located in a small city (population about seventy thousand) in Illinois. Apex produces a variety of small products for large-machine producers (e.g., bearing rings, piston rings, etc.). They are the largest employer in the community. Recently, the environmentalist and antipollution movement has caught on in this somewhat out-of-the-way mid-American community, and Apex has found itself with some new problems, most particularly concerning a small river that flows by the main plant.

You will each take the role of one of three persons in one of two groups of three; the three in one group will be management employees of Apex while the three in the other group will be members of a local environmental action group.

Joe Turner is Production Manager of the largest production department of Apex. He has been a resident of the community for a number of years.

Ray Jones is Manager of Apex's R & D group. He's been working for Apex for two years now.

Jim Black was appointed Manager of Consumer Relations for Apex last year. Prior to this he was Assistant Manager of Personnel for five years.

Jane Lerner is Chairperson of the Environmental Action Group's Water Pollution Committee. She has chaired this committee for two years, since joining ENACT as one of the original organizers in the community.

Ralph Fischer is a member of the ENACT Water Pollution Committee. He joined ENACT a year ago and runs a small business in town.

John Clark is also a member of the ENACT Committee. He's been a teacher in the local high school for three years, moving into the community after graduation from the University of Michigan.

CASE OF THE POLLUTED STREAM

Role for Joe Turner, Production Manager

You've been trying your best to implement Ray Jones's new methods to reduce noxious waste emission from your production line into the stream that flows by the factory. It's a tough job, and these environmental action people don't understand any of it and don't seem to want to. You think they'd like to see your company go out of business. The community's economy would be in even worse shape than it is now, since the Apex Company is the major employer in this area. Maybe they'd deserve it, too.

CASE OF THE POLLUTED STREAM

Role for Ray Jones, Research and Development Group Manager

You've given Joe some new plans and production methods in the past year to reduce the water pollution in the local stream, but there are lots of bugs that keep coming up and need to be worked out. These damn activists talk like you're trying to destroy the world. It's just a little, insignificant stream, anyway, and you *are* trying to solve the problem, but they won't listen.

CASE OF THE POLLUTED STREAM

Role for Jim Black, Consumer Relations Manager

The Apex Company has been working hard this past year to eliminate pollution in a local stream, but it's not easy, and it seems like the local environmental action group (ENACT) just won't believe anything you say, though you've repeatedly tried to tell them the full story. All they do is organize rallys and boycotts against the company. You figured that a meeting between some of them and some of your people who are on this problem (Joe Turner from Production and Ray Jones, R & D manager) might show them that the company really is responding.

CASE OF THE POLLUTED STREAM

Role for Jane Lerner, Chairperson, Environmental Action Group Water Pollution Committee

For two years now you've been trying to get the Apex Company to stop polluting the stream running by their factory. It's important because it feeds into a nearby swampy wildlife refuge area. Since all they've done is talk and talk, your group has been actively organizing in the community for the past six months. And *now* the company wants to talk again, but knowing their past action (that is, words only) you're going to let them know that they're not taking you in any more!

CASE OF THE POLLUTED STREAM

Role for Ralph Fischer, Member, ENACT Water Pollution Committee

Being a businessman, you can sympathize with the pressures being put on the Apex Company, but they've had plenty of time to take some action on eliminating pollution in the stream by their factory. All they've given are promises — two years' worth! They keep trying to put you off with excuses and rationalizations and don't understand the basic environmental issues. After your recent rally, they seem to be running scared, and Mr. Black, their new consumer relations man, set up a meeting between some of them and your committee. You don't really expect anything more from today's meeting than more glib promises, though.

CASE OF THE POLLUTED STREAM

Role for John Clark, Member, ENACT Water Pollution Committee

After you organized that rally, the Apex Company saw that your group was for real. Now, it looks like they want to pacify you and quiet things down, but you're determined to show them that your group is going to step up the pressure even more. All they want is the buck, and that's where you're going to get to them — in their profits. Your boycott plans are going forward full blast.

C.   **The Fishbowl Technique**

1.   *Purpose.* This is a technique. It is best used when different groups and their members have learned to work openly with their interface problems and have little or no fear of expressing exactly how they see the situation and what they feel about it but still want to prepare for their problem solving work by hearning and seeing how members of the other group are viewing the problems and issues between them. As with the Merger Group Exercise this technique can be used with groups of different sizes, but is most often successful with smaller, more cohesive groups.

2.   *Materials needed.* An appropriate meeting room with movable chairs, newsprint pads and markers, masking tape to post each of the "fishbowl" products.

3.   *Steps in using the design.*

    a.   State purposes of the session.

    b.   Give instructions on how to work.

    c.   Have first group begin work in "fishbowl."

    d.   Have first group stop and second group begin work in "fishbowl."

    e.   Have groups merge to set priorities for further work.

4.   *Deriving learnings and deciding on next steps.* Once again — as in the case with the Merger Group Exercise — at this point the total group is ready to begin to move through the full set of steps required for effective problem solving. The group can work as a whole or break into mixed subgroups to develop tentative solutions for the whole group to evaluate and finally decide on which to adopt and try for a time.

5.   *Support materials.*

THE FISHBOWL TECHNIQUE

The technique is based on the proposition that it is often easier and more useful to talk to other members in one's own group about frustrations and problems that have not been well formulated or stated than it is to talk to a larger group where one's group is only one of two or more groups involved. A "fishbowl" allows each group to do this beginning work with itself, while the other group listens and observes. This procedure can be arranged in a number of different ways; several of these are described in this chapter. One arrangement that is commonly used is for one group to draw its chairs into the middle of the room to form a circle, with members of the other group pulling their chairs away and forming another circle around the outside of the room. Thus, one group is inside the "fishbowl," while the other is sitting outside in a larger circle that facilitate its observations and learnings about how the members of the group see and feel about the problems.

The power of this technique is that it allows each group to get things visibly "on the table" — with full disclosure of who is feeling strongly about certain problems and where the resources are within the other group to develop a mutually satisfactory solution to test operationally. There is clearly more risk involved in this technique, compared to the Merger Group Exercise, but groups can move faster using the Fishbowl Technique once they have become accustomed to working openly and authentically on problems. Both of these techniques help to ensure that good work is done in surfacing problems before the more careful task of problem definition is begun. They ensure that the first problem that is offered is not taken as "the problem," but many are offered as candidates for the use of the time of the two groups.

OTHER INTERGROUP PROBLEM IDENTIFICATION METHODS

There are several other variations on the above methods that might be used to initiate a problem solving process between groups. Briefly, some are:

1. *Problem-surfacing tapes.* Each group discusses problems it has with the other group, and this session is taped. Groups then exchange tapes, and each begins to develop a list of inter-group problems to be solved with the other group. The groups then get together to decide which problems to work on first, and how they will work.

2. *Dyadic problem surfacing.* The two groups break into pairs, each pair including one member from each of the two groups. Each dyad then produces a list of problems it feels are present at the interface of the two groups. Pair products are then compared.

3. *Oral confrontation.* Instead of asking one group to sit inside a circle where members can be observed as they work to identify problems, one group can be asked to move together physically and face the wall so they cannot see who in the other group is talking about a problem he has with them. Problems are posted. Groups are asked to exchange places and the process moves ahead.

4. *Shouting confrontation.* When there is a great deal of anger present and a high need "to say it as it is" to the other group, two groups may be formed (e.g., adults and teenagers) with first one and then the other telling the other group how they feel about them and the way they see it. Shouting and the full verbal expression of feelings are legitimate. After feelings have been vented, the groups are invited to begin working, using one of the intergroup problem-surfacing methods described in this chapter to develop a list of problems they now feel they might be able to handle.

5. *Complex-system problem identification.* When system boundaries are more complex, as in a community or city, heterogeneous groups, composed of at least two members from different interest groups, can meet to list problems they see in the total community. This type of inter-group merger technique can often be the start-up vehicle through which the various group interests come together around solutions for the whole community.

These variations indicate ways in which the risk of confrontation can be varied depending on the emotional states of the groups and on their readiness to work effectively in problem solving. Their value — and that of the two principal techniques — is considerably enhanced when the groups using them are familiar with the small-group problem solving techniques we have presented in other chapters. It is essential that the genuinely difficult problems that each of these methods are bound to surface be *dealt* with — worked on — by the organization that risks itself in opening up issues.

It is also important to understand that none of these techniques can be "laid on" in a group or intergroup setting by a consultant, change agent, or manager. By this we mean that they should be natural outgrowths of the needs of the system at a particular time in the process of system development, most often after good diagnosis of group or organizational needs. The techniques in this kind of action process may be identified or named by a consultant, but quite often they never are, resulting instead from process suggestions made by him or the system members themselves.

II. CONCEPTUAL SUPPORT MATERIALS: CONFLICT MANAGEMENT

APPROACHES TO CONFLICT MANAGEMENT

Types of Conflict

Whether conflict occurs between individuals or groups, it can be classed in one of *three basic categories.* The *first* type of conflict exists due to miscommunication or misunderstanding. For example, a child says, "I'm going over to Johnny's house," and his mother replies loudly, "Oh no you're not, you're going to clean your room!" "But . . ." the child responds, to be interrupted by the parent's command, "Now get upstairs, and no argument!" The boy goes upstairs muttering, "What a dope . . ." because he meant he would be going to Johnny's after finishing his clean-up chore, or perhaps, because he just finished the job. In other words, there is no real conflict at all; if the two parties had listened to and understood one another, they would have quickly found that the conflict was entirely due to misunderstanding. A similar type of easily resolvable conflict occurs from lack of information – again a communication problem. Managers A and B may engage in heated, and pointless, conflict simply because their common superior has not adequately defined certain job responsibilities of one or the other. This type of role ambiguity is generally uncomfortable for the person or persons involved and often leads to unnecessary conflict.

While conflict due to miscommunication or misunderstanding is fairly common, it is also fairly easy to deal with. A *second*, and more frequent, type of conflict is more difficult to handle. Many conflicts are substantive, that is, the result of "real" problems, problems of substance. Often the substantive problem of resource allocation leads to serious conflicts. In an organization such situations range from issues such as which secretary gets a new typewriter or which driver gets a new truck, through interdepartmental conflicts among managers, each of whom wants a bigger share of the budget, to the executive level, with vice-presidents in conflict over which long-range programs to support and which to drop. Other substantive conflict problems involve, for example, assignment of tasks, coordination between individuals and groups, and allocation of responsibilities among workers or managers.

Conflicts in this second category can generally be worked on and creatively resolved through a problem solving process. Solutions tend to be within one of two frameworks – structural or behavioral. *Structural* solutions resolve conflict by removing the basis for conflict. For example, two groups in conflict over the use of certain equipment or facilities may be told to provide schedules to a third party, who will work out nonconflicting assignments. Even interdependent individuals or groups can sometimes have their situation restructured so that total physical separation is possible. This solution would often involve some redesigning of the actual work process, but with no contact there can be no conflict. *Behavioral* solutions are usually more difficult to reach, because the negative feelings that the conflicting parties have developed toward one another must first be dealt with. These feelings hinder effective communication and understanding. Only when the parties can clearly communicate with and understand one another can they work through their problems and resolve the conflict. While this framework is more difficult to apply, it is often the only possible approach, since conflicting individuals or groups are often highly interdependent within the organization and cannot simply be separated and kept from contact. The results of effective, problem solving-based conflict resolution can be very positive, too.

The *third* type of conflict, emotional or value-based conflict, is often impossible to resolve. The basis for conflict is not fact or substance, although the conflict situation may involve a substantive problem. The basis for the conflict lies in the values of the parties and the feelings each has, based on those values. For example, Mr. Smith, a liberal senator, is backing an education appropriation bill that includes a provision for free hot lunches for children from poor families. He believes that it is the responsibility of the government to provide basic living essentials such as food, shelter, and medical care to those who cannot afford them. He cites the Constitution (Preamble and Article 1, Section 8, Paragraph 1) in support of his belief. Mr. Jones, a conservative senator, is strongly opposed to this provision. He believes that government is not obliged to and should not attempt to care for the poor, that such activities should be administered through various charitable agencies. Senator Smith's argument that the Congress is charged "to promote the common welfare" is invalid according to Senator Jones, since the legislation in question applies only to certain low-income persons, not to all persons. As should be obvious, both Smith and Jones are interpreting the Constitution in light of their personal *values* and *feelings.* Agreement between them is not possible, unless one or the other changes his values, which is not likely. One way to achieve partial agreement, however, is by appeal to still "higher" values the parties hold in common. In the above case, for example, some compromise agreement is likely since both Smith and Jones believe that the government has a basic responsibility to assist public education. Other than change or appeal to a higher-order common value, the only nondestructive way to handle such conflicts is through the participants' "agreeing to disagree." Such agreement is facilitated when the parties in conflict understand and respect one another.

A Framework for Conflict Management

Blake, Shepard, and Mouton (1964) have created a useful framework for classifying approaches to conflict management. They start with three sets of premises that managers may believe: (1) conflict is not inevitable but agreement is impossible; and (2) conflict is inevitable and agreement is impossible; (3) conflict is not inevitable, but does frequently occur, and when it does, agreement is possible.

These alternative premises seem to be based on two situational factors: task interdependency and interaction processes. Let us look first at task interdependency. An organization may require two persons or, more often, groups to coordinate their efforts, because of the nature of their tasks, e.g., each is responsible for a part of a larger task. While interdependency is, as most organizational variables, a matter of degree, we can oversimplify and refer to situations in which the parties are interdependent in that efforts must be coordinated and situations in which there is no necessary interdependence. To add a larger dimension of reality, we can note that often interdependence can be varied, within certain limits. Sometimes it is quite possible to make two units that have been highly interdependent completely independent, or, at least, to change the situation so that little or no direct contact is needed between the two units. Generally, in complex organizations, interdependence among units is a fact of life. It must, however, be remembered that the assumptions managers might make about interdependence may bear little resemblance to the *real* situation. And, given a choice between high and low interdependence situations, when both are possible, the assumptions made, in Blake, Shepard, and Mouton's terms, can act as a "self-fulfilling prophecy."

Interaction process can be seen as determining whether one views agreement as possible or impossible. Dutton and Walton (1966) developed a model of interunit interaction process consisting of three factors: (1) the type of joint *decision-making process* used by the two units (bargaining/win-lose versus problem solving); (2) *interaction patterns* between members of the two groups (formal, limited, versus informal, frequent); and (3) *attitudes* of members in one group toward members of the other group (negative versus positive). These three factors have interactive, causal effects and form two basic patterns: decision making via bargaining/limited-formal interaction/negative attitudes, and decision making via problem solving/frequent-informal interaction/positive attitudes. The first pattern is termed "distributive," the second "integrative." The conflict-management pattern between two units can be described on a dimension from high distributive to high integrative. The two patterns arise in large part out of the assumptions people make about conflict, and are highly self-reinforcing. That is, once two units are in a highly distributive (or integrative) type of pattern, it is hard to get out. Win-lose conflict leads to limited interaction with the "enemies" and bad feelings toward members of the other group. Bad feelings reinforce limited interaction, and both of these factors lead toward a motivation to "get even," which involves the bargaining/win-lose decision-making dynamic. A similar type of reinforcement process supports an integrative pattern.

Let us now substitute the two situational factors we have identified for the terms used by Blake, Shepard, and Mouton, and look more closely at the dynamics that take place in the three situations that are identified.

When no necessary interdependence exists but a distributive pattern holds (conflict not inevitable/agreement impossible), a set of strategies is used that centers on withdrawing from the situation. After all, if conflict is unnecessary and all the parties can do is argue, why bother? The other two situations are more complicated. If interdependency is acknowledged, but the distributive pattern dominates (conflict inevitable/agreement impossible), the actions will depend on the stakes involved. If there is little to be gained (or lost), the parties may simply leave the conflict to work itself out, or even settle it by chance (a coin flip). However, when the stakes are greater, a third-party judge may be called in to resolve the conflict, perhaps someone higher up in the hierarchy. When a great deal is at stake, a win-lose battle may result, with both parties fighting it out, using whatever tactics they can, to the bitter end.

The third, and rather different, set of strategies is used when interdependency is recognized (or seen as potentially existing), and the integrative pattern exists. When conflicts are quite minor, a strategy of "peaceful coexistence" can be used — "Okay, we disagree, but let's just agree to disagree, for now." When the stakes are moderate, a compromise-bargain may be worked out between the conflicting parties. After all, each can get something and give up something without much pain. When stakes are high, a collaborative problem solving process becomes worth the effort. If effective, all parties can gain.

These strategies cover six basic behavioral approaches to conflict management: (1) withdrawal from the situation or isolation of the parties; (2) smoothing over the conflict, pretending it really isn't there; (3) compromising or splitting the difference; (4) third-party judgment by some impartial outsider; (5) forcing or fighting an all-out battle to decide who wins the conflict; (6) confronting the conflict and the problems that underlie the conflict and attempting to collaboratively solve these problems. Occasionally compromise bargaining results in benefits for both parties, and sometimes withdrawal-isolation has positive effects, but the most *generally* positive approach is through confrontation and problem solving.

The set of situational contingencies and the conflict-management strategies and behaviors we have defined and discussed are summarized in the following chart (Table 8-1).

TABLE 8-1   Contingency Factors That Determine Approaches to Conflict Management

TASK STRUCTURE FACTORS	NO NECESSARY INTERDEPENDENCY	INTERDEPENDENCY	POTENTIAL INTERDEPENDENCY
INTER-ACTION PROCESS ASSUMPTION	DISTRIBUTIVE	DISTRIBUTIVE	INTEGRATIVE
HIGH STAKES	WITHDRAWAL (AVOIDANCE)	WIN-LOSE BATTLE (FORCING)	PROBLEM-SOLVING COLLABORATION (CONFRONTATION)
MODERATE STAKES	ISOLATION (AVOIDANCE)	THIRD-PARTY JUDGMENT (FORCING) (COMPROMISE)	SPLITTING THE DIFFERENCE – BARGAINING (COMPROMISE)
LOW STAKES	IGNORANCE-INDIFFERENCE (AVOIDANCE)	FATE (AVOIDANCE) (FORCING)	PEACEFUL COEXISTENCE (SMOOTHING OVER)

SIGNIFICANCE OF OUTCOMES (left axis)

LEVEL OF ACTIVITY INVOLVED — ACTIVE ← — — — — → PASSIVE (right axis)

REFERENCES

Argyris, C. (1964) *Integrating the individual and the organization.* New York: Wiley.

Blake, R. R.; Mouton, J. S.; and Sloma, R. L. (1965) The union-management intergroup laboratory. *Journal of Applied Behavioral Science* 1: 25-57.

**Blake, R. R.; Shepard, H. A.; and Mouton, J. S (1964) *Managing intergroup conflict in industry.* Houston, Texas: Gulf.

Blumberg, A., and Wiener, W. (1971) One from two: Facilitating an organizational merger. *Journal of Applied Behavioral Science* 7: 87-102.

Burke, R. J. (1970) Methods of resolving superior-subordinate conflict: The constructive use of subordinate differences and disagreements. *Organizational Behavior and Human Performance* 6: 393-411.

Dalton, M. (1959) *Men who manage.* New York: Wiley.

Dutton, J. M., and Walton, R. E. (1966) Interdepartmental conflict and cooperation: Two contrasting studies. *Human Organization* 25: 207-221.

Golembiewski, R. T., and Blumberg, A. (1968) The laboratory approach to organizational change: "Confrontation design." *Academy of Management Journal* 11: 199-210.

Harrison, R. (1972) Role negotiation: A tough minded approach to team development. In *The social technology of organization development*, eds. W. W. Burke and H. A. Hornstein. Washington, D.C.: Learning Resource Corp./NTL.

Kahn, R. L., and Boulding, E. (1964) *Power and conflict in organizations.* New York: Basic Books.

**Kahn, R. L.; Wolfe, D. M.; Quinn, R. P.; Snoek, J. D.; and Rosenthal, R. A. (1964) *Organizational stress: Studies in role conflict and ambiguity.* New York: Wiley.

**Lewin, K. (1948) *Resolving social conflicts.* New York: Harper.

**Lorsch, J. W., and Lawrence, P. R., eds. (1972) *Managing group and intergroup relations.* Homewood, Ill.: Irwin.

McNeil, E. B., ed. (1965) *The nature of human conflict.* Englewood Cliffs, N.J.: Prentice-Hall.

Pondy, L. R. (1967) Organizational conflict: Concepts and models. *Administrative Science Quarterly* **12: 296-320.

Pondy, L. R. (1969) Varieties of organizational conflict. *Administrative Science Quarterly* **14**: 499-505.

Rogers, C. R. (1951) *Client-centered therapy.* Boston: Houghton Mifflin.

Seiler, J. A. (1963) Diagnosing interdepartmental conflict. *Harvard Business Review* **41(5): 121-132.

Sherif, M. (1966) *In common predicament: Social psychology of intergroup conflict and cooperation.* Boston: Houghton Mifflin.

Sherif, M., ed. (1962) *Intergroup relations and leadership.* New York: Wiley.

Stagner, R., ed. (1967) *The dimensions of human conflict.* Detroit: Wayne State University Press.

Walton, R. E. (1968) Interpersonal confrontation and basic third-party functions. *Journal of Applied Behavioral Science* **4**: 327-344.

**Walton, R. E. (1969) *Interpersonal peacemaking: Confrontations and third-party consultation.* Reading, Mass.: Addison-Wesley.

Walton, R. E. (1970) A problem-solving workshop on border conflicts in Eastern Africa. *Journal of Applied Behavioral Science* **6**: 453-489.

Walton, R. E., and Dutton, J. M. (1969) The management of interdepartmental conflict: A model and review. *Administrative Science Quarterly* **14**: 73-84.

Walton, R. E.; Dutton, J. M.; and Cafferty, T. P. (1969) Organizational context and interdepartmental conflict. *Administrative Science Quarterly* **14**: 522-542.

**References preceded by a double asterisk are those judged most basic or important.

CHAPTER NINE

Evaluation: Helping People Learn How to Determine the Effects of Actions

May 1: "This is really the answer! It's sure to work."
July 1: "Well, give it time; I've got this gut feeling . . ."
September 1: "Gee, I guess all we can do is try again . . ."

INTRODUCTION

Most people would agree that experience can be a hard teacher, but the common saying to the effect that experience is the best teacher is often untrue; experience can be a rather poor teacher at times. The cat that jumps onto a hot stove may never jump on a stove again, thus missing out on all the tempting food left uncovered, when the appropriate lesson is "avoid the stove when you can feel warmth coming from it." But *that* lesson can be learned only by examining the action and determining exactly what went wrong ("jumped before approaching stove to determine warmth level").

In this chapter our aim is to help people learn how to plan for evaluation of their experience, in the context of Integrated Problem Solving. For good evaluation planning, a group must attend to three things: First, it must determine what the evaluation measures will be — the quantitative criteria for determining success or failure. Second, there must be an assignment of action responsibilities — who will do what — a timetable, and a plan for coordinating, when this is necessary. Finally, there must be acceptance of and commitment to carry out evaluation actions by individual group members.

This chapter is primarily concerned with *planning* for evaluation, Phase V of the problem-solving model presented in Chapter One, and only secondarily with *carrying out* an actual evaluation. This "real" evaluation could produce the greatest degree of learning, but is only possible (in full detail) when a real-life group is working on real problems. However, the second learning design in this chapter, which is highly adaptable to various classroom and training group situations, does provide some experience in evaluation planning *and* action. For "real" groups in organizations, the second design in Chapter Ten can also be used for learning evaluation design skills.

I. SPECIFIC SKILL-DEVELOPMENT AND LEARNING DESIGNS

A. Design for Learning to Plan Evaluation Actions

1. *Purpose.* This design provides practice in designing an evaluation process. It is for use with groups that have already committed themselves to actions that need to take place in order

to move toward attaining goals they have set earlier. This design is aimed at practicing the skills of designing and planning for the evaluation of such actions.

2. *Materials needed.* Paper and pencils, newsprint and markers, role materials (from prior exercise).

3. *Steps in using the design.*

    a. Give lecture on evaluation.

    b. Review the earlier design and problem solution developed from it.

    c. Define and develop "criteria measures."

    d. Stop action to select criteria measures.

    e. Have groups develop detailed evaluation plan.

    f. Have groups prepare newsprint lists of criteria and plan.

    g. Have class review and critique group products.

    h. Discuss problems with and learnings about evaluation design.

4. *Deriving learnings.* Some of the more important questions that should be raised in step h, above, are:

    — Is there a trade-off between the quality of a criterion measure and the ease of obtaining evaluation measures? How can a balance be struck?

    — How detailed and specific must the solution-action plan be before it is reasonable to plan for evaluation? How much does solution specification affect evaluation planning?

    — How is a "good" evaluation measure chosen? On what basis?

    — What if the criteria are clear but cannot be measured?

    — Is a bias in evaluation measurement possible, intentionally or unconsciously, when the person responsible for some action also is responsible for evaluating the effects of that action? How do we get around this, if it is a problem?

5. *Support materials.*

NOTE ON EVALUATION DESIGN

Many groups attempting to follow rational problem solving steps assume that it is enough for them to decide upon the solution to their problems. For them, problem solving is *finding* answers and no more. Other groups understand that solutions won't magically get implemented all by themselves. Somebody has to do something; someone has to take specific responsibilities and set time schedules. For these groups, solutions get implemented — sometimes even the *wrong* solutions become long-term answers to goals that were originally set. There are many mechanisms and processes in our organizational life that are used because "things have always been done that way." Who cares if some of them don't work very well, or if we feel a little uneasy about them. As long as things are going along fairly smoothly why rock the boat? By now the point should be obvious: problem solving is really not finished until groups *evaluate* whether or not the solutions they have been implementing really work. Only by doing so can they be assured that they either have the "right" answer or need to try new solutions or take new directions toward their goals.

But how does a group prepare itself to do good evaluation? Our proposition is that for every goal or objective set by a group there must also be established a set of *measurable criteria* that will be used both during and at the close of the action-implementation phase of the problem-solving process. This is the first step in designing evaluation and it presupposes that the group has developed a set of adequately specified actions, along with commitments by those who are to carry out the actions, and a timetable. When criteria of evaluation are determined, the group must repeat the process it went through in developing action plans: determine how the criteria are to be measured (actions needed), who is to take these actions (assignment of and commitment to action responsibilities), and when (timetable).

B.   Design for Learning to Carry Out Evaluation

1.   *Purpose.* In a limited way, a classroom or training-group situation can be used for practicing some of the skills involved in planning and carrying out evaluation; this is the purpose of the present design, which is concerned with evaluation of goal attainment. That is, rather than starting with a problem, the group begins by setting goals. This design could, then, directly follow one of the designs in Chapter Seven on goal setting. While the goals might be long range, such as learning goals for a semester course, we have found it particularly useful to focus on immediate goals. This requirement means that group members must plan and carry out an immediate evaluation of goals set for a particular session, which can be done using either individual or group goals, set at the beginning of the session and evaluated at points during the session and at the end.

2.   *Materials needed.* Newsprint and markers, or chalkboard.

3A.   *Steps in using the design: One session.*
   a.   Review purposes and problems of evaluation.
   b.   Review purpose of present session.
   c.   Consider individual purposes.
   d.   Share ideas with the group.
   e.   Define and write out specific personal goals. Begin groups.
   f.   Stop action to review goals.
   g.   Apply goal measurement ideas.
   h.   Share current evaluations of goal attainment.
   i.   Repeat application steps and derive learnings.

3B.   *Steps in using the design: Several sessions.*
   a.   Continue from previous activity.
   b.   Give brief lecture on problem solving in second or third session.
   c.   Develop evaluation criteria in following session.
   d.   Conduct final evaluation at closing session of class.

4.   *Deriving learnings.* Some significant questions for discussion after attempting an evaluation of actions are:
   — What are the implications of this evaluation regarding possible or desirable changes in our goals or action plan?
   — Did the evaluation measures give a clear reading of the degree of accomplishment or the real effects of actions? If not, what other measures are needed?

— Is interim evaluation always possible or useful? Are there situations in which only a final evaluation is needed?

— Can evaluation criteria and measures be redefined and modified as the action plan is being carried out? Would this affect the action plan in any way?

II. CONCEPTUAL SUPPORT MATERIALS: EVALUATION

PITFALLS IN EVALUATION

Planning and carrying out a good evaluation of a problem solution is probably the hardest and most neglected part of problem solving. Often, people assume that once a solution is developed the problem is solved (of course, this assumption also ignores the issues of carrying out the actions involved in the solution plan) or that it will be obvious whether or not the problem is solved. Thus, the two most obvious pitfalls are *failure to develop criteria measures* and *failure to make detailed evaluation plans.* These pitfalls can be avoided by remembering to ask two questions: (1) How will we know if we're on track, if the solution is working as planned? (2) How will we know when the problem is actually solved?

There are other, less obvious, pitfalls. An important one is caused by human biases, which may be conscious or unconscious. A subordinate who has committed himself in front of his supervisor to the achievement of a specific goal will not want to look bad if the goal is not attained, and will also very likely have a high degree of personal ego investment in achieving that goal. Thus, this subordinate might actually fudge the figures a bit, to make a so-so result look a little more impressive. Or, he might simply overlook certain evaluation data, honestly unaware of his oversight. Human bias in evaluation — seeing what we would like to see instead of what is really there — is a serious pitfall and is not easy to avoid or resolve. Perhaps the most general solution is to have evaluations carried out by persons other than those who are responsible for the solution actions (and the success or failure of those actions). This solution, however, is not always possible, and often the persons who can most easily carry out accurate evaluations are those who carried out the actions being evaluated.

A second nonobvious and serious pitfall has to do with causality. Both researcher and manager alike fall into this problem with almost equal ease and frequency. The problem is this: "We went through a careful, deliberate problem solving process, we arrived at an experimental solution, we planned carefully for both action *and* evaluation, these plans were carried out, and the results are . . ." *But,* how does one *really* know that it was the actions we carried out that *caused* the result(s)? Unless one is a sophisticated, trained researcher, one usually forgets even to ask this question. Furthermore, due to the multiple, complex actions and events within and impinging upon real-world organizations, even the trained researcher, carrying out experimental work, is unable to say with absolute certainty, "It was actions 'A' and 'B' that led to these good [or poor] outcomes." And, since few of us are trained researchers, we are often quite unaware that this causality issue even exists! What can we do about it, though? *First,* be aware that some outside factors may be producing (or affecting) the results. *Second,* look for any such factors you can identify before taking action, and see if you can, at least, keep track of them. Then, you'll have a chance of saying, "We really do think it was these actions that produced our results, and not . . ."*

Finally, the most general pitfall, and the hardest one to do anything about, arises from the fact that evaluation takes time and effort, in planning and action. It is reasonable to ask how much effort should be spent, for there is no sense in investing more time and energy in evaluation than such efforts can possibly return in benefit to the group or organization. If we know, for example, that a solution is working moderately well, and that it would work better with modifications but we also know that the cost of developing such modifications, through further evaluation

---

*For an extensive treatment of this pitfall see Campbell (1957).

research, would be so great as to wipe out the value of any potential increase in effectiveness, then it would be foolish to conduct such evaluation. Such a problem is, however, rare. Much more often the issue is whether or not *any* time and effort should be invested in evaluation, and to this question the answer is invariably "yes."

REFERENCES

Benedict, B. A.; Calder, P. H.; Callahan, D. M.; Hornstein, H. A.; and Miles, M. B. (1967). The clinical-experimental approach to assessing organizational change efforts. *Journal of Applied Behavioral Science* 3: 347-380.

**Blalock, H. M., Jr., and Blalock, A. B., eds. (1968) *Methodology in social research.* New York: McGraw-Hill.

**Campbell, D. T. (1970). Considering the case against experimental evaluations of social innovations. *Administrative Science Quarterly* 15: 110-113.

**Campbell, D. T. (1957). Factors relevant to the validity of experiments in social settings. *Psychological Bulletin* 54: 297-312.

Campbell, D. T. (1969). Reforms as experiments. *American Psychologist* 24: 409-429.

**Campbell, D. T., and Stanley, J. C. (1963). *Experimental and quasi-experimental designs for research.* Chicago: Rand McNally.

Caplan, N. (1968). Treatment intervention and reciprocal interaction effects. *Journal of Social Issues* 24 (1): 63-88.

**Caro, F. G. (1969). Approaches to evaluation research: A review. *Human Organization* 28(2): 87-99.

Caro, F. G., ed. (1971). *Readings in evaluation research.* New York: Russell Sage Foundation.

Fairweather, G. W. (1967) *Methods for experimental social innovation.* New York: Wiley.

Fisher, R. (1960) *Design of experiments.* 8th ed. New York: Hofner.

Freeman, H. E., and Sherwood, C. C. (1965) Research in large-scale intervention programs. *Journal of Social Issues* 21 (1): 11-28.

Seashore, S. E., and Bowers, D. G. (1970). The durability of organizational change. *American Psychologist* 25: 227-233.

Suchman, E. A. (1967) *Evaluation research.* New York: Russell Sage Foundation.

Williams, W. (1969) Developing an evaluation strategy for a social action agency. *Journal of Human Resources* 4 (4): 451-465.

**References preceded by a double asterisk are those judged most basic or important.

CHAPTER TEN

Integrated Problem Solving

"I've been in analysis for twelve years now, and it's helped me tremendously . . . of course, I've a ways to go yet . . ."

INTRODUCTION

The above quote could easily be slightly rewritten and attributed to an executive speaking about a consultant hired by the firm, or a poor person referring to a social worker. In all these cases, we would agree that the client has probably benefited from the helping relationship. However, in all three cases the helper has failed in what we believe is a critical part of the helping process: none of these clients has learned to deal with his or her own problems independent of the helper. In fact, they have all probably become increasingly dependent on the helper and *less* able to solve their own problems. Surely, this is a better state than having problems and never solving any of them. Furthermore, this condition of dependency upon a helper may, to some degree and in some cases, be unavoidable. For example, severely retarded persons in a permanent-care facility will always need helpers. Yet, even in such an extreme example, these persons will usually have *some* learning capacity and should have the opportunity to learn to solve *some* of their own problems, however small these problems may seem to us. However, the therapist, consultant, or social worker referred to above would, in general, have no good reason for making the clients more and more dependent on outside help. In most real-life situations people can — and should — learn to solve their own problems, to whatever extent possible.

The preceding eight chapters focused on the skills needed to solve problems and on learning how to help others develop these skills. This final chapter is aimed more specifically at the intervention skills needed by an effective helper and on structured ways for group members and leaders to learn problem-solving skills. The first learning design is, in a sense, a test, since the helper-consultant will have to use most of the skills covered in the past eight chapters to give effective help. The second learning design presents a method for learning to use the problem-solving process described in Chapter One, with or without a consultant-helper.

Following this chapter are two appendices. The first is an organizational simulation game, which involves application and practice of the skills developed in this book. While Design B in this chapter has a similar focus, the ORGS simulation provides a much more sophisticated, detailed, and adaptable vehicle for skills integration. When an appropriate time block is available (or can be arranged) we strongly recommend use of the ORGS simulation as a capstone class session.

The second appendix, on the development and use of role-play methods, will be useful for classes in which the development of consultation skills is a major goal.

I. SPECIFIC SKILL-DEVELOPMENT AND LEARNING DESIGNS

A.   Design for Practicing Acting upon Perceptions as a Consultant with a Client Group

1.   *Purpose.* The purpose is to practice consultation skills on the spot, in a simulated problem solving group. The conceptual framework that is used is found in the reading titled "Acting upon Perceptions," in part 5 of this design.

2.   *Materials needed.* Needed are: a table around which the "client" group and the "consultants" may sit, newsprint and markers or a chalkboard, chairs for observers, and role-play materials (in part 5).

3.   *Steps in using the design.*
      a.   Propose the conceptual framework.
      b.   Decide on the specific case to work on.
      c.   Have group members select roles.
      d.   Start role play.
      e.   Stop action to discuss interventions.
      f.   Continue action with additional stop-actions.
      g.   Have new consultants take over, resume action.
      h.   Derive learnings from the activity.

4.   *Deriving learnings.*   In order to gain a more complete cognitive understanding of the dynamics at work in the perception-to-action problem-solving process of the consultant, the group may find it valuable to discuss some of the forces at work that influence the ability of the consultant to make successful interventions with a client group. (See part 5 for a background discussion of these issues.) Some specific questions that could be raised are:

      — Did consultants actually consider several alternative intervention possibilities before selecting and trying one?

      — What are some important cues that signal group support or rejection of the consultant's intervention?

      — Did the consultants do anything that would make the client group members less receptive to interventions? What can a consultant do to increase receptivity?

      — When an intervention does not produce the intended results, should the consultant simply try again with another, different, intervention or intervention method? How should this decision be determined?

5.   *Support materials.*
ACTING UPON PERCEPTIONS: A CONCEPTUAL FRAMEWORK

Learning when and how to act and then acting upon perceptions is a major task in the process of learning to become a helper, consultant, or change agent. In this discussion "action" is defined as the change agent's verbal suggestion of an appropriate strategy for group action (in terms of the group's interaction process).

Change-agent interventions may take place at different levels in the total help-giving effort with a client system. That is, some interventions may be complete designs that plan for organization development and change over a long period of time. Other interventions may involve a small segment of the organization; such interventions would be less complicated suggestions and could lead to immediate trial by individuals or by a small group. In both kinds of intervention strategies, however, the change agent uses the same process of diagnosing needs, deciding upon relevant interventions to meet those needs, and then acting in some way to help the client system. Although the process is similar, the time pressures for action are not. On the one hand, when major system interventions are desired, it is obvious that much time must be spent collecting data, analyzing, planning, designing, carrying out the design, and evaluating results. On the other hand, in small groups within the client system, the change agent in an ongoing consultant role to the group must often make quick and accurate decisions about action and then intervene to suggest an appropriate strategy for group movement toward a goal.

In the case of large-system designing, the educational process for the change agent requires acquisition of content knowledge of the field of system change, followed by opportunities to use this knowledge with actual client systems – first as an assistant and then in a major leadership role. The consultant working in a small goal-oriented group operates in much the same way. Not only is content knowledge of the change field needed, but the consultant also needs to practice intervening by offering suggestions for help. Unfortunately, there are few opportunities in the purely educational setting to practice acting upon perceptions one has about the need for help in a real client system group. How then can a change-agent student learn to act upon perceptions and to check out with others whether or not the actions determined were correct? A first step in this process of learning would be to participate in practice opportunities that simulate real client groups at work, in which the consultant acts and is critiqued by observers.

Consider the change agent's consultant role to a small group. What happens in this setting as the change agent thinks about the process and about how the group can be helped to move toward its goal? Although in ordinary situations of this kind the change agent may seem to act somewhat instinctively, reacting to needs of the group, it is probable that over a period of time as a change agent this person has learned to act upon perceptions, after much practice to insure that these perceptions are generally correct. Attempting to analyze the change agent's actions, we might find that, *in sequence:*

1)   the change agent/consultant receives many messages from the group, both about the process of group interaction and also about the task at hand and group progress or lack of progress toward the goal;

2)   the change agent evaluates some of these messages as relevant and important to group movement and some as not so important;

3)   the change agent further decodes and analyzes those messages considered important and decides whether or not action is called for;

4)   if a positive decision to intervene is made, the change agent mentally reviews a variety of potential interventions;

5)   the change agent chooses a particular course of action and decides also upon the method of intervening;

6)   the change agent acts upon the perception by verbally intervening in the group discussion process, making a suggestion for movement or proposing a course of action;

7)   the change agent receives and evaluates the reaction or lack of reaction to the intervention from members of the group;

8)   and, finally, this group feedback to the intervention is filed mentally for future refinement and use in other consulting relationships.

The more completely the change agent understands this process the more effective he or she will become as a facilitator of goal-oriented group action. The important point, of course, is *acting* upon perceptions, for without action there is no help. Equally important, the developing change agent must be given opportunities to practice and then repractice acting upon perceptions in groups. Such practice cannot be done in real client groups, where the costs of failing are high both to the change agent and to the client. The change agent in training can, however, practice acting upon perceptions in low-risk settings, such as a planned simulation exercise of a client group in action. Opportunities such as this need to be provided if developing change agents are to bridge the gap between *what* they know to be potentially useful intervention strategies and *how* they need to behave to put these strategies into action.

FACTORS IN EFFECTIVE INTERVENTIONS

There are a variety of personal and situational characteristics that will determine the effectiveness of specific consultant interventions ("micro-interventions"). Some of these relate directly to the knowledge and skills of the change agent, for example:

- content knowledge of intervention strategies and behavioral science concepts;
- content knowledge of the client system's field;
- skills in group listening and observation, being aware of the messages being sent between individuals and among group members;
- skill in decoding, analyzing, and interpreting these messages.

Other factors concern the personal characteristics of the change agent, particularly in relation to the client group, such as:

- anxiety the consultant may feel about his or her skill as a change agent;
- the values the consultant holds, in general and as a change agent, and the degree to which these values are similar to those of (or shared by) client group members;
- age, sex, and perceived status in relation to client group members.

Finally, some factors that determine intervention effectiveness are based primarily on the relationships between the change agent and some or all client group members, such as:

- the degree to which the group is supportive of the consultant's efforts, which may depend on whether or not the change agent has a particular ally in the group, a co-consultant, or an "internal" change agent associate;
- the power that the client group may have over the change agent;
- the degree of risk client group members feel exists in implementing the change agent's intervention proposals.

Some or all of these factors will be important in determining the effectiveness of any specific change agent micro-intervention in working with a client group. The change agent/consultant in training must learn to take into account these and other factors in making an intervention decision.

On the following pages are background and role-information sheets for two role plays that may be used with this learning design. For the ABCO Case, it is important that you read your role carefully, since there are many details. It is also important that you read *only* your own role; reading the other roles prior to the session would destroy the reality of the situation, and its value for skill practice.

THE BUS PROBLEM

Background

Fourth-, fifth-, and sixth-graders are bused every day to the Adams School. On the particular bus in question there are, on the average, twenty-five to thirty children riding to and from school. Seven to ten of the children are black and the rest white. Several times in the last three weeks some of the children have returned home with stories of yelling and fighting on the bus. Mrs. Alberts and her neighbor Mrs. Bridges, both of whom are black, are disturbed with the treatment their little girls have received. They (and they're sure other parents too) are concerned with the failure of the bus driver (Ned Smith, who is fifty-five years old and white) to control the white children and keep them from beating up on their little girls. Mrs. Alberts has called the PTA president, George Kashe, the local banker, who in turn has arranged a meeting with Dr. Storey, assistant principal of the school. Mrs. Alberts has also taken it upon herself to call a friend of her husband's at the local university, who has been doing some community work, and asked him to come to the meeting. He has agreed to come and bring one of his colleagues with him.

THE BUS PROBLEM

List of Roles

Mrs. Alberts, parent of a nine-year-old girl

Mrs. Bridges, parent of a ten-year-old girl

George Kashe, PTA president

Dr. Storey, assistant principal

Ned Smith, bus driver

One or two other parents on invitation of George Kashe

Dr. Worth, consultant friend of Mrs. Alberts

Sallie Field, consultant

ABCO MANUFACTURING COMPANY*

Background

ABCO came into existence toward the end of the Second World War, organized by two electronics engineers, James Armes and Wesley Burney, to produce electronics equipment for the government (communications and radar gear, in particular). Practically all work was performed on government contracts, on a "cost plus" basis. After the war, Armes and Burney were able to redirect the firm's efforts toward the growing radio-TV industry, producing mainly large electronics items such as TV broadcast transmitters. In addition, they began to supply the manufacturers of consumer equipment (radios, TVs) with small parts and components, although this line was just getting started when the Korean conflict arose. Again, the firm turned to producing equipment for use by the armed forces.

As the Korean war drew to a close, the government contracts again disappeared. Armes and Burney felt that they didn't have the degree of technical sophistication or resources to compete for government contracts on the space and missile program, which was just getting started and seemed a high-risk venture in any case. They returned to producing for the electronics-entertainment industry, planning to rebuild slowly their market there and move on into the small-component area they had started to get into earlier. However, they found competition stiff on both fronts from industry giants such as RCA and GE. Practically all their work was on single-order items for radio and TV stations, which required special design. Due to their experience, and with hard work, they could underbid larger companies on a number of such orders.

The firm had grown rapidly when organized, slowed in the early 1950s, and expanded again during the war to about two hundred line workers, plus supervisors and managers. Now, growth was very slow indeed. In fact, it was all Armes and Burney could do just to keep what business they had, and this took considerable effort and work — even on technical matters — on their part. In 1967, after about ten years of effort, they decided they'd had enough. The company went public, stock was sold, and a group of professional manager-executives was hired to run the firm. The founders stayed on as technical consultants, but after a couple of years they moved to jobs with other firms.

The new management consisted of a president, a vice-president for manufacturing and product development, a sales manager, and a personnel director. All except the personnel director were hired from outside the company. The president was responsible to a newly created Board of Directors. After two years, in 1969, the position of vice-president for sales was created. The board felt that marketing was a severe problem, so they hired a man from outside to build a strong sales force.

After this management group had been in office four years, it was clear that things were no better and, in fact, somewhat worse. Except for the success of the vice-president for sales in developing a sales force and generating some market attention, the firm was clearly headed downhill, with problems in all other areas, particularly production. Thus, in 1971, the board discharged the president and vice-president for manufacturing. The vice-president for sales was retained. Shortly thereafter the personnel director was promoted to a new position, vice-president for personnel and industrial relations.

---

*This case is an extensive modification of one prepared by Norman R. F. Maier, "The President's Decision," published in *Supervisory and Executive Development* by N. R. F. Maier, A. R. Solem, and A. A. Maier (New York: Wiley, 1957. Science Editions, 1966). Modified and used by special permission.

Two years later, in 1973, the situation seems somewhat improved; true, there had been no dramatic turnaround of the company's position, yet all of the top managers agree that they are at least moving in the right direction. Of particular concern at this time is the issue of whether to build a new plant and expand. The vice-president for personnel, Russ/Ruth Haney, has also involved an organizational consultant (with the president's agreement) to help look at management problems.

It is at this point that we will observe a meeting that the president has called for top management. It is 3 P.M. on a Friday. Since the organizational consultant is in the plant today, (s)he will also be present.

ABCO MANUFACTURING COMPANY

Summary of Individuals' Backgrounds

John Ward: Age thirty-nine; BA, CPA. Served as Controller of ABCO for three years, giving financial advice to the President. Named President in 1971 when the Board of Directors fired the previous top management. Has been President two years.

William/Wilma Carson: Age thirty-three; high school diploma and two years of college. Joined the company at age twenty-three as a line supervisor, promoted regularly, became Plant Superintendent in 1967 when ABCO first reorganized. Promoted to Vice-President for Manufacturing and Product Development two years ago (1971), when the top management was replaced.

James Jackson: Age twenty-nine; BA, MBA (Marketing). After graduation, worked two years as Assistant Sales Manager of a division of a large electronics manufacturer; hired as Vice-President for Sales four years ago; the only member of the prior top-management group who was retained.

Russ/Ruth Haney: Age thirty-two, BA. Has been with the firm for ten years; joined after graduation from college as Assistant Personnel Manager; promoted to Personnel Director five years ago by the former President. Promoted to a new position, Vice-President for Personnel and Industrial Relations, by Ward one and one-half years ago.

Ray/Rae Coombs: Age twenty-eight, Ph.D. (Organizational Behavior). Assistant Professor of Management at the nearby state university; has been involved in organization consulting for the past four years. Has considerable small-group training experience. Has worked with business and government organizations.

ABCO MANUFACTURING COMPANY

Role for John Ward, President

You are President of the ABCO Manufacturing Company and have held this position for the past two years. In your previous position as Controller you advised the President on various fiscal and policy matters, and gained a close knowledge of the inner workings of the company. As President, your duties are much broader and more complex. You now have final responsibility for policy formulation and execution in such diverse fields as procurement, manufacturing, sales, finance, product development, personnel, public relations, and various other aspects of business operation. Thus, to a large extent the progress of the company and your own success or failure as President depend on your making wise decisions. You get a certain amount of credit when things go well, but you also take the rap when they go wrong.

One of the most difficult problems you have had to deal with since you became President is whether to expand operations. Within the company and among your close business associates there are conflicting views on the matter. Those who are opposed to expansion contend that real estate and building values are seriously inflated and that the costs of new equipment are out of line. A further argument is that the television and other electronics sales are highly sensitive to economic conditions. Since company reserves are low, you would have to obtain the necessary funds through stock sales or mortgage loans and the present financial condition of the company does not place it in an advantageous position for such financing. Further, it would be some time before returns from expansion would begin to pay off to any great extent and an early business slump could wreck the company.

At the same time, there are a number of people in the company who favor immediate expansion. However, all of them tend to see things in terms of their own particular area of the business and none are in a position to have a broad, overall perspective on things. Nevertheless, in casual discussions of the matter they have come up with some impressive facts and arguments in favor of setting up a new plant. One contention, for example, is that the present four-story, thirty-year-old building is not adapted for modern straight-line production methods. Not only is it expensive to heat and light, but it lacks the flexibility needed for efficient changeovers to meet the production requirements of various orders. In addition, it has been necessary to turn down two or three large orders in the past because of insufficient capacity to meet production deadlines. Then there is the further contention that a lack of growth is damaging to morale and that good people tend to become discouraged and leave to go with larger or faster-growing companies, where opportunities are greater.

Over the past several months you have tried to keep an open mind to both points of view and despite the risks of expanding you were becoming convinced that on a long-term basis expansion was the better course to follow. True, you have been making headway toward getting the company back on its feet, but as things are it is a slow, uphill struggle. Nevertheless, you felt that under the unfavorable circumstances you were making as satisfactory progress as could be expected.

Despite your best efforts over the past two years, the Board of Directors informed you late yesterday that they had voted to give you one more year in which to show some significant results or else resign. You had known previously that certain members of the board were becoming impatient. However, this action was totally unexpected and came as a real shock. Obviously, expansion is out of the question if results have to be shown within a year. It would take longer than that to make the necessary financial and other arrangements to construct a new plant and get it into operation.

The only possible course of action is to play it safe and hope for the best. With a few good breaks and strict belt-tightening throughout the organization, it may be possible to demonstrate the desired results within the deadline set by the board. Certainly this is not the time to take chances. Your decision not to expand must be announced immediately. As a first step, you have called a meeting of your three vice-presidents for 3 P.M. Your purpose is to check with them to see whether anything has been overlooked in arriving at your decision.

Also attending this meeting will be Dr. Ray/Rae Coombs, an organization development consultant from the state university. Haney, Vice-President for Personnel and Industrial Relations, suggested that an outside consultant could be helpful in developing your group of top people into a more effective team, and you therefore have contracted with Dr. Coombs an arrangement whereby (s)he spends three days a month in the company. This has gone on for one month so far. Most of Coombs's time has been spent in interviews and discussions with you and your vice-presidents, though (s)he has also run a small survey among lower-level supervisors and has been sitting in on meetings. So far, (s)he hasn't really said much in the meetings (s)he's attended. However, with Coombs's expertise and knowledge of organizations, it may be that (s)he can be of assistance to you today in getting the group to understand and accept your decision and back you up on it.

ABCO MANUFACTURING COMPANY

**Role for William/Wilma Carson, Vice President,
Manufacturing and Product Development**

You are the vice-president of the ABCO Company in charge of manufacturing and product development. When you moved into this job from plant superintendent two years ago you had high hopes of streamlining operations and have been able to accomplish a good deal. For years the previous management had refused to spend money on manufacturing facilities and instead followed a penny-pinching practice of patching and fixing and making you do the best you could with inferior, outmoded equipment and methods. Through your influence with Ward, you have been able to make a number of changes in layout and methods. By careful shopping around you have been able to get good buys on several pieces of secondhand but fairly modern equipment. In addition, you have set up a new product-development laboratory. This is a must if the company is to compete with the larger companies and their staffs of research people, both in bringing out new products and in working out designs to simplify manufacture. The company is slowly getting back on its feet and in large part this is due to the reduced unit costs you have been able to achieve in manufacturing.

However, you have gone just about as far as you can in this direction, and what is needed now is a new, modern plant. The present four-story building was satisfactory for its purpose thirty years ago, but with the newer, integrated assembly-line procedures all operations should be on one floor. The layout of the present building is awkward for moving things along from one process to the next and creates a lot of needless delay in changeovers when you have new orders to fill. Also it is costly to light and heat and the construction isn't strong enough to support some of the new heavy equipment on the upper floors, where you can use it to the best advantage. Repeatedly you have urged Ward to expand into a new, modern building and purchase new equipment, and although he has always given you a fair hearing you cannot get him to commit himself. Ward is a good accountant, but he doesn't know the manufacturing end of the business too well and he seems to be a fence rider. This may be because he was not experienced in administrative work before he became President. As Controller he learned company operations from a fiscal angle but he merely advised the former President and did not have to make the final decisions himself. Now that he is on the firing line and has to stand or fall on his own judgment he seems to have difficulty in making up his mind about things. You have given him the best advice you can and you want to help him move things along faster, but he has to make up his mind to expand or else the company will no longer be able to meet competition.

Ward has called a meeting with you and the other two vice-presidents in his office for three o'clock today. He has these meetings at fairly frequent intervals. You don't know what he has on his mind but you hope he has finally agreed to go ahead with the new plant. Almost anything would be an improvement over the one you now have.

ABCO MANUFACTURING COMPANY

Role for James Jackson, Vice-President, Sales

You are vice-president in charge of sales and came to the ABCO Company four years ago. Previous to that you were one of the assistant sales managers of a division of one of the large electronics manufacturing companies. Stepping into the vice-presidency of the ABCO Company meant quite an increase in salary and responsibility and it seemed that here was a real opportunity to do a good job and make a name for yourself. Five years ago the company had no real sales organization and was losing ground rapidly. Thus, one of your first moves was to build from the ground up in an effort to recapture the market and expand further. This took a lot of work and you had a struggle to win over the old management to your ideas. Now there are sales offices in most of the principal eastern cities where ABCO products are in demand by manufacturers, and a fairly strong organization has been built up. The reorganization two years ago had its advantages in that John Ward gave you more freedom to operate than you had enjoyed previously. In some ways he is doing a fair job as President, but seems to be rather unimaginative. He always gives your ideas a fair hearing but in the end he seems to shy away from new advertising campaigns. During the past two years he has taken the steam out of some of your best promotional ideas by simply delaying action on them until too late. One of the things you have been pushing, for example, is an expansion of plant facilities. This would give you a big advantage because in the past years you have lost several big orders when Carson said that (s)he couldn't possibly meet the deadline set by the customers. There may have been something to what Carson calls "unreasonable deadlines" in one or two instances; however, it begins to look more and more as though Carson isn't fast enough on his/her feet to make the necessary changeovers in manufacturing and Ward refuses to push him/her. Carson seems to be Ward's "fair-haired boy." With a new, modern plant there could be no more excuses and you could take advantage of the breaks when big orders come in. It would help a lot too if those in charge of product development would get to work. They have been set up for two years now and despite the ideas for new or modified products that your salesmen have been funneling in to them, they haven't shown any progress. A small company like this must frequently have new and better products to put on the market if it is to compete for new markets. That way the newspapers and trade journals give you a lot of free publicity and the salesmen have a chance to get a foot in the door of potential new customers. The main thing, however, is to get a new plant so that larger orders can be handled. Turning down the big ones as you had to do several times in the past is what hurts, and it demoralizes your sales force.

Ward has been receptive enough to your arguments for expansion and there has been increasing evidence lately that he is ready to take action on the idea. Today at three o'clock there is to be a meeting in his office with you and the other two vice-presidents. Apparently Ward is about to announce plans for the new plant because his secretary told you over the phone that Ward wanted you to review in your mind all of the pros and cons on the matter of expansion prior to coming to the meeting.

Dr. Coombs, the organizational consultant hired by Ward and Haney, the Personnel Vice-President, will probably be at the meeting too, since (s)he is here for the day. In the private interview you had with Coombs you got the impression that (s)he felt there was not enough trust and openness among the top-management group. Maybe this meeting will show how a really effective top team can function.

ABCO MANUFACTURING COMPANY

Role for Russ/Ruth Haney,
Vice-President, Personnel and Industrial Relations

You are vice-president in charge of personnel and industrial relations, and have held this position since you moved up from the job of Personnel Director a year and a half ago. All of the usual personnel services, such as recruitment, hiring, promotions, training, and contract negotiations are handled through your office. On a policy basis, you have set up your office to serve three main functions. One is to prevent as many personnel problems as possible and assist the supervisors with those that arise. Second, you advise the President, John Ward, on personnel matters. Third, you are responsible for maintaining a competent work force that gets along well and does a good job.

One of the things you were able to get under way as Personnel Director was an individualized program of training and work experiences for promising young college recruits, and even though the conservatism of the previous management stymied their progress in many ways, you were able to obtain a few good people each year. Then, when the reorganization took place two years ago, a considerable number of these people were able to move up a notch. This left a number of vacancies at the trainee level, which you were able to fill by going out to the colleges. However, you are again faced with the same problem you had previously. The company isn't growing and many of the people you brought in a few years back who were not ready to move up at the time of the reorganization are becoming impatient. Further, you cannot hold out much promise to new college recruits. At present, there just isn't any place for them to move up in the company, and there won't be any new opportunities unless the company expands its operations. Meanwhile, some of your best people are disheartened and are leaving. Competing companies are picking them off one by one. If this attrition is allowed to continue, the management at the middle and lower levels will be second-rate again in a few years. Unless the company can offer good people some inducements to stay, there will be crippling losses in many of the key positions, and the company simply cannot afford that and stay in competition. As far as you can see, expansion is absolutely essential if the company is to keep these people.

This was one reason, really the major reason, you worked so hard to convince Ward to enter a contract with Dr. Ray/Rae Coombs, an organizational consultant out of the state university. The survey (s)he did among lower- and middle-level managers provides some hard data to support your feelings and worries about losing these people. Furthermore, it seems like Ray/Rae has been able to get a pretty good picture of this problem, as well as of how the top-management group works, from the interviews (s)he's had and from attending some meetings.

John Ward has sent word that there is to be a meeting at three o'clock in his office and that Carson, Jackson, and Coombs will be there. Since Carson is in charge of manufacturing and Jackson is in charge of sales, it looks as though Ward may be ready to announce plans for the new plant. Unless there is some such development, it will be hopeless to try to keep your best people. With the concrete information that Coombs has obtained, you're hopeful that (s)he will be a major help in getting these points across to Ward.

ABCO MANUFACTURING COMPANY

Role for Ray/Rae Coombs, Organizational Consultant

About two months ago Russ/Ruth Haney, Vice-President of Personnel of the ABCO Company, contacted you about the possibility of doing some consulting for that firm. After a couple of meetings with Haney and John Ward, President of the company, you agreed to spend three days a month in the company, for a period of three months, at a per diem rate of a hundred and fifty dollars, with a review of the relationship at the end of that period. You explained to them that while you would be doing some survey work your primary immediate aim would be to conduct in-depth interviews with all top-management personnel, since from your discussions with them one of the major problems seemed to be the functioning of top management as an effective team.

Haney explained that the major practical problem the company was currently faced with was the issue of expansion. Your interviews pretty much confirmed this. All three vice-presidents, Haney, Carson (manufacturing and product development), and Jackson (sales), were quite concerned about the company's future and saw it dependent on immediate efforts to expand operations by getting into a new plant. A small survey of middle- and lower-level managers strongly confirmed Haney's fear that many good people would be leaving the company if it became apparent that no upward movement was possible, which would be the case if the expansion were not made.

While this certainly seems to be a major and immediate problem, you are more concerned about the way problems like this are generally dealt with. The top-management group does not seem to function as a real and cohesive team; this impression was confirmed by your observation of a couple of their meetings. Although Ward does schedule meetings fairly frequently, he does not really make good use of the group, compared with your estimate of the potential. He primarily uses the meeting as an information-gathering device, hearing out each person and, it seems, listening to and understanding their ideas and arguments. He does not, however, deal with them as a group or involve the group in any real decisions. This is particularly unfortunate, since Ward himself is very hesitant to make major decisions. If he used the group in that way, he'd probably find it easier to make these decisions and he'd also be able to get the group's support for decisions.

On the issue of expansion, for example, Ward knows that his three vice-presidents all favor such a course of action, but is not aware of the real strength of their feelings, which would be evident if they knew where each other stood on the problem (which, at present, is not the case).

Today Ward has called a meeting in his office with the vice-presidents, which you will attend. While you have pretty much kept quiet at the other meetings you've attended, you feel that this might be an appropriate time to get into the issue of turning the top management into a smoothly functioning team, rather than an aggregate of individuals. If you can show Ward how to use and involve the group in this issue of expansion, you feel that some good progress would be made toward this goal. While it's possible that Ward has made a final decision on this matter, if you could get him to hold off on any announcement and try to involve the group in a decision, you think it would be possible to get this group functioning as a real problem solving team.

ABCO MANUFACTURING COMPANY

Instructions for Observers

On the basis of what you already know about the ABCO Company and the top executives, you probably have formed certain impressions about the situation. Most of the things you have learned so far are factual in nature. However, you also know that these facts may be relatively unimportant except as background and that the attitudes, feelings, and personalities of these people (as well as their relationships with each other) may be much more important in determining what happens in this meeting. It is important to observe the *feelings* about the facts that are indicated and not be misled by the actual words spoken, if you are to sense the developments as they occur in the role playing. It is in developing sensitivity to feeling that one becomes a good observer. The following questions are designed to give you certain clues about what to watch and listen for:

1.   a)   Observe how Ward opens the discussion. Does he seem at ease?
     b)   Did he state a problem with all relevant facts for open discussion?
     c)   Does he seem open-minded?

2.   a)   What are Ward's reasons for calling this meeting?
     b)   How do the other members react to his views?
     c)   To what extent is he accepting of their views or responses?
     d)   What evidence is there, if any, that Ward is feeling defensive?

3. a) To what extent is this a problem solving discussion? If not, why not?
    b) What do you think is the real problem here?
    c) What does Ward do to help or hinder the group?

4. Do any of the participants seem stubborn? Why?

5. Note any behaviors that indicate a member is holding back relevant information.

6. What evidence is there to indicate that fear or threat are influencing the relationships of the various persons in the discussion?

7. a) How is the consultant helping or hindering the discussion?
    b) Identify and try to categorize and classify each intervention the consultant makes.
    c) Observe the consultant's timing and whether or not the interventions meet what you perceive to be the needs of the group.

B.   Design for Learning to Use the Problem Solving Process in Groups

1.   *Purpose.* In this, our final learning design, we propose a method for small groups to learn and practice the actual ongoing steps of problem solving. We have organized the phases of problem solving that were outlined and discussed in Chapter One into a questionnaire. We call this instrument "Six Phases of Integrated Problem Solving"; a copy can be found in part 5 of this design. We propose that groups can use the questionnaire in at least two different ways.

First, in both the classroom and in real organizations it can be used to *learn* and *practice* the steps of problem solving. This, then, is the primary aim of the final learning design.

The *second* major use of the questionnaire is as a monitoring tool to observe and give feedback on the progress of a real group in action. This procedure could be undertaken either by appointed observers or by all of the group members themselves. If the questionnaire is used in this way, the group should provide adequate opportunity for the members to give and receive feedback concerning their actions. As we have seen from earlier designs in this book, such feedback should be used both *during* and at the *end* of the group problem solving activity. When used in this way the primary functions of the questionnaire are to monitor, support, and increase a group's effectiveness at solving ongoing problems in its particular organization. Thus, the questionnaire may become a useful *support mechanism* for the continuing process of group problem solving.

But first (and before the questionnaire can be used as a support mechanism), we return to the primary purpose of this last learning design: to learn and practice the actual steps of group problem solving.

2.   *Materials needed.* In part 5 of this design, you will find a copy of the Integrated Problem Solving questionnaire. Following the questionnaire is a description of "Camp Bigfoot," along with the roles needed for that exercise. Newsprint, marking pens, masking tape, and a room with movable chairs are also needed.

3A. *Steps in using the design: Classroom*

    a.   State the learning goals.

    b.   Explain and discuss Integrated Problem Solving.

    c.   Divide the class into small work groups.

    d.   Have everyone read the background information, assign roles and start the role play.

    e.   Stop to look at Phase I questions.

    f.   Have the groups resume work on the problem.

    g.   Stop to look at Phase II questions.

    h.   Have the groups resume work on the problem.

    i.   Stop to look at Phase III questions.

    j.   Have the groups resume work on the problem.

    k.   Stop to look at Phase IV questions.

    l.   With the entire class, review evaluation planning needs – Phase V.

    m.   Lead the class in a critique of their problem solving process, using some of the questions in Phase VI.

3B. *Steps in using the design: Organizations.*

   a.   State the purpose of the meeting.

   b.   Choose the problem to work on.

   c.   Discuss Integrated Problem Solving.

   d.   Have the group divide into observers and problem solvers.

   e.   Arrange the work setting.

   f.   Have the group begin the problem solving work.

   g.   Stop to look at Problem Definition.

   h.   Resume work on the problem.

   i.   Continue stop-action and work periods.

   j.   Discuss and critique the work of the session.

4.   *Deriving learnings.* For both learning designs, in the classroom and in a real organizational group, it is important to spend a period of time critiquing the action and deriving learnings from the experience. Some questions that both groups might deal with during this period are:

   — How can we use the questions in Phase VI of the questionnaire to suggest processes that might be applied in other groups (and in our own group the next time we meet)?

   — What do we see as being the two or three *most* important processes or procedures that have to take place to achieve effective group problem solving?

   — What kinds of skills are needed to do good group problem solving, in addition to just knowing the steps in the process?

   — How could we use the questionnaire to help us while we're actually working on the problem, rather than only after we complete a particular phase?

   And specifically for real organizational groups:

   — How should we retain, disseminate, and perhaps continue the work we have started here today? What are our next steps as a group?

   — In our subsequent meetings can we agree to spend a few minutes at the end critiquing what we have done? Could we, in fact, appoint two of our members as process observers to help us with this task during, as well as following, the discussion?

5.   *Support materials.* On the following pages is the "Six Phases of Integrated Problem Solving" questionnaire instrument. Unlike most questionnaires, which are intended to measure people's opinions and attitudes, this instrument is designed to be a procedural aid in an actual group problem solving discussion. Following the questionnaire are roles for a problem solving simulation exercise.

SIX PHASES OF INTEGRATED PROBLEM SOLVING
I. Problem Definition: Exploring, Clarifying, Defining

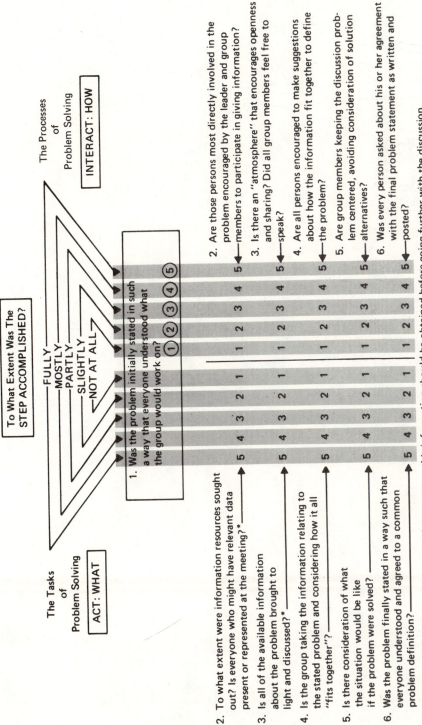

The Processes of Problem Solving

INTERACT: HOW

The Tasks of Problem Solving

ACT: WHAT

To What Extent Was The STEP ACCOMPLISHED?

FULLY — MOSTLY — PARTLY — SLIGHTLY — NOT AT ALL

1. Was the problem initially stated in such a way that everyone understood what the group would work on?

INTERACT: HOW

2. Are those persons most directly involved in the problem encouraged by the leader and group members to participate in giving information?

3. Is there an "atmosphere" that encourages openness and sharing? Did all group members feel free to speak?

4. Are all persons encouraged to make suggestions about how the information fit together to define the problem?

5. Are group members keeping the discussion problem centered, avoiding consideration of solution alternatives?

6. Was every person asked about his or her agreement with the final problem statement as written and posted?

ACT: WHAT

2. To what extent were information resources sought out? Is everyone who might have relevant data present or represented at the meeting?*

3. Is all of the available information about the problem brought to light and discussed?*

4. Is the group taking the information relating to the stated problem and considering how it all "fits together"?

5. Is there consideration of what the situation would be like if the problem were solved?

6. Was the problem finally stated in a way such that everyone understood and agreed to a common problem definition?

* If additional information is found to be necessary, this information should be obtained before going further with the discussion.

Use the next page to record, in detail the final problem statement

II. Problem Solution Generation: Brainstorming, Elaborating, Creating

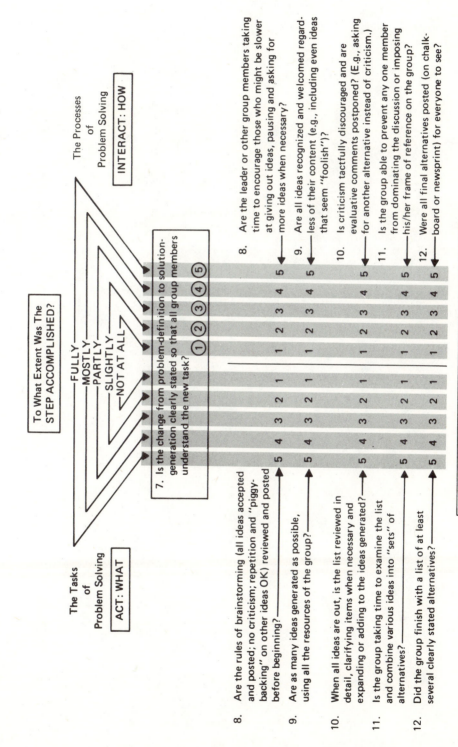

The Processes
of
Problem Solving

INTERACT: HOW

To What Extent Was The
STEP ACCOMPLISHED?

FULLY
MOSTLY
PARTLY
SLIGHTLY
NOT AT ALL

The Tasks
of
Problem Solving

ACT: WHAT

7. Is the change from problem-definition to solution-generation clearly stated so that all group members understand the new task?

① ② ③ ④ ⑤

8. Are the leader or other group members taking time to encourage those who might be slower at giving out ideas, pausing and asking for more ideas when necessary?

5 4 3 2 1   1 2 3 4 5

9. Are all ideas recognized and welcomed regardless of their content (e.g., including even ideas that seem "foolish")?

5 4 3 2 1   1 2 3 4 5

10. Is criticism tactfully discouraged and are evaluative comments postponed? (E.g., asking for another alternative instead of criticism.)

5 4 3 2 1   1 2 3 4 5

11. Is the group able to prevent any one member from dominating the discussion or imposing his/her frame of reference on the group?

5 4 3 2 1   1 2 3 4 5

12. Were all final alternatives posted (on chalkboard or newsprint) for everyone to see?

5 4 3 2 1   1 2 3 4 5

Use the next page to record the list of solution alternatives

8. Are the rules of brainstorming (all ideas accepted and posted; no criticism; repetition and "piggybacking" on other ideas OK) reviewed and posted before beginning?

9. Are as many ideas generated as possible, using all the resources of the group?

10. When all ideas are out, is the list reviewed in detail, clarifying items when necessary and expanding or adding to the ideas generated?

11. Is the group taking time to examine the list and combine various ideas into "sets" of alternatives?

12. Did the group finish with a list of at least several clearly stated alternatives?

III. Ideas → to → Actions: Evaluating, Combining, Selecting

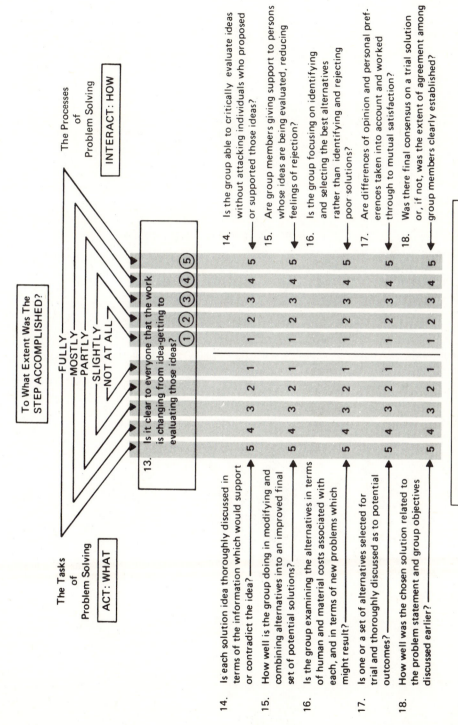

The Tasks
of
Problem Solving

ACT: WHAT

The Processes
of
Problem Solving

INTERACT: HOW

To What Extent Was The
STEP ACCOMPLISHED?

FULLY
MOSTLY
PARTLY
SLIGHTLY
NOT AT ALL

13. Is it clear to everyone that the work is changing from idea-getting to evaluating those ideas?

① ② ③ ④ ⑤

14. Is each solution idea thoroughly discussed in terms of the information which would support or contradict the idea?

5 4 3 2 1   1 2 3 4 5

14. Is the group able to critically evaluate ideas without attacking individuals who proposed or supported those ideas?

15. How well is the group doing in modifying and combining alternatives into an improved final set of potential solutions?

5 4 3 2 1   1 2 3 4 5

15. Are group members giving support to persons whose ideas are being evaluated, reducing feelings of rejection?

16. Is the group examining the alternatives in terms of human and material costs associated with each, and in terms of new problems which might result?

5 4 3 2 1   1 2 3 4 5

16. Is the group focusing on identifying and selecting the best alternatives rather than identifying and rejecting poor solutions?

17. Is one or a set of alternatives selected for trial and thoroughly discussed as to potential outcomes?

5 4 3 2 1   1 2 3 4 5

17. Are differences of opinion and personal preferences taken into account and worked through to mutual satisfaction?

18. How well was the chosen solution related to the problem statement and group objectives discussed earlier?

5 4 3 2 1   1 2 3 4 5

18. Was there final consensus on a trial solution or, if not, was the extent of agreement among group members clearly established?

Use the next page to record, in detail, the final trial solution

IV. Solution Action Planning: Planning, Assigning, Coordinating

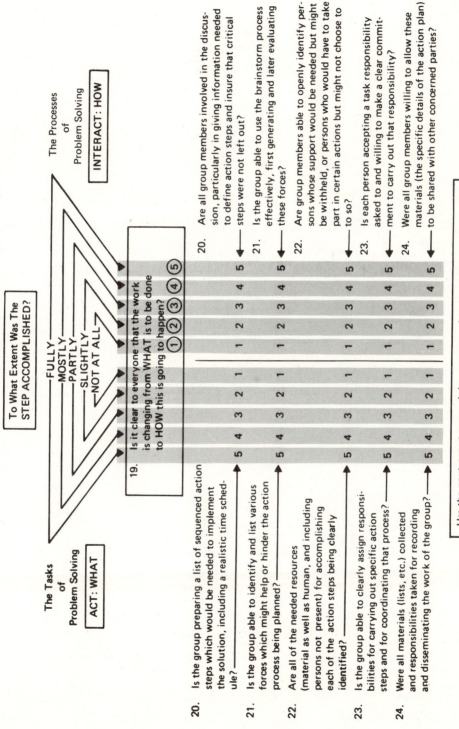

The Tasks
of
Problem Solving

ACT: WHAT

The Processes
of
Problem Solving

INTERACT: HOW

To What Extent Was The
STEP ACCOMPLISHED?

FULLY
MOSTLY
PARTLY
SLIGHTLY
NOT AT ALL

19. Is it clear to everyone that the work is changing from WHAT is to be done to HOW this is going to happen?

① ② ③ ④ ⑤

20. Is the group preparing a list of sequenced action steps which would be needed to implement the solution, including a realistic time schedule?

5 4 3 2 1   1 2 3 4 5

20. Are all group members involved in the discussion, particularly in giving information needed to define action steps and insure that critical steps were not left out?

21. Is the group able to identify and list various forces which might help or hinder the action process being planned?

5 4 3 2 1   1 2 3 4 5

21. Is the group able to use the brainstorm process effectively, first generating and later evaluating these forces?

22. Are all of the needed resources (material as well as human, and including persons not present) for accomplishing each of the action steps being clearly identified?

5 4 3 2 1   1 2 3 4 5

22. Are group members able to openly identify persons whose support would be needed but might be withheld, or persons who would have to take part in certain actions but might not choose to to so?

23. Is the group able to clearly assign responsibilities for carrying out specific action steps and for coordinating that process?

5 4 3 2 1   1 2 3 4 5

23. Is each person accepting a task responsibility asked to and willing to make a clear commitment to and carry out that responsibility?

24. Were all materials (lists, etc.) collected and responsibilities taken for recording and disseminating the work of the group?

5 4 3 2 1   1 2 3 4 5

24. Were all group members willing to allow these materials (the specific details of the action plan) to be shared with other concerned parties?

Use the next page to record the sequence of action steps agreed to, who accepted responsibility for each step, and the time schedule for actions.

V. Solution Evaluation Planning: Describing, Monitoring, Contingency Planning

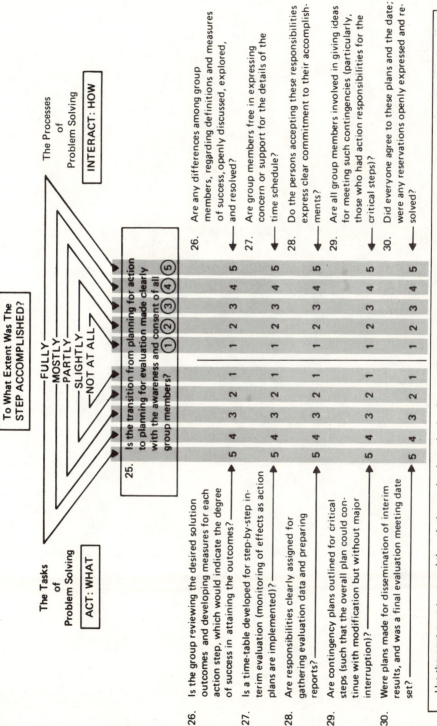

26. Is the group reviewing the desired solution outcomes and developing measures for each action step, which would indicate the degree of success in attaining the outcomes?

27. Is a time-table developed for step-by-step interim evaluation (monitoring of effects as action plans are implemented)?

28. Are responsibilities clearly assigned for gathering evaluation data and preparing reports?

29. Are contingency plans outlined for critical steps (such that the overall plan could continue with modification but without major interruption)?

30. Were plans made for dissemination of interim results, and was a final evaluation meeting date set?

26. Are any differences among group members, regarding definitions and measures of success, openly discussed, explored, and resolved?

27. Are group members free in expressing concern or support for the details of the time schedule?

28. Do the persons accepting these responsibilities express clear commitment to their accomplishments?

29. Are all group members involved in giving ideas for meeting such contingencies (particularly, those who had action responsibilities for the critical steps)?

30. Did everyone agree to these plans and the date; were any reservations openly expressed and resolved?

Use the next page to record the solution evaluation criteria, the specific evaluation plan (actions, timetable, and responsibilities) and the final evaluation meeting date.

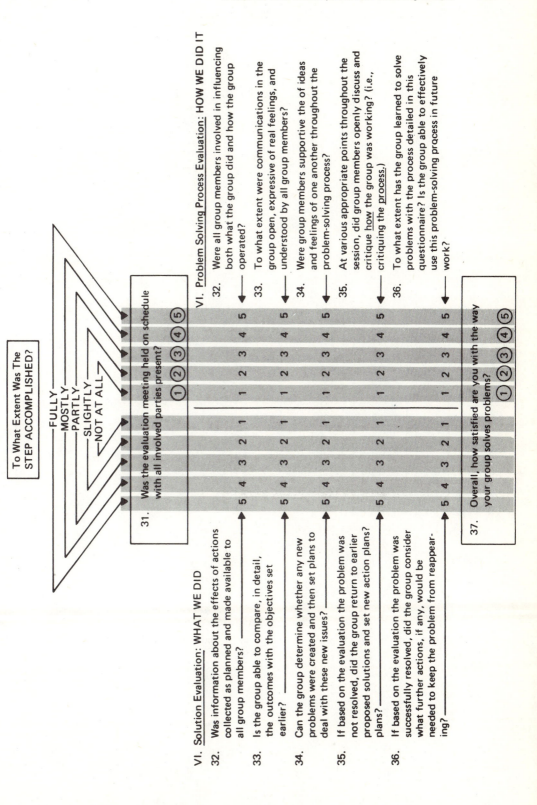

To What Extent Was The STEP ACCOMPLISHED?

FULLY
MOSTLY
PARTLY
SLIGHTLY
NOT AT ALL

31. Was the evaluation meeting held on schedule with all involved parties present? ①②③④⑤

VI. Solution Evaluation: WHAT WE DID

32. Was information about the effects of actions collected as planned and made available to all group members?

33. Is the group able to compare, in detail, the outcomes with the objectives set earlier?

34. Can the group determine whether any new problems were created and then set plans to deal with these new issues?

35. If based on the evaluation the problem was not resolved, did the group return to earlier proposed solutions and set new action plans? plans?

36. If based on the evaluation the problem was successfully resolved, did the group consider what further actions, if any, would be needed to keep the problem from reappearing?

VI. Problem Solving Process Evaluation: HOW WE DID IT

32. Were all group members involved in influencing both what the group did and how the group operated?

33. To what extent were communications in the group open, expressive of real feelings, and understood by all group members?

34. Were group members supportive the of ideas and feelings of one another throughout the problem-solving process?

35. At various appropriate points throughout the session, did group members openly discuss and critique how the group was working? (i.e., critiquing the process.)

36. To what extent has the group learned to solve problems with the process detailed in this questionnaire? Is the group able to effectively use this problem-solving process in future work?

37. Overall, how satisfied are you with the way your group solves problems? ①②③④⑤

CAMP BIGFOOT*

Background

Camp Bigfoot is nestled in a valley in the Sasquatch Mountains. It is one of several camps sponsored by the State Department of Natural Resources for high-school-age boys and girls. Its purpose is twofold: to provide summer jobs and to teach about the natural environment through an organized program of environmental education. The nearest big city is a hundred miles away. The camp is residential and lasts for eight weeks. Most of the forty campers are from white lower-middle-class families and come from several small towns up the valley. Four campers are of Spanish surname, and are the only campers who come from the big city. It is now the end of the second week of camp. Today's staff meeting is the first one since the campers arrived. In the week prior to camp there was not much time for the staff to meet as a whole, since there were so many things that had to be done to get the physical plant in shape for the arrival of campers.

*Case prepared by Jerome Johnston and David Lingwood of the Center for Research on Utilization of Scientific Knowledge, Institute for Social Research, The University of Michigan.

CAMP BIGFOOT

Role for Camp Director (Male)

As far as you can tell, everything is just fine in camp. The campers are happy and the staff seems to be working out quite well. You have heard a few staff complain about some minor problems on the work sites, but nothing to become concerned about. You are frequently away from camp checking on various administrative matters.

You feel good about yourself. You have run a DNR camp for the last two years and have done a very good job. You have good relations with your staff, though some of the girls on the staff might occasionally resent a joking remark about how the females can't do a man's job. You always mean them in jest, and hope that they take the comments in that vein. Secretly, however, you really don't think that girls *can* do a man's job.

Your philosophy of running a camp is this: a productive camp is a good camp. You know that your project manager is most concerned about the "value return" figure that is calculated at the end of the summer, and you know that this is based on the amount of work the campers accomplish.

CAMP BIGFOOT

Role for Coordinator of Work Projects

You are very concerned about the amount of work the crews are accomplishing — or rather, not accomplishing. Because of vehicle failure, the crews frequently arrive late on the job. When they do arrive, they often don't have the right tools, and the tools they do have don't function very well. The projects you're working on are far away from the camp, thus a lot of time is spent transporting the work crews to the sites. In an effort to get more work accomplished you have been pushing the crew leaders to urge the campers on to greater productivity.

CAMP BIGFOOT

Role for Environmental Education Instructor

You are concerned that the campers aren't getting enough EE instruction. You feel guilty that you yourself haven't been able to conduct enough classes for the campers, and you feel that you should be getting out to the work sites more often to discuss the environmental implications of the projects. You have been with the camp for several years, and you know a lot about the messy details of running it. Accordingly you are always having to do things other than EE in order to keep the camp running smoothly. You have a state chauffeur's license, but the Work Coordinator does not, so you frequently have to shuttle campers back and forth to the work sites.

CAMP BIGFOOT

Role for Tool Clerk

Last summer you were a camper, and this year you have returned as an aide. Your job is to keep all the tools in good repair. The problem is that you don't know how to do the job. Nobody has shown you how to sharpen an ax properly, or fix a broken posthole digger. You are afraid to tell anyone because they might fire you if they find out you can't do your job. What you would really like is for someone to show you how to do your job right. Everyone's just so damned busy they don't seem to have time to help or supervise you.

CAMP BIGFOOT

Role for Group Living Counselor

You have noticed some problems with the campers. When they come back to camp they seem really tired, like they have been pushed a little too hard. So, they aren't really interested in evening recreation activities. There also seem to be some problems with the Spanish campers getting along with others. Their background seems so different that there are frequently problems getting them to do things with the rest of the campers. They seem to want to stick by themselves. Otherwise, there are no problems that you can detect.

CAMP BIGFOOT

Role for Work Leader #1 (Male)

You have a good group of kids and they really put out a lot for you. The Work Coordinator has been putting pressure on you to have your kids get more work done, and they don't like him too much for this. You've responded to the pressure, but you dislike having to push the kids; it makes you appear to be the "bad guy." Incidentally, you are wondering when the kids are going to get some Environmental Education instruction. You would like to do some yourself, but you need a little guidance from the EE instructor, since this is not really your bag. You're a little bothered by the fact that each morning your work crew leaves camp later than you would like, because they never seem to find the right tools; when they do, they're not in good repair.

CAMP BIGFOOT

Role for Work Leader #2 (Male)

You have a good group of kids, although there are frequently some disagreements between the Spanish and white campers. The Work Coordinator has been putting pressure on you to have your kids get more work done, and the kids don't like him much for this. You've responded to the pressure, but you dislike having to push the kids; it makes you appear to be the "bad guy." Incidentally, you are wondering when the kids are going to get some Environmental Education instruction. You would like to do some yourself, but you need a little guidance from the EE instructor, since this is not really your bag. You're a little bothered by the fact that each morning your work crew leaves camp later than you would like, because they never seem to find the right tools; when they do, they're not in good repair. Also, the vehicles break down every other day, it seems.

CAMP BIGFOOT

Role for Work Leader #3 (Female)

You have a good group of campers, although there are frequently some disagreements between the Spanish and white campers. Several things are bothering you right now. You are not a women's lib advocate, but you have noticed how the other male work leaders act as though you can't do anything physically difficult. All you would like is for them to be a little less chauvinistic about it and . give you women (staff and campers) a chance to try the harder jobs. You are somewhat irked by the Camp Director; although he is a very nice guy generally, he drops comments that indicate that he really doesn't think that females can do a man's job. You would like to teach the campers Environmental Education, but you don't feel you know enough. You would like the EE instructor to help you so that you could instruct the campers on the work sites.

II. CONCEPTUAL SUPPORT MATERIALS: INTEGRATED PROBLEM SOLVING

THE CONSULTANT AS TEACHER OF THE INTEGRATIVE FUNCTION

This chapter has emphasized several critical facets of consultant activity, on a specific, immediate, behavioral level. First, the consultant in working with a group makes specific interventions. That is, the consultant stops the task work and, in one way or another, says, "Wait a minute, now, let's look at what's going on here . . ." While the obvious purpose is to help the group work more effectively, the more important function of such intervention is to help group members learn to intervene in their own group task work when necessary. Second, the consultant can help the group by giving it a problem solving framework and helping it learn to use this framework. Finally, the consultant can help the group members learn to monitor their own use of the framework. Design B presents an important way of helping a group learn to use a good problem-solving framework.

To be considered a fully effective helper, the consultant must not only put these things together but must go still further. The consultant must, in the context of work with a real client, integrate some of the process intervention skills (the focus of Design A) within a problem solving framework (Design B), so that the client actually learns to use problem solving processes and procedures, as well as how to integrate the monitoring process into task-oriented problem solving work. This means being an effective teacher, fulfilling and modeling the integrative function. This is asking a great deal; it is complex and difficult work, and requires skills on the conceptual and behavioral levels (and, of course, the integration of these skills). The aim in this book has been the development of such skills, and the aim of this chapter is to begin learning to integrate the skills.

SMALL GROUP PROBLEM SOLVING

In a classic paper, Maier (1967) presented a concise outline of the assets and liabilities of problem solving groups. Briefly, he stated that in problem solving, groups possess four assets and four liabilities, as compared with individuals.

Assets

- A group has more information than any one individual. While one person may know more than any other group member, the others will still have at least some additional relevant information.

- Since individuals will take certain, different, approaches to a problem, the members of a group are likely to push one another out of "ruts in thinking."

- When the persons who must carry out a decision are also involved in arriving at the decision their commitment to the action is increased. Whatever the objective quality of the decision, it is likely to work better than a decision that is not accepted by those who must implement it.

- When those who will carry out the decision are involved in making it there is no need for time-consuming effort on the part of supervisors to communicate the details of the decision. Misunderstandings are also far less likely to occur.

Liabilities

- Pressure to conform may silence minority opinions. This reduces the flow of significant information and can lead to adoption of a poor decision.

- A solution that has received at least fifteen more positive than negative comments tends to be adopted, regardless of its quality. In fact, a solution can be pushed to acceptance by a small but vocal minority. Certain individuals may even learn to manipulate the entire group.

- One individual can, in a variety of ways, attain dominance over the group. An appointed leader, in particular, is likely to dominate group problem solving discussions, but any group member might do the same.

- When group members differ in their solution preferences the discussion may degenerate into a win-lose argument. The goal of solving a problem is then subordinated to individuals' desires to see "their" solutions "win."

Neutral Factors

In addition, certain factors can be either assets or liabilities, depending on the skill of the group leader.

- Disagreement has been shown to lead to creativity or to bad feelings, depending on whether the leader is able to develop a group atmosphere in which differences are seen as valuable and are accepted and used to generate new ideas.

- Differences may arise when group members are unknowingly looking at different problems. When the leader is able to help the group define an area of mutual interest and then define the specific problem or problems, the group is able to use its differences productively.

- Groups may make riskier decisions than individuals, in certain circumstances. Risk is not necessarily bad, but must be understood and taken into account in solution-action plans if the probability of an effective solution is to be maximized.

- Group decisions require more time than do decisions made by supervisors alone. This can be a serious problem when quick action is imperative. Pushing the group to finish its discussion can result in a loss of contributions and frustration on the part of members, yet allowing a discussion to go on and on will lead to boredom and withdrawal.

Group Processes

Maier (1963) defines three leadership discussion approaches. Two of these, "tell and sell" and "tell and listen," are based on a model of *persuasion.* The third, problem solving, is quite different, being based on a *joint collaborative* model of group interaction. The salesman-leader has the solution; the only problem is in gaining the acceptance of subordinates. The problem solving leader does not push for a predetermined solution; he comes to the group looking for ideas rather than selling them.

These two processes can be compared by using an interesting physical analogy, the starfish. A starfish is a rather primitive organism. It has no brain, as such. The legs, or "rays," are almost like five discrete individuals. The organism is, however, integrated by a nerve ring that connects the five rays. When the nerve ring is cut, the animal can still function. One dominant ray may move and the others follow, with a degree of coordination. However, one or more of the other rays may *not* follow. In that case, the starfish is at best immobilized; at worst it is literally torn apart. Maier (1967) suggests that the leader of an effective problem solving group acts as a nerve ring, thus eliminating or minimizing the liability factors and turning most or all of the neutral factors into assets. Instead of exerting pressure on the group, like a "dominant ray," the leader acts as an *integrator.* He is

> . . . receptive to information contributed [by the group members], accept[s] contributions without evaluating them . . . summarize[s] information to facilitate integration, stimulate[s] exploratory behavior, create[s] awareness of problems of one member by others, and detect[s] when the group is ready to resolve differences and agree to a unified solution [p. 247].

In addition, the leader may provide the group with problem-relevant information, as long as he does not imply a solution. In sum the leader must focus on group *process*, avoiding any direct involvement in the *content* work of the group.

INTEGRATED PROBLEM SOLVING

Maier's work, as briefly summed up above, has been of great importance in identifying the elements of the problem solving process and determining how people can learn to use it. However, we wish to carry his argument still further and, in part, disagree with his conclusions.

Maier feels that the role of the leader in effective problem solving groups is essentially different from that of any group member or subordinate. While it is certainly true that the leader is in a different position from most other group members (see Likert, 1967), it is not necessary to assume that the leadership role in the small-group problem solving meeting is so greatly different from the membership role.

In this book, the aim has been to help individuals learn effective group problem solving behaviors. In an effective problem solving group it is not only the leader who attends to group process and gives direction; *all* group members can participate in this activity. The more skilled *every* group member is in observing and acting on group process the more effective all members will be in contributing to the group's task or content work. And, the more effective the group will be in solving problems.

Physical analogies are invariably imperfect. Integrated Problem Solving is not based on the leader serving as a nerve ring. Rather, the nerve ring in an integrated problem solving group is a nonphysical *process*, contributed to by all group members.

The approach presented in this book is a logical extension of earlier work (Maier, 1970). As groups within and outside of organizations become more transitory, more temporary (Bennis and Slater, 1968), it will become increasingly important for the skills of Integrated Problem Solving to be shared by all members of a problem solving group. To a considerable extent, this goal must be achieved in organizations by skilled leaders, administrators, and managers, who can help their groups learn to operate using more effective problem solving processes. We hope this book will help facilitate that outcome.

REFERENCES

**Argyris, C. (1962) *Interpersonal competence and organizational effectiveness.* Homewood, Ill.: Irwin-Dorsey.

**Argyris, C. (1970) *Intervention theory and method.* Reading, Mass.: Addison-Wesley.

Bennis, W. G.; Berlew, D. E.; Schein, E. H.; and Steele, F. I. (1973) *Interpersonal dynamics.* 3rd ed. Homewood, Ill.: Dorsey.

Bennis, W. G., and Slater, P. E. (1968) *The temporary society.* New York: Harper & Row.

Bouchard, T. J., Jr. (1969) Personality, problem solving procedure, and performance in small groups. *Journal of Applied Psychology* 53: 1-29.

Dyer, W. G. (1972) *Modern theory and method in group training.* New York: Van Nostrand Reinhold.

Fordyce, J. K., and Weil, R. (1971) *Managing with people.* Reading, Mass.: Addison-Wesley.

Harrison, R. (1970) Choosing the depth of organizational intervention. *Journal of Applied Behavioral Science* 6: 181-202.

Havelock, R. G., and Havelock, M. C. (1973) *Training for change agents.* Ann Arbor, Mich.: Institute for Social Research, The University of Michigan.

Kepner, C. H., and Tregoe, B. B. (1965) *The rational manager.* New York: McGraw-Hill.

Likert, R. (1967) *The human organization.* New York: McGraw-Hill.

Lippitt, R. (1959) Dimensions of the consultant's job. *Journal of Social Issues* **15: 5-12.

Maier, N. R. F. (1967) Assets and liabilities in group problem solving: The need for an integrative function. *Psychological Review* **74**: 239-249.

**Maier, N. R. F. (1963) *Problem solving discussions and conferences.* New York: McGraw-Hill.

Maier, N. R. F. (1970) *Problem solving and creativity in individuals and groups.* Belmont, Calif.: Brooks/Cole.

Maier, N. R. F.; Solem, A. R.; and Maier, A. A. (1957) *Supervisory and executive development.* New York: Wiley. (Science Editions, 1966.) (Revised and reissued as *The role-play technique.* La Jolla, Calif.: University Associates, 1975.)

Sashkin, M.; Frohman, M. A.; and Kavanagh, M. J. (1976) *Organization development: Theory, approaches, and management.* Homewood, Ill.: Irwin.

Schein, E. H., and Bennis, W. G. (1965) *Personal and organizational change through group methods.* New York: Wiley.

**References preceded by a double asterisk are those judged most basic or important.

APPENDIX I

Integration of Skills Through Simulated Organizational Behavior

Skills that are learned through experiential training, as is true for most of the learning designs in this book, must be practiced repeatedly if they are to be integrated into the normal behavior of an individual. While there are many ways of practice that can lead to such integration, this appendix presents an example of one approach for practicing and integrating behavioral skills — an organizational behavior simulation game.

The simulation experience serves as an important link between the initial learning of specific skills and their application in the course of everyday behavior. The specific learning designs detailed in this book are "micro-exercises" in that each one concentrates on the development of one or a few specific skills by creating situations in which the use of those skills is necessary or appropriate. In most cases the situation is controlled in the sense that the activity focuses on one specific skill (or one specific set of skills) with all other factors being held constant. This kind of situation is of necessity somewhat different from the "real life" situations individuals face in the course of their experiences in groups and organizations.

In contrast, the simulation game provides a "macro-exercise" in which a number of skills are involved, without providing specific cues as to the skill to be used. As such, it is one step closer to real life and is a useful learning experience as the individual attempts to integrate the broad range of skills he or she may have learned through an experiential-based training course or program. The simulation game, then, forms a link between specific experiential skill learnings and real-world behavior.

In the following pages, a simple organizational behavior simulation will be presented. First, some of the characteristics and advantages of simulation will briefly be outlined. Second, background and instructions needed to plan and conduct the simulation will be provided. This will be followed by a list of potential modifications to the game, each of which adds a different dimension to the experience. Fourth, the materials needed for the basic simulation game will be provided. The final section is a brief list of additional relevant readings on simulation gaming.

SKILLS INTEGRATION THROUGH SIMULATION GAMES

Simulation games provide the opportunity for individuals to function as if in a real group or organizational situation. They combine the validity of a real-world situation with the learning opportunities of an in-class experiential exercise. Four major elements are needed in order to produce this realistic but artificial situation:

1.   An environment must be created that approximates the "real world" along certain dimensions.

2.   Within that environment the roles (or potential roles) of participants must be structured. These are also approximations of real-world roles.

3.   A model must exist that provides for some kind of payoff to participants (or groups of participants), based on their performance in the simulated environment.

4.   Participants must engage in activities (within the framework of the model) that require the application of certain kinds of skills.

The game we will shortly describe is constructed to give participants an opportunity to apply different skills related to individual, interpersonal, and group behavior in an organizational situation. It has a number of positive features as a learning tool:

- The simulation allows for the application of a number of different skills, rather than just one specific skill.

- The simulation puts the participant in a situation where he or she must diagnose situations and make choices about what skills to use and how.

- The structure of the simulation creates intense pressures for task performance, which puts blocks in the way of process-oriented activities similar to the blocks that exist in real-life situations.

- The simulation model provides hard measures of effectiveness that allow participants to see the relationship between their own skill applications and the effectiveness of the groups to which they belong.

- Within the general structure, there is enough freedom to allow different issues to arise from the interaction (such as conflict among group members, role ambiguity, etc.). These in turn require use of additional skills.

- By its very nature, the game is highly involving and the participants quickly become motivated to perform within role.

- Because of the similarity of simulation and real-life activities, the experiences and learnings of the simulation activity have high face validity for participants.

Given this very general overview of simulation games and their use in the development of skills integration, it becomes obvious that there is a need for an effective yet relatively simple simulation game that can be used for skills integration in a wide variety of circumstances and that involves a wide variety of skills. The outline of such a game follows.

THE ORGANIZATIONAL ROLE-PLAY GAME SIMULATION (ORGS)

The game presented here, ORGS, was designed as an exercise that could easily be run without specialized materials or equipment. The objective was to develop a simulation that could be run as part of a college course, a training program, or other similar learning activities.

The basic game was designed for use in three particular learning settings. First, it was designed to be used in a graduate-level course on interpersonal behavior for managers. The game provides the opportunity for participants to apply skills of communication, conflict resolution, giving and receiving feedback, goal setting, decision making, and other aspects of group leadership. Second, it was intended for use in an undergraduate course in group behavior in organizations. By creating groups within simulated organizational settings, the game provides real behavior for the students to study. Third, the game was conceived for use in a program for training change agents and helpers who would apply their skills in organizations. The game creates organizations into which interventions can be made. It thus creates an opportunity to develop and practice intervention skills. These three settings, of course, are not the only applications for the simulation; they are presented as examples of the different purposes for which the game might be used.

The structure of the simulation calls for teams made up of participants who must develop interdependent roles in order to perform tasks effectively. In the game, two or more teams of participants compete with each other. Each team starts with the same amount of money. Teams buy components, assemble them into finished products, and then sell the products (for a profit, they hope). During this repeated cycle of events, the teams must deal with a variety of issues that are common to most organizations, including developing organizational structure, defining organizational roles, allocating resources, and making strategy decisions. At the same time, certain kinds of interpersonal process issues are inherently involved in the initial sequence of events. In one way or another, each team must deal with issues relating to communication patterns, group norms, feedback, leadership style, decision making, and other such concerns.

Given this basic thrust, the game can be used for a variety of purposes. In this section, the basic game will be described. Following that, a list of possible modifications to the game will be presented. These modifications allow the person running the game to change the nature of the simulation so that certain issues become emphasized.

The Basic Game

The basic game creates the structure for competitive teams to function for a series of game rounds. Theoretically, the game can be run for any number of people. For purposes of explanation, a group of fifteen (three groups of five participants each) will be used. The key points of running the game are as follows:

Materials. The basic materials for the game include the instrumentation sheets and a few reusable accessories that can easily be purchased. The instrumentation is discussed below and includes the following sheets (found at the end of this appendix), which can be duplicated for use in the game:

Form A — General Instructions
Form B — Parts Price List
Form C — Parts Order Form
Form D — Product Quality Standards
Form E — New Product Announcement Memo
Form F — Tractor Production Diagram and Parts List
Form G — Airplane Product Diagram and Parts List
Form H — Car Product Diagram and Parts List

In addition, the following materials are needed for the basic game:

— Play money (about a thousand dollars in different denominations for the basic ten-round game)

- Tinkertoys (two of the "Giant Engineer" sets for each fifteen participants)
- A whistle (or some other sound device to indicate beginning and ending of rounds)
- Various signs (to indicate team work and conference areas, vendor store and marketplace; can be made on newsprint)

Staff. The basic game requires three people in leadership roles. One person takes the primary role of running the game while the other two work at the vendor store and marketplace tasks. It is important that the staff be thoroughly briefed on the mechanics of the game and have enough time to get their materials set up. It is often useful to have the staff go through a round of purchasing components, assembling them, and selling the products. This helps to familiarize them with the game and also work out any problems with procedures or physical arrangements.

Room arrangement. Any number of different arrangements could be used, but one setup of tables that has been found to be workable is as follows:

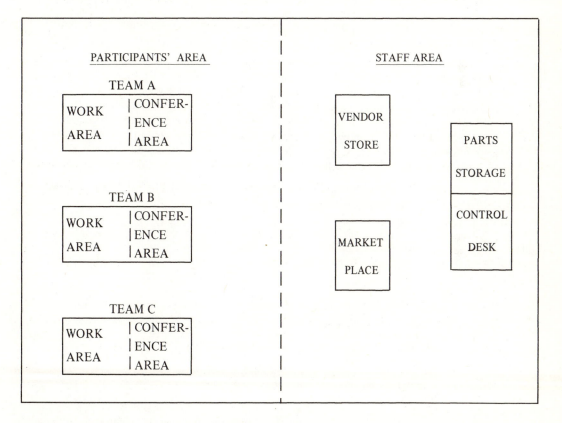

Basic structure. The activity of the game takes place in rounds. Each round in the basic game is ten minutes long. Each round is followed by a conference period that usually lasts about five minutes. The beginning and ending of rounds is indicated by blowing a whistle (or making some other kind of loud noise using a buzzer, gong, bell, etc.). During the round, the teams use the part of their tables marked "work area." During the conference periods they are to move to the part of their tables marked "conference area," leaving all materials in the work area. This arrangement is important so that the work and conference periods will be used for their intended purposes and so that no team can gain from misuse of conference periods. Experience with the game indicates that ten rounds is generally sufficient to have the major desired experiences take place. With briefing time included, the ten work rounds (each followed by five minutes of conference time) take about three hours to run. This calculation does not include any time for postactivity discussion for the purpose of extracting specific learnings.

Starting the game. Before the game starts, teams should be formed and roles assigned. In the basic game, there are three roles: president, manager (at least one per team), and technician (all remaining team members). Once the teams have assembled at their tables (conference areas), the introduction sheet (Form A) should be handed out and time permitted for teams to read and go over the sheet. Once this has been done, the person conducting the game reads the following introductory statement:

> In a few minutes we will be starting the first round of the ORGS Simulation Game. Each working round will last ten minutes. During that time you will be working in the location marked "work area." Other time periods will be used for conferences, for planning, and for discussing working arrangements. During that time, you will work in the area marked "conference area."

> The beginning and ending of rounds will be marked by the blowing of a whistle [or other sound] like this [blow whistle]. When starting a working round, all announcements (distribution of materials, new-product announcements, etc.) will be made exactly after the blowing of the beginning whistle. When the ending whistle is blown for each round, *all work must stop.* Transactions that have already begun at the marketplace and vendor store tables will be completed but all other activity will cease and all personnel should move immediately to the conference area. No papers, plans, order forms, materials, etc., should be taken to this area and violations of the rules will be fined.

> We will be running for ten rounds. The computation of team results will be on the basis of *cash only* at the end of the tenth round.

> Do you have any questions?

After answering any questions, blow the whistle to start the first working round and distribute the following packet of materials to each team:

> — A hundred dollars in play money
>
> — Parts Price List (Form B, one copy each team)
>
> — Parts Order Form (Form C, about thirty copies each team)
>
> — Product Quality Standards (Form D, one copy each team)
>
> — New Product Memo (Form E, one copy each team)
>
> — Tractor Product Diagram (Form F, one copy each team)

Game operation. In each team, the general sequence of events will probably be as follows. First the team will study the diagram of the tractor. Next, the team will use the diagram and the parts price list to fill out an order form. The order form will be taken to the "vendor store" desk, where one of the staff members will fill the order. The parts will be taken back to the work area and the team will attempt assembly. Once the product is assembled, one member will take it to the "marketplace" desk, where the staff member will examine the product, make a quality decision (based on the standards in Form D) and, if the decision on quality is acceptable to the seller, pay the appropriate price. In most cases, teams do not get through an entire cycle in the first round.

After the teams have worked out their major operating problems (about the third or fourth round) the two other products can be introduced right after the whistle beginning the round. A copy of the New Product Memo (Form E) with the airplane or car diagrams attached (Forms G and H) is given to each team.

As the rounds continue, it is often useful to have a place (for example, a chalkboard or prepared newsprint) where announcements (of parts changes, etc.) can be posted and the round number can be kept track of.

At the beginning of the tenth round, announce that this will be the last round. Only cash assets will be counted at the end of the game. Teams may sell parts back to the store, but all transactions must be done during the tenth round, not after it.

Potential problems. As the game gets into gear, the pace generally becomes very fast. It is therefore important for the staff to plan ahead and be aware of potential problem areas. The simulation retains its validity for the participants only as long as the model continues to work as promised. Two frequent problems involve having enough materials and attempts by participants to "subvert" the game. First, it is important to have enough of the necessary forms and parts on hand. This is particularly true of the Parts Order Forms (Form C), which tend to get used up quickly, and the Tinkertoys. The game can continue only if finished products are disassembled by the staff and parts put back into the supply area. If there are not enough Tinkertoys, the stress on the game staff increases and lines begin to form at the supply desk. Second, it is important to prevent subversion of the game rules by participants. When game subversion, as opposed to specified production activity, is rewarded a host of issues arises that may be very realistic but very different or off-target from the purpose for which the game is being used. For this reason it is probably useful to keep parts out of sight, since the most typical subversive attempt is to buy up all of the scarce parts. Having enough Tinkertoys can also prevent this occurence.

Deriving learnings. As with any other experiential learning activity, much of the payoff comes in the postactivity discussion, or "processing," of the experience. After the tenth round, a number of different approaches can be used. In general, it is probably useful to have the teams discuss the simulation by themselves first and then at some later point attempt to generate and list some more general observations or learnings. The process discussion can also focus on different issues — feelings of members during the game, types of decision making, communication patterns, etc.

Modifications

The set of procedures that has just been outlined constitutes the basic simulation. As described, it can be used effectively and applied to a number of different situations. The potential of the game, however, is increased by the possibility of making modifications. Following is a list of possible modifications that can be made in the game. The list is far from complete, but it gives an idea of the range of things that can be done. Care should, however, be taken in the use of modifications. Each time a modification is added, the nature of the game is changed and different behavioral issues are emphasized. Therefore, thought should be given to the purpose and consequences of any change, particularly when several modifications are made at the same time. Possible modifications include:

1. *Process sessions.* Several of the conference sessions can be used for process discussions by the teams themselves. In this case, it is probably advisable to lengthen somewhat the conference period.

2. *Feedback.* Group process can be affected by feedback on how well the teams are doing. This can easily be done by posting the cash on hand and value of inventory (at cost) of each team at the end of rounds. This can be done at selected rounds or at the end of each round.

3. *Survey feedback.* With relatively little effort, an attitude survey can be constructed with a few questionnaire items relating to satisfaction, motivation, task characteristics, role clarity, and other related issues. The survey could be administered during one of the conference periods, results tabulated by the staff, and feedback of data given during the next conference period. As with survey-feedback programs in organizations, a variety of activities could accompany the feedback itself.

4. *Organizational consultant.* A participant (either internal or external to the specific team) could be designated as organizational consultant and would be free to make various interventions for the purpose of helping the team members learn to work together more effectively, make decisions, set goals, etc. This modification would be particularly useful in programs for training practitioners.

5. *Additional products.* The Tinkertoy manual contains numerous other products. Additional products could be interjected into the game to highlight the decision-making aspects of the simulation. Use of additional products is advisable, for example, when the market is made to fluctuate, via announcements that only a certain number of a specific product will be purchased or when the market prices of items are changed.

6. *Team rewards.* As a means of heightening involvement, rewards could be provided for winning teams. (In the past a twelve-pack of beer has been used successfully.) In certain cases, participants have been asked to chip in cash (usually a nominal amount like twenty-five or fifty cents) with the pot going to the winner. This modification increases the salience of winning (and losing) and helps facilitate discussion of the feelings that go along with winning and losing.

7. *Individual rewards.* With a slight reworking of the process structure of the game, pay for employees could be built into the simulation. Rewards could then be tied to highest individual net worth as well as highest team net worth at the end of the game. The introduction of pay adds to the differentiation of managerial and nonmanagerial roles and introduces a whole set of issues around compensation.

8. *Manager preparation.* In the basic simulation, the different roles are not highly differentiated in practice (with the frequent exception of the company president). If increased role differentiation is desired, managers could be briefed first and could play a pregame round before workers enter the room, thus giving the managers some "expert" power (in addition to their "legitimate" power) and emphasizing the difference between managers and workers.

9. *Turnover.* The potential for turnover could be built in, highlighting satisfaction issues. All technicians would be called out of the room and told they are now free to go to any firm they want to. When combined with the pay modification, this modification builds in bargaining and wage negotiation as major issues.

10. *Structure changes.* During the game, a different organizational structure could be introduced on either a voluntary or mandatory basis. Process discussion could focus on how the change in formal structure affected changes in relationships, effectiveness, etc.

11. *Leadership changes.* Leadership issues could be highlighted by introducing various changes. For example, all the presidents might be removed and given observer roles. Other possibilities include making the presidents into technicians. Process discussion could then focus on issues of succession, legitimacy, style differences, etc.

12. *Mergers.* Following the initial ten rounds, the teams could be merged into one large company. Without any guidance different teams may respond to the merger differently. Processing could focus on issues that arise when formerly competing groups now must cooperate. Other issues raised by this modification include issues of restructuring, increased coordination problems, etc.

13. *Larger teams.* The complexity of all the issues could be increased by using larger teams (perhaps ten to fifteen per team) and dealing with the process issues that come about with increased size.

14. *Change of pace.* It is also possible to experiment with the pacing of the game (length of work and conference rounds) to test the effects of different time periods.

Summary

The directions, materials, and modification suggestions provided here enable the user to create a variety of different simulation activities. It is hoped that this information will make it possible for simulation games to be used more widely in learning programs where the emphasis is on the integration of skills related to group and organizational issues. It should again be emphasized that in a simulation, as in most experiential learning, the payoff comes in the postactivity discussion of the experience. Through reflection, abstraction, and conceptualization, learnings are crystalized and the true value of the activity is realized. The procedures and instrumentation here do no more than create the situation for experiences that can then be "processed."

This fairly simple simulation is one example of a growing literature of simulation gaming. For those who are interested, a few key sources of information about this technique have been provided in the reference list at the end of this appendix.

Simulation, like any other behavioral-training methodology, is a tool to facilitate learning. By the creation of environments and roles that approximate the real world, a simulation game aims at integrating skills and promoting the successful transfer of skills from the classroom or seminar room into real organizational settings.

Instrumentation

The following pages contain the various forms needed for running the basic simulation. They are ready for use and can be copied as is.

Form A — *General Instructions:* given out to teams before the first round and also used for briefing staff.

Form B — *Parts Price List:* used as a source for prices for making up orders and figuring margins.

Form C — *Parts Order Form:* used for submitting parts orders; requires computation of cost and signature of the company president. These should be saved by the staff in case of disputes over transactions.

Form D — *Product Quality Standards:* given to each team for their information; used by staff at marketplace to judge products.

Form E — *New Product Announcement Memo:* cover memo announcing the introduction of a new product.

Form F — *Tractor Product Diagram and Parts List.*

Form G — *Airplane Product Diagram and Parts List.*

Form H — *Car Product Diagram and Parts List.*

ORGANIZATIONAL ROLE-PLAY GAME SIMULATION
• ORGS •

General Instructions

OVERVIEW: YOU ARE ABOUT TO PARTICIPATE IN A COMPETITIVE MULTI-GROUP SIMULATION EXERCISE. THIS EXERCISE SIMULATES AN ORGANIZATION ENGAGED IN THE PRODUCTION AND SALE OF PRODUCTS. BY CREATING SUCH AN ORGANIZATION, WE CAN LOOK AT BEHAVIORAL ISSUES IN A SETTING SIMILAR TO REAL LIFE.

Purpose: Each team will compete to maximize profit by the end of the game. Profit is made by purchasing components, assembling products, and selling those products in accordance with the rules listed below.

Rounds: The game time will be divided up into a number of rounds. Each round will last exactly ten minutes. During the round, members of each team are allowed to write purchase orders, purchase products, assemble and test products, and sell products.

In Between Rounds: During the period between rounds, no work may be performed (work being defined as activities normally done during the round). When the round ends, all members of the team move from the space indicated as "work area" to the space indicated as "conference area." All tools, components, work sheets, order forms, etc., are to be left in the work area. *Teams attempting to do work in between rounds will be heavily fined.*

Company Structure: Each team (company) will be structured as follows: One person shall serve as president, two other individuals shall serve as managers, and the remaining people shall serve as workers (technicians). Assignment to these roles may be made ahead of time. Beyond the assignment of roles, the structure of the team is up to each individual team.

Products: Products to produce will be provided in the form of a product diagram and parts list, which will be handed out at the beginning of the game. As the game progresses, more products may be introduced. Teams are free to produce any of the available products, given constraints of cash, time, and individual skill level.

Buying Components: Each product diagram includes a parts list. A price list of all parts also will be provided. All orders for parts must be written up using the parts order form provided. Parts can be obtained at the desk marked "vendor store." To obtain parts the company representative must submit a correctly filled out parts order form and the appropriate amount of money (cash bucks).

Producing: Products are to be assembled in the work area, according to the diagrams provided.

Selling Products: Products for sale should be presented at the desk marked "marketplace." Products will be examined and upon quality rating (top quality, workable quality, low quality) a price will be paid. Top-quality and workable quality prices are indicated on the product diagrams; low-quality products will not be accepted.

ORGANIZATIONAL ROLE-PLAY GAME SIMULATION
• ORGS •

Parts Price List

PART	PRICE PER PART IN BUCKS

RODS:

ORANGE	1 buck
PURPLE	1 buck
GREEN	2 bucks
YELLOW	1 buck
BLUE	1 buck
RED	1 buck

WOODEN TURNINGS:

SPOOL (BASIC ROUND PIECE)	2 bucks
BG (SPOOL WITH LARGE HOLE)	1 buck
W (MULTIPLE-HUB SPOOL)	2 bucks
WHEELS	3 bucks

PLASTIC HARDWARE:

CAPS	2 bucks
POINTS	1 buck
BEARINGS	4 bucks
WINDBLADES	1 buck

ORGANIZATIONAL ROLE-PLAY GAME SIMULATION
• ORGS •
Parts Order Form

PART NAME	PRICE	QUANTITY	COST
Orange Rod			
Yellow Rod			
Blue Rod			
Red Rod			
Green Rod			
Purple Rod			
Spool (Basic Round Piece)			
BG (Spool with Large Hole)			
W (Multiple-Hub Spool)			
Wheels			
Bearings (Orange Plastic)			
Caps			
Points			
Windblades			
Total Number of Pieces and Total Cost of This Order			

Round Number_____ Company_____
Order Computed by_____ Company President_____

- -

Time Order Submitted at Desk_____

Check When Filled (_____)

ORGANIZATIONAL ROLE-PLAY GAME SIMULATION
• ORGS •

Product Quality Standards

HIGH-QUALITY PRODUCTS: ALL COMPONENTS ARE ASSEMBLED CORRECTLY AND ALL ASSEMBLIES ARE PERFECTLY PUT TOGETHER (E.G., ALL PARALLEL LINES ARE PARALLEL, ETC.). WHERE THERE ARE WORKING PARTS (WHEELS ON THE CAR AND TRACTOR, HYDRAULIC LIFT ON THE TRACTOR) THESE PARTS MUST WORK. ALL ASSEMBLIES ARE TIGHT AND DO NOT FALL APART. PRODUCTS SHOULD SIT ON THE TABLE EVENLY.

WORKABLE-QUALITY
PRODUCTS: ALL COMPONENTS ARE ASSEMBLED CORRECTLY BUT MAY NOT BE UP TO THE HIGH-QUALITY STANDARDS. THEY SHOULD BE FULLY ASSEMBLED, HOWEVER, WITHOUT SUBASSEMBLIES FALLING APART. PARTS NEED NOT WORK AND THE PRODUCT NEED NOT SIT ON THE TABLE EVENLY.

LOW-QUALITY PRODUCTS: ALL PRODUCTS NOT OF THE ABOVE QUALITY WILL BE JUDGED LOW-QUALITY PRODUCTS.

NOTE: ALL PRODUCTS ARE JUDGED *AS DELIVERED.* THIS MEANS NO REPAIR WORK ALLOWED AT THE MARKETPLACE. PRODUCTS THAT ARE NOT OF THE DESIRED QUALITY MUST BE TAKEN BACK TO THE WORK AREAS. IF THE SELLER DOES NOT LIKE THE QUALITY RATING, HE/SHE IS FREE TO NOT SELL THE PRODUCT AND ATTEMPT TO REWORK IT TO A HIGHER QUALITY.

ORGANIZATIONAL ROLE-PLAY GAME SIMULATION
• ORGS •

. New Product Announcement

MEMO TO: PRESIDENTS OF ALL COMPANIES
FROM: PRODUCT DEVELOPMENT STAFF
SUBJECT: NEW PRODUCTS

ATTACHED YOU WILL FIND DIAGRAMS AND PARTS LISTS FOR PRODUCT(S) THAT ARE NOW READY FOR PRODUCTION. AT THIS TIME YOU ARE FREE TO PRODUCE THIS PRODUCT OR ANY COMBINATION OF PRODUCTS FOR WHICH YOU HAVE DIAGRAMS.

ORGANIZATIONAL ROLE-PLAY GAME SIMULATION
• ORGS •

Product Diagram and Parts List

PRODUCT: TRACTOR WITH HYDRAULIC LIFT

TOP-QUALITY PRICE: 99 BUCKS

WORKABLE-QUALITY PRICE: 89 BUCKS

PARTS LIST:
- — 3 caps
- — 7 orange rods
- — 2 red rods
- — 2 W (multiple-hub spool)
- — 2 blue rods
- — 6 yellow rods
- — 5 bearings
- — 3 green rods
- — 4 wheels
- — 9 spools

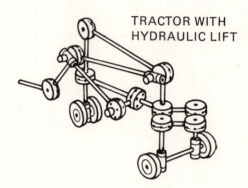

TRACTOR WITH
HYDRAULIC LIFT

ORGANIZATIONAL ROLE-PLAY GAME SIMULATION
• ORGS •

Product Diagram and Parts List

PRODUCT: AIRPLANE

TOP-QUALITY PRICE: 88 BUCKS

WORKABLE-QUALITY PRICE: 78 BUCKS

PARTS LIST:
- — 2 wheels
- — 5 yellow rods
- — 10 spools
- — 3 blades
- — 4 green rods
- — 4 bearings
- — 8 orange rods
- — 5 blue rods
- — 1 point

AIRPLANE

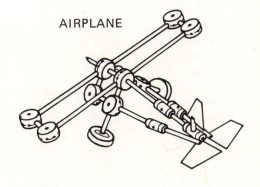

ORGANIZATIONAL ROLE-PLAY GAME SIMULATION
• ORGS •

Product Diagram and Parts List

PRODUCT: CAR

TOP-QUALITY PRICE: 70 BUCKS

WORKABLE-QUALITY PRICE: 62 BUCKS

PARTS LIST:
- 4 blue rods
- 4 wheels
- 5 orange rods
- 2 caps
- 2 red rods
- 4 yellow rods
- 4 bearings
- 6 spools

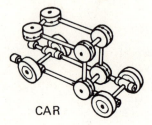

CAR

REFERENCES

Abt, C. C. (1970) *Serious games.* New York: Viking.

Babcock, S. S., and Schild, E. O., eds. (1968) *Simulation games in learning.* Beverly Hills, Calif.: Sage Publications.

Bass, B. M. (1963) Experimenting with simulated manufacturing organizations. In *Stimulus determinants of behavior,* ed. S. B. Sells. New York: Ronald Press. Pp. 117-196.

Cohen, K. J.; Dill, W. R.; Kuehn, A.; and Winters, P. (1964) *The Carnegie Tech management game: An experiment in business education.* Homewood, Ill.: Irwin.

Croft, C. J.; Kibbee, J.; and Nanus, B. (1961) *Management games.* New York: Reinhold.

Guetzkow, H. S., ed. (1962) *Simulation in social science: Readings.* Englewood Cliffs, N. J.: Prentice Hall.

McKenny, J. L. (1967) *Simulation gaming for management development.* Boston: Harvard University Graduate School of Business Administration.

Learning to Use
Role Play Methods

INTRODUCTION

The techniques of role playing have been used extensively in this book. Role playing is one of the most involving of experiential learning methods, and has been used a great deal in training programs in schools, business, industry, and government over the past twenty-five years.* We will briefly review four basic types of role play and then provide designs for learning to create and use two of these types.

Sociodrama. This is a method for diagnosing problems rather than learning skills. Those involved in a particular problem gather and share all the information they have concerning the problem. These data are used to develop roles for the people involved in the problem (who may not be present) and a key or critical situation example is defined. Group members then take the roles they developed and act out the situation, with some of them observing the action. After some period of time, the role play is stopped and the players and observers analyze what happened in order to identify the problem or problems in the situation. They can then determine what other information is needed and who else should be involved in a problem-solving meeting.

Empathy training. Much research[†] has shown that people can develop a better understanding of how others feel by acting out the role of the other person in a role play. This is a particularly useful technique in conflict situations, when the two parties (or groups) each develop their *own* role(s) and these roles are then acted out by the *other* party(ies), in a defined, simulated situation. Thus, each party gets the basic experience of how the *other* feels, which facilitates communication and interaction between them for the purpose of working on and solving their mutual problems.

Anticipatory practice. All of us experience, to some degree, a kind of stage fright when we know we must face some difficult problem situation in the near future but are rather uncertain of how we should act or what could happen (Perls, 1969). This anxiety can be greatly reduced by trying out a variety of alternative actions in a role-play simulation of the situation. First, the situation is defined in detail. Then, there is a brainstorm to generate action alternatives. One or more alterna-

---

*For more detailed discussion of the historical development of role-play methods, see Corsini, Shaw, and Blake (1961) and Sashkin (1971).

†For example, Elbing (1967) and Speroff (1953).

tives are then tried out in the simulated role-play situation by the person(s) who will be involved in the upcoming real situation. Finally, the role players and observers review what happened and determine which action alternatives seemed to be most effective. These actions can then be re-practiced, and the person(s) who will soon be involved in the real situation can develop an action plan for dealing with that situation.

Skill training. Of all the purposes for which role-play methods are used, this is probably the single most common function. A role-play situation, complete with specific written roles (which could be quite short — a sentence or two — or quite long — two or three pages) is prepared in advance, designed to bring out some particular behavioral skill (such as sharing information, nondirective group leadership, or interviewing). In general, participants should *not* be involved in the development of the role-play situation, since the situation should be somewhat different from any of their normal work activities in order to avoid "overinvolvement" in the details of the role play, which could result in missing the skill focus. (Of course, there are circumstances in which a very real role-play situation would be desirable, for diagnosis, anticipatory practice, or to get the group involved in working on a specific problem. Sometimes, but not generally, these aims can be combined with a specific skill-learning focus.) Usually, the situation would be described in some detail to the role players, who would then be given individual prepared roles. Depending on the size of the group, there might be only one role play or several groups might simultaneously be involved in the same role play (Maier and Zerfoss, 1952). In either case, observers would be used for later discussion of what took place. The role play can be stopped while in progress, for critique by observers, or can continue to some conclusion. Sometimes it is useful to repractice the role play, after discussion of the behavioral skills that are important in the situation.

I. SPECIFIC SKILL-DEVELOPMENT AND LEARNING DESIGNS

Following are two general learning designs, one for helping people learn to use role playing for anticipatory practice, the other for learning to design skill-training role plays.

A.   Design for Learning to Help Others Use Anticipatory Practice Role Playing

1.   *Description.* This design can be used for training students and consultants to use anticipatory practice role plays or can be applied directly to a real group. The design is basically a framework; the user and participants can easily develop some content problem to explore within this framework. When used for anticipatory practice role plays, the teacher or consultant should avoid particularly serious issues, since such content will tend to draw the group away from process learning. With real client groups, however, serious problems may be attacked with this technique, since meaningful, real success experiences will reinforce the clients in applying the technique themselves. *But* the consultant should take care that the client group is ready to deal with such problems, in terms of their openness toward and trust of one another. Ideally, the group should be small, no larger than fifteen, at most twenty persons. At least two hours will be needed.

2.   *Materials needed.* Newsprint and markers, movable chairs, possibly a table.

3.   *Steps in using the design.*

    a.   Briefly explain the technique and aim of anticipatory role playing.

    b.   Have the group brainstorm possible problems to work on (real problems) and select one of these to try first.

c.   Have the person who suggested the problem describe the situation, giving as much detail as seems useful (the other people involved, the nature of the situation, what apprehensions and uncertainties (s)he has about the situation, etc.). If there are others in the group who are involved in the situation, they too should contribute (this is particularly likely in a real organizational group). Those not directly involved in or aware of the situation should ask questions for clarification of details. This discussion should not take longer than fifteen or twenty minutes.

d.   Have the group create a role for each person involved in the anticipated situation (e.g., a department meeting, a confrontation with a supervisor, a discussion with a spouse or child, etc.). The roles can be initiated by brainstorming the characteristics, feelings, and knowledge of each role-person. (The person who suggested the problem will usually play him or herself.) Then, each item is reviewed so that the group develops an overall role-image for each role-person.

e.   Have group members take as many roles as have been developed; there should be at least as many observers as role players. Any remaining group members can serve as "alter egos," identifying with one of the role players. Since the person who suggested the problem situation plays him or herself, it is generally very useful for this person to have at least one alter ego, to whom he or she can turn for advice when needed.

f.   "Set the scene," reviewing the nature of the situation for all group members. Then signal the role players to begin.

g.   You or a group member should interrupt the action whenever a critical point arises, that is, when some particularly useful or dysfunctional action has been taken by the person who is practicing in the anticipated situation (the person who suggested the problem). The person may be given advice or suggestions and the incident "replayed." This should happen at least several times during the role play. The person who is practicing may also stop the action to ask advice of the alter ego. This action phase will usually last thirty to forty minutes, but could take up to one hour.

h.   When the situation is played out to some conclusion, or when it is clear that no further progress can be made, end the role play. At this point, the person who was practicing, who has the real problem, should share his/her learnings, plans for the actual situation, and present feelings about the situation. Observers might be asked to give feedback on this person's behavior. The group could discuss how they feel about the probable effects of the action plan the practicing person has in mind.

i.   Have the group, finally, consider the technique of anticipatory practice role playing (see step 4, below).

4.   *Deriving learnings.* Whether the group was a real client group or a classroom group, several questions concerning the use of this technique should be discussed after the role play is over and the results have been reviewed. Some of these questions are:

– What other situations could this technique be helpful with?

– When is it desirable *not* to use anticipatory practice role playing?

– What are the key points to remember if I'm trying to show someone else how to use this technique?

– Can I use the technique on my own, alone? How?

B.   Design for Learning to Help Others Design and Use Skill-Training Role Plays

1. *Description.* Creating a skill-training role play is a skill in itself. The effective use of such role plays also requires certain skills. This design would be primarily useful for students or consultants-in-training, persons who want to learn to design specific skill-learning role plays for use with clients. Of course, many structured exercises and prepared role plays exist, and some of these are very broadly useful (such as Maier's [1952] "New Truck" role-play case). Still, any consultant, trainer, or teacher will occasionally come up against some specific situation involving a client need that cannot be satisfied by using one of the "old, familiar" skill-training or role-play designs. In such instances, it is important to have the skill of designing a role play specifically aimed at some particular client need. This learning design will take between two and three hours to work through. It is particularly important to separate the two skill elements involved: *first,* the skill of designing a role-play situation, and, *second,* the skill of conducting a role-play skill-training session. The group size should be at least ten; this design can be adapted for use with groups of up to about thirty persons.

2. *Materials needed.* Newsprint and markers, movable chairs, large room (if group is larger than fifteen), ditto masters and a ditto machine (if available), guideline sheets (on the following pages).

3. *Steps in using the design.*

   a.   Review the role-play skill-training method, perhaps giving a brief lecture.

   b.   Have the group brainstorm a list of skills for which it would be interesting to develop role-play skill-training situations.

   c.   Form small groups of four or five around the skills on the list. (A group of six should be used *only* if there are eleven people in all.) If at all possible, form an even number of groups.

   d.   Have everyone turn to the "General Guidelines for Designing" on the next page, and review each point with the total group before starting. In particular, remind everyone that his or her "client/user" will be other persons in the class. This should enable each small group to develop a *relevant* role play. (If a duplicating machine is available, the groups can write the roles on masters and duplicate enough copies for the entire class.)

   e.   Give each group thirty minutes to design a role play. The role play will be tried out on one of the other groups.

   f.   After thirty minutes, halt the design period. Review the "General Guidelines for Directing Role-play" (p. 291). Ask the groups to discuss the guidelines and develop a plan for trying out the role play on one of the other groups. This planning discussion should take no longer than ten to fifteen minutes.

   g.   Have the groups pair up. One group should lead the other in actually using the role play it developed. One member leads the role-play exercise, another observes the leader, making notes on how well the leader follows the directing guidelines, and the other group members observe the second group as it goes through the role-play exercise, taking notes on how well the roles seem to come across and whether the skill they designed the role play to focus on is really brought out, either in action or by omission. This activity should take no more than twenty minutes. After the role play, the leader should conduct a discussion with the other group members, just as though they were an actual client training group.

    h.   With the help of the observers, have the two groups spend about fifteen to twenty minutes reviewing the role play and its use — how well it was constructed, whether the leader was effective in directing the participants, whether the skill focus came out as intended, etc.

    i.   Repeat steps g and h, with the group that had served as "client/user" now trying out *its* role play on the other group.

    j.   Reconvene the full group to share and compare learnings about role-play design and conduct.

4.   *Deriving learnings.* Some relevant questions for the group to consider in the final discussion are:

    — What are the skills involved in creating a role play?

    — What are the skills needed to lead effectively a role-play skill-training session?

    — What are the characteristics of a well-prepared role?

    — How can client/users in a role-play skill-training session be encouraged to experiment with or try out their skill learnings in real situations?

5.   *Support materials.* Following are two guideline lists, one dealing with designing, the other with conducting, skill-training role plays.

GENERAL GUIDELINES FOR DESIGNING ROLE PLAYS FOR SKILL TRAINING

1.   *Determine the specific skill(s)* that is (are) to be the focus of the training exercise. The skill should be defined as clearly as possible (e.g., "communication between superior and subordinate"; "sharing information among peers"; "giving effective feedback"; "sharing leadership functions in a small group discussion"; etc.).

2.   *Determine the user population.* Is this exercise to be used with industrial supervisors? Students in public health administration? Define *who* will be trained using this exercise.

3.   *Develop a situation.* The situation should be realistic, not contrived. However, the situation should *not*, in general, be taken directly from the work setting of the client or user population. In other words, it should be realistic and analogous to situations the users might really be involved in but should *not* be a specific example of such a user situation. This is in order to avoid getting hung up on minor details of the situation, which would diffuse the learning impact of the exercise. Of course, the situation may or may not involve a work setting — it could be a discussion between or among friends, married couples, parent and child, in a social group, etc.

4.   *Define the problem* in the situation, the issue(s) that the role players have to deal with. The problem should be set up so that the role players *must* use the skill the role play is designed to focus on if they are to solve the problem effectively.

5.   *Determine the appropriate number of persons needed* in the role play. Observers are always desirable, but some skill-training situations involve dyadic (one-to-one) skills, others involve skills important in small groups of three or more persons. Here, the type of client/user work situation should be taken into account, in terms of work-group size.

6.   *Write a description of the situation* to be used as introductory background material for the role players. There should be enough detail to give a feel for the situation, but don't give

away any key points that should come up during the role play. A paragraph or two is about the right length.

7. *Discuss the specific roles to be written* for each role person. What should this person be like? What characteristics and background should he or she have? How does this person feel about the other person(s)? About the situation? About the problem?

8. *Write out each role,* using full sentences and simple words. Also prepare an instruction sheet for the observer(s), cuing them on what key points to look for during the role play. The roles may be as short as a sentence or two or as long as a page or two; a paragraph or two is the average. All roles should be about the same length.

GENERAL GUIDELINES FOR DIRECTING ROLE PLAYS IN SKILL TRAINING

1. *Describe the situation* briefly and clearly, even if prepared, written roles are used. Cover all essential facts and give enough information for the participants to get a feel for the situation.

2. Unless everyone is participating in the role play, *select the role players.* A volunteer who gives a "bad" performance could lose face before his or her peers. When everyone is participating, distribute roles randomly, but do *not* give a person who has a specific real problem (which you are aware of) a role that involves this same problem, and do *not* place persons with real-life status differences (such as a supervisor and subordinate) in a role play together in which they would take similar or reversed status (unless you have a specific reason for doing this).

3. *Brief the actors.* Allow plenty of time for reading, if written roles are used. Ask if there are any questions. It is helpful to check for participant understanding; *always* do this when verbal, rather than written, briefings are used. Tell the role players to make up facts or information that they forget or that was not covered in their roles, but which seems necessary. Participants might sometimes be given a few suggestions on how to behave.

4. *Assign tasks to the audience or observers.* This might be done in private, if you're telling the observers to watch for something in particular. Explain to the audience, if there is one, the role of the alter ego, if used.

5. *Set the scene.* Label props and show role players where to stand and move to. A brief introduction can help set the mood. Use imagination freely to define the physical situation.

6. *Start the action.* When several groups are involved, all should start at the same time.

7. *Cut the role play.* Don't continue too long. Often, a group will arrive at a natural end point, but if they're bogged down push them a bit and cut the action when no further progress is being made. Just a few minutes of onstage action can provide data for a long discussion, so don't overload the audience. You can also stop the action, discuss what happened, and start again, either from the beginning or with some parts "erased."

8. When the role-play action is over, in an onstage role play, *thank the role players, using real names.* This removes them from the role, and they can better dissociate themselves from "failures."

9. *Discuss what happened.* The more views the better, but try to keep the group on track. With several groups, review and compare the different outcomes. Ask observers for their reports on specific issues. In general, (a) determine what happened; (b) discuss how the outcomes could have been better; (c) try to trace the way the situation and interaction developed, why

the role players behaved as they did; and (d) try to identify what could have been done differently, by whom, to bring about a better outcome.

10. If possible, *repractice.* Try out some of the ideas developed in the discussion, perhaps with a new set of role players, or with everyone involved in multiple small groups.

REFERENCES

Blake, R. R.; Shepard, H. A.; and Mouton, J. S. (1964) *Managing intergroup conflict in industry.* Houston, Texas: Gulf.

Bray, D. W., and Grant, D. L. (1966) The assessment center in the measurement of potential for business management. *Psychological Monographs* **80**(17). Whole No. 625.

Chesler, M., and Fox, R. (1966) *Role-playing methods in the classroom.* Chicago: Science Research Associates.

Corsini, R. J. (1960) Role playing: Its use in industry. *Advanced Management* **25**(2): 20-23.

Corsini, R. J.; Shaw, M. E.; and Blake, R. R. (1961) *Role playing in business and industry.* New York: Free Press.

Culbertson, F. M. (1957) Modification of an emotionally held attitude through role playing. *Journal of Abnormal and Social Psychology* **54**: 230-233.

Elbing, A. O. (1967) The influence of prior attitudes on role playing results. *Personnel Psychology* **20**: 309-321.

Gibb, J. R. Defensive communication (1961) *Journal of Communication* **11**.

Janis, I. L., and King, B. T. (1954) The influence of role-playing on opinion change. *Journal of Abnormal and Social Psychology* **49**: 211-218.

King, B. T., and Janis, I. L. (1956) Comparison of the effectiveness of improvised versus non-improvised role-playing in producing opinion changes. *Human Relations* **9**: 177-186.

Klein, A. F. (1959) *How to use role-playing effectively.* New York: Association Press.

Lewin, K. (1958) Group decision and social change. In *Readings in social psychology.* 3rd ed., eds. E. E. Maccoby, T. M. Newcomb, and E. L. Hartley. New York: Holt, Rinehart, & Winston.

Maier, N. R. F. (1967) Assets and liabilities in group problem solving: The need for an integrative function. *Psychological Bulletin* **74**: 239-249.

Maier, N. R. F. (1952) *Principles of human relations.* New York: Wiley.

Maier, N. R. F. (1970) *Problem solving and creativity in individuals and groups.* Belmont, Calif.: Brooks/Cole.

Maier, N. R. F. (1963) *Problem solving discussions and conferences.* New York: McGraw-Hill.

Maier, N. R. F., and Sashkin, M. (1971) Specific leadership behaviors that promote problem solving. *Personnel Psychology* **24**: 35-44.

Maier, N. R. F.; Solem, A. R.; and Maier, A. A. (1957) *Supervisory and executive development: A manual for role-playing.* New York: Wiley. (Science Editions, 1966; revised and reissued as *The role-play technique.* La Jolla, Calif.: University Associates, 1975.)

Maier, N. R. F., and Thurber, J. A. (1969) Limitations of procedures for improving group problem solving. *Psychological Reports* **25**: 639-656. (Monograph Supplement 1-V25).

Maier, N. R. F., and Zerfoss, L. F. (1952) MRP: A technique for training large groups of supervisors and its potential use in social research. *Human Relations* **5**: 177-286.

Miller, A. G. (1962) Role-playing: An alternative to deception? *American Psychologist* **27**: 623-636.

Moreno, J. L. (1923) *Das stagreif theater.* Potsdam: Kiepenhaven.

Moreno, J. L. (1953) *Who shall survive?* New York: Beacon Press.

Pelz, E. B. (1958) Some factors in "group decision." In *Readings in social psychology.* 3rd ed., eds. E. E. Maccoby, T. M. Newcomb, and E. L. Hartley. New York: Holt, Rinehart, & Winston.

Perls, F. S. (1969) *Gestalt therapy verbatim.* Lafayette, Calif.: Real People Press.

Piaget, J., and Inhelder, B. (1969) *The psychology of the child.* New York: Basic Books.

Sashkin, M. (1971) *Supervisory leadership in problem solving groups.* (Doctoral dissertation, The University of Michigan, 1970.) Ann Arbor, Mich.: University Microfilms No. 71-4719.

Scott, W. A. (1957) Attitude change through reward of verbal behavior. *Journal of Abnormal and Social Psychology* **55**: 72-75.

Speroff, B. J. (1953) Empathy and role-reversal as factors in industrial harmony. *Journal of Social Psychology* **37**: 117-120.

†